THE
LOSS OF THE
BISMARCK

THE
LOSS OF THE
BISMARCK
AN AVOIDABLE DISASTER

Graham Rhys-Jones

Naval Institute Press
Annapolis, Maryland

To Rowland Rhys-Jones

First published in Great Britain in 1999 by Cassell & Co., Wellington House, 125 Strand, London WC2R OBB

Published and distributed in the United States of America and Canada by the Naval Institute Press, 291 Wood Road, Annapolis, Maryland 21402-5034

Library of Congress Catalog Card No. 99-74684

ISBN 1-55750-533-0

This edition is authorized for sale only in the United States, its territories and possessions, and Canada.

Edited and designed by Roger Chesnau/ DAG Publications Ltd.

Printed and bound in Great Britain

Contents

List of Illustrations   7

Preface   9

1   Ends and Means   13

2   Operation 'Berlin': The Experiment Begins   33

3   Operation 'Berlin': The Experiment Continues   55

4   Planning for 'Exercise Rhine'   72

5   Break-Out   90

6   'An Unlucky Hit'   111

7   The Admiralty Intervenes   132

8   A Stale Datum   147

9   The Riddle is Solved   172

10   The Final Ordeal   193

11   The Search for Lessons – and Scapegoats   211

Appendix: A Technical Controversy   235

Bibliography   241

Glossary   245

Index   249

Illustrations

Plates *(between pages 128 and 129)*
Erich Raeder in the uniform of Grand Admiral
Günther Lütjens on appointment as Fleet Commander
Raeder inspecting ships of the surface fleet
The battlecruisers *Scharnhorst* and *Gneisenau*
Lütjens arrives in Brest after Operation *'Berlin'*
The *Gneisenau*, Lütjens' flagship during Operation *'Berlin'*
HMS *Ramillies* in the Mediterranean
Admiral Somerville with his Chief of Staff on board the *Renown*
Admiral Tovey on board his flagship, December 1940
Admiral Wake-Walker, Flag Officer First Cruiser Squadron
Helmut Brinkmann of the *Prinz Eugen*
General-Admiral Alfred Saalwächter, CinC Group West
The *Bismarck* in the North Sea, 21 May 1941
The *Bismarck* approaching Grimstadtfjord, 21 May 1941
Flying Officer Suckling's photograph of the *Bismarck* in Grimstadtfjord
Captain H. St J. Fancourt talking to a Swordfish crew at Hatston
HMS *Norfolk* leaving Isafjord for her station in the Denmark Strait
Able Seaman Alfred Newall, the first man to sight the *Bismarck*
HMS *Hood* during a maintenance period in Scapa Flow
HMS *Prince of Wales* at anchor in Scapa Flow
The *Bismarck* in action with the *Hood* and the *Prince of Wales*
Captain J. C. Leach of the *Prince of Wales*
Captain R. M. Ellis on the bridge of the *Suffolk*
825 Squadron Swordfish on the deck of the *Victorious*
The famous 'Stringbag'
Admiral Somerville with Captain L. E. H. Maund

825 Squadron, key players in the *Bismarck* drama
HMS *Rodney* in Atlantic weather
HMS *Nelson* exercising her secondary armament
Phillip Vian, Captain (D) 4th Destroyer Flotilla
The *Prinz Eugen*, Brest, summer 1941
The *Prinz Eugen* during the Channel break-through, February 1942
Brinkmann addressing his ship's company on leaving the *Prinz Eugen*
The pattern of things to come

Maps

Operation *'Berlin'*: Phase I   42
Operation *'Berlin'*: Phase II   58
Break-out of *Bismarck* and *Prinz Eugen*   100–1
The battle off Iceland: approach to contact   118
Loss of contact and search plans, 24–25 May 1941   156
Search plans and movements, 25–26 May 1941   186–7

Preface

Staff and War Colleges aim first and foremost to expand the mind. They take in middle-ranking officers whose perspectives are essentially specialist and send them out after a year of reflection and study with some broader understanding of the higher conduct of war. The new graduate will have read the works of the principal military theorists and discussed them at length in seminar; he (or she) will have examined certain aids to rational decision making, studied the operational doctrines of national armed forces and those of potential enemies, and analysed the conduct of selected campaigns through the medium of historical case studies. Case studies are a vital element in the mix. To mine a single historical episode in the hope of unearthing enduring lessons or 'principles' is almost certainly misguided; the real benefit comes from the process of analysis itself. Defining a military problem, finding out who knew what and when, seeing how participants interpreted (or misinterpreted) the facts before them, identifying and evaluating the choices open to the commanders concerned – these things help to sharpen the forensic skills of those who may, one day, have to carry high responsibilities themselves. They encourage a disciplined and analytical approach to the conduct of war.

This book started out as a case study and was part of a series. It began as a lecture to faculty and students at the US Naval War College in Newport, Rhode Island, and appeared soon afterwards as a short essay in the *Naval War College Review* under the title 'The Loss of the *Bismarck*: Who was to Blame?'. If this book is preoccupied with the thoughts and decisions of admirals and headquarters staffs and neglects the perspectives of those who saw these events from the cockpit of an aircraft or through the eye-pieces of a rangefinder it is merely betraying its origins.

The choice of this particular historical episode was partly accidental. I had been looking at German archive material in the War College Library and had been struck by the diligence with which German commanders, educated in the Prussian tradition, had recorded their impressions of events. (The German *Kriegstagebuch,* or War Diary, provides a unique insight into a commander's mind.) But the history of German surface ship operations in the spring of 1941 had seemed a particularly rich archaeological site to dig in. It had seemed likely to throw light on some of the evergreen problems of maritime warfare, on problems of space and force density, on the riddle of enemy intentions (few commanders are gifted with second sight), and on the psychological pressures arising from the possibility of catastrophic failure. These issues had seemed worth exploring for their own sake; they were some of the more important factors that distinguished the art of the admiral and that of the general. Equally importantly, the episode had been recognisably modern. The age of Fisher, Jellicoe and Beatty was not quite dead. In the spring of 1941, speed and gunpower still mattered; success or failure could still turn on relative velocity and visibility distance just as it had at Scarborough, the Dogger Bank and Jutland twenty-five years before. But the aircraft and the electronic revolution were beginning to transform the conduct of war at sea. Admirals were no longer peering through telescopes; they were sifting the air waves for their clues to enemy dispositions and intentions. This was a context that the modern professional could appreciate and identify with.

I had concentrated, mainly, on the key choices made by commanders at sea during the spring of 1941 and on the consequences of those choices. But the search for cause and effect had led inevitably to the higher levels of command which had launched the *Bismarck* operation in the first place. Admiral Raeder's role had called for the closest scrutiny. (The naval bureaucracy in Berlin had been the driving force behind Operation 'Rheinübung' from first to last.) I had therefore devoted a good deal of space to Raeder's reading of strategic trends, to the pressures on the naval hierarchy arising from the Germans' inexorable drift towards continental engagement, and to the lessons that they had drawn from the maritime war so far. But the Admiral's motives had remained enigmatic. Some important ingredient had been missing, though my mainly American audience had been too polite (or too bemused) to mention it. I have since come to realise that the missing element was doctrine. The German naval leadership had been seized with a 'vision'. Pre-war theorists had offered a radical solution to the problem of war with Britain and their ideas had acquired a special status. Doctrine (or dogma) had taken the helm and nothing was going to divert it from its course. This more complete study of Operations '*Berlin*' and '*Rheinübung*' will, I hope, make good this omission.

My debt to the Naval War College cannot be overstated. My particular thanks must go to Rear-Admiral Ronald J. Kurth and to Rear-Admiral Joseph C. Strasser Jr, Presidents of the Naval War College during my four years in Newport first as the Royal Navy's representative on the War College faculty and later as a research fellow. Without their active support and sponsorship this book could not have been written. I owe an equal debt of gratitude to Captain Tim Somes, Chairman of the Operations Department, who did so much to encourage my own (latent) interest in the theory of maritime operations and whose influence on the operational thinking of a generation of serving officers has been far-reaching. I must also record my thanks to Frank Uhlig Jr, former editor of the *Naval War College Review*, for his unfailing interest in my line of research and for his helpful guidance.

I would like to express my thanks, too, to Captain Dr Werner Rahn for his advice on German sources, to *Herr* Helmut Bögler for his expert translations of German source material and for his perceptive commentaries an Admiral Lütjens' war diaries and to my nephew James Gibbs for his help with German documents and photographs. Then there are the unsung heroes of the Public Record Office, of the Imperial War Museum, of the National Archives in Washington and of the *Bundesarchiv* in Koblenz, on whose dedication and efficiency any researcher ultimately depends. My sincere thanks go to them all. My final tribute must go to my wife. She has suffered a good deal during the course of this project but has borne my obsession with her usual tolerance and good humour.

A Note on Terminology

When writing about the German Navy for an English-speaking readership, it is never easy to know whether to use German ranks, titles and organisational terms or whether to use English-language equivalents. I have chosen the second course. The rank of *Korvettenkapitän* strikes no immediate chord with the British or American reader. The title *Führer* is well understood, and one can get away with *Reichsmarschall* (just) – but probably not with *Befehlshaber* or *Seekriegsleitung*. I have used the terms 'Commander-in-Chief' and 'Naval War Staff', or simply 'Naval Staff'. I hope that German readers will overlook this lack of precision. I have followed the same guidelines when dealing with German naval conventions: in general, I have followed British usage.

Times are expressed in terms of the twenty-four-hour clock (for example, 1600 rather than 4 p.m.); this procedure was common to both navies. The times given in the text are the times that were being kept by the ship or shore authority concerned. Zone times should not bother the reader. For most of '*Rheinübung*' (the sortie of the *Bismarck* and the *Prinz Eugen*) both navies kept the same time – Zone-2 (British Double Summer Time or German Summer Time).

Positions are expressed in latitude and longitude or as a bearing and distance from a well known geographical point. German ships reported their positions in grid (for instance, AJ 6159). (It took British intelligence some time to work it out.) I have used grid positions occasionally when quoting German signals. The general position should be clear from the text.

Direction is expressed in degrees (measured clockwise from true north). Relative bearings (as viewed from the bridge of a ship) follow the British convention – 'port bow', 'starboard quarter', and so on – qualified by the terms 'fine' or 'broad' to give an idea of the size of the angle. The German equivalent, 'angle of training', is not used.

Distances are expressed in nautical miles (1nm = 6,080ft). Speed is in knots (nautical miles per hour). Gun ranges are given in yards (British ships) and metres (German ships). The difference between the two matters to gunnery officers but it need not excite the general reader.

I have tried to avoid the excessive use of naval expressions; those who run into difficulties may find the Glossary at the back of the book helpful.

Graham Rhys-Jones

1

Ends and Means

In the autumn of 1940 the German Naval High Command reopened its campaign against the British war economy with all the strength that it could muster. A return to established doctrine was long overdue. For months past, the Navy had seen its strategic prescriptions set aside and its energies dissipated in operations of secondary importance.

Looking back, it was possible to see that Hitler and the naval leadership had differed on the conduct of the war almost from the beginning; but early differences had been ones of emphasis and not of principle. The gap had widened as the war had entered its first winter and as plans for the spring offensive (*Fall 'Gelb'*) had come to dominate thinking in Hitler's headquarters. (Grand-Admiral Raeder had warned Hitler against the dangerous influence of 'continental ideas' and had complained that he was being left to conduct the campaign against British supplies 'practically single-handed'.[1]) But naval protests had done little to restore a maritime perspective to German strategy. Hitler's decision at the beginning of March to prepare for a surprise invasion of Norway and Denmark (*Fall 'Weserübung'*) had forced the Navy to suspend operations against the British economy altogether. The Navy had then found itself drawn into the direct confrontation with British sea power that it had hoped (and planned) to avoid. The *Führer* had congratulated the Navy on its 'splendid achievement'. But the tally of losses during five days of bitter fighting had been hard for a small navy to bear: the brand-new cruiser *Blücher* sunk in Oslofjord; a second cruiser damaged then sunk off Bergen; a third cruiser torpedoed in the Skagerrak; the pocket-battleship *Lützow* (prime candidate for an early return to ocean warfare) crippled by a British submarine; and ten modern fleet destroyers, half the Navy's total, trapped and sunk in the northern port of Narvik. And the battle for Norway had barely begun. German garrisons, isolated in northern Norwegian ports, were calling for immediate reinforcement by sea. A return to that primary strategic mission, to the task that guaranteed the Navy's independent status, had become a distant prospect.

The Navy had still been preoccupied with the untidy aftermath of '*Weserübung*' when Hitler had opened his offensive in the West. It had watched from the side-lines as German armies had breached Allied defences along the Meuse, expelled the British Expeditionary Force from the continent of Europe and forced the French government into a separate and humiliating peace. Hitler's intuitions had been right. The Anglo-French coalition, a nightmare scenario for a generation of German strategists, had collapsed like a house of cards. All that remained was to bring an obstinate though isolated and essentially powerless enemy to terms.

As the implications of this dramatic (and unexpected) turn of events became clearer, Grand-Admiral Erich Raeder, the amenable state servant and consensus builder who had steered the Navy through the shoals of German politics for a dozen testing years, had recognised that the British crisis was as much economic as military and that a concerted attack on the British war economy had taken on a wholly new significance. Britain's commercial and industrial heartland lay under the threat of German air power. The port of London, which, on German estimates, handled up to 40 per cent of British import volumes, faced closure. It had become possible to envisage that the entire system of supply and distribution could be reduced to a state of paralysis. In early July Raeder had called once again for a concerted sea, air and mining offensive against British imports and against her main commercial centres. The 'man in the street', he had told Hitler, had to be brought face to face with the realities of war.[2]

The *Führer* had listened carefully, but he had been tempted by schemes that seemed more direct and more immediately decisive. On 16 July he had issued his directive on preparations for the invasion of England ('*Seelöwe*') and Raeder, reluctant to present himself as an obstacle to the plan of the moment, had found himself immersed in the intricacies of a project that he knew was beyond the Navy's powers. Through August and into September, Navy and Army staffs had argued about cargo space, loading schedules, tides, intervals between assault and follow-on echelons, and, above all, about the width of the invasion front. And, throughout this time, the *Luftwaffe* had directed its air campaign against targets that were wholly inconsistent with Raeder's concept for a 'siege' of England.

Yet '*Seelöwe*' had never enjoyed Hitler's unqualified support. During wide-ranging discussions with his military chiefs on 21 July, he had accepted that a cross-Channel invasion would be an 'exceptionally daring undertaking'; and he had speculated on the motives that might lie behind Britain's continued and irrational resistance. An American declaration of war had seemed unlikely; financial losses as a result of the Great War had run to tens of billions of dollars. The British might be looking to Moscow to bale them out, but this, too, had seemed unlikely: Stalin might be unenthusiastic about German successes but he was in no condition to start a war. If an intervention by the United States and Russia could be ruled out, it followed that a conclusion to the war with Britain was in no sense urgent. Germany's military and economic position was sound; there were no parallels with the circumstances of 1918. If all necessary conditions for the launch of '*Seelöwe*' had been met by mid-September, the operation could go ahead; if not, it could be postponed until spring 1941 and other plans put in its place.[3]

Something of the nature of these 'other plans' began to emerge during a new round of military conversations at the end of the month. There was much discussion about naval force levels during the coming winter. (Raeder had forecast the arrival of the *Bismarck* and *Prinz Eugen* and had demanded additional resources for his U-boat programme.) The Chief of the Army General Staff had wanted to support Italian operations in Tripoli and develop a thrust towards Suez. Hitler had favoured an attack on Gibraltar.[4] None of the participants, it seems, had been ready to set out their proposals in detail. But, at his next meeting with the *Führer*, Raeder had been able to put his hopes and fears for the future in a much more coherent form. Stripped of its geopolitical jargon, Raeder's case amounted to this: that American attitudes were hardening; that an indefinite continuation of the war would push Britain and her Dominions into an ever-closer alignment with the United States; and that, before long, Germany would find herself in conflict not with Britain alone but with a formidably powerful Anglo-Saxon block. The military priorities for Germany and her Italian ally were clear: they needed to consolidate their position in the Mediterranean by expelling the British and enhancing the security of the French West African colonies; and they needed to accelerate the maritime war against Great Britain by every possible means.[5]

It had become clear by the date of this meeting that the conditions prescribed for the launch of *'Seelöwe'* were unlikely to be met. On 10 September Hitler had postponed a decision. He had done so again on 14th. He had then started to look for a way out that would preserve some shred of German prestige. A shift in the focus of Göring's air campaign had offered a glimmer of hope but it had faded quickly; on 19 September, the Supreme Command had put an end to the deployment of invasion shipping and ordered the dispersal of existing concentrations. These moves were to be made without alerting the enemy to a change of plan – or so the Supreme Command had hoped.

As the postponement of *'Seelöwe'* moved from probability to virtual certainty, Raeder returned to the strategic analysis that he had put forward so cogently at the beginning of the month. Germany, he urged, needed to wage war against Great Britain 'with all the means at her disposal and without delay before the United States can intervene effectively'. The Axis position in the Mediterranean had to be made safe; the threat of American, British or Gaullist intervention in North-West Africa had to be countered and the maritime campaign stepped up.[6] In the weeks that followed, he turned more and more to the possibilities of naval warfare. U-boats were continuing to achieve high rates of success, although their effectiveness was likely to decline with the coming of autumn weather. Auxiliary cruisers operating in distant waters were producing 'very good results'. The pocket-battleship *Admiral Scheer* had completed her refit; she would be deployed to the South Atlantic shortly. The new strategic bases on the French Atlantic coast indicated a 'definite concentration' of naval force. He would deploy destroyers for operations against Britain's north–south supply lines and establish fuelling bases on the coast of Spain. As battleships and heavy cruisers became available during the course of the winter, he would begin 'extensive operations' in the North Atlantic. The enemy supply and convoy system would be 'greatly affected'.[7]

* * *

The ocean campaign that Raeder was preparing for (and which he had alluded to in that mid-October meeting) had figured prominently in the Navy's calculations for nearly two years. It had been the pre-war Navy's radical solution to the 'British question' and, for a brief period, it had guided every aspect of naval planning. At the outbreak of war, the leadership had turned to it in circumstances of extreme difficulty and the idea had continued to beckon throughout the spring and summer of 1940 when the leaders had been preoccupied with other things. Now they could turn to it again in conditions that seemed to offer genuine chances of success.

The decision to shift to a strategy that focused on the enemy's maritime economy rather than on his fighting strength had not been easy. Raeder and his senior colleagues were men steeped in the ethos of the Imperial Navy. Their professional instincts had been those of Tirpitz and Hipper (Raeder had served under both), and the lessons of 1914–18 and of the Weimar period had done little to modify them. In the new climate created by Hitler's arrival, Raeder had set parity with France and Italy as his policy goal and started to convert a modest building programme into something that potential enemies (and potential allies) would recognise as a modern fighting fleet. In March 1934, he had added U-boats and aircraft carriers to his building programme and doubled the number of cruisers. He had then lobbied for large increases in the tonnage and armament of the next pocket-battleships in his building schedule, Ships 'D' and 'E'; they would emerge later as the *Scharnhorst* and *Gneisenau*, battlecruisers with a standard displacement of more than 30,000 tons and a main armament of nine 28cm (11in) guns.[8] But like all aspiring navies of the period, the resurgent *Kriegsmarine* would be built round the nucleus of a battle fleet. In July of the same year Raeder had ordered his Construction Department to prepare plans for Ship 'F', a fast battleship, the equal of anything afloat.

Ship 'F' is so central to this story that it is worth pausing to consider the main features of her design. Although official sources would admit to a displacement of 35,000 tons only (the capital ship limit set by the Washington Naval Treaty of 1922), Ship 'F' would emerge with a standard displacement of nearly 42,000 tons and a full load displacement of over 50,000 tons. She would thus outweigh the *King George V* and the *Washington*, her near contemporaries in the Royal Navy and the United States Navy respectively, by nearly 5,000 tons.[9]

The extensive use of welding, a technique pioneered in the earlier *Deutschland* (pocket-battleship) class, had produced a hull that was relatively light for its dimensions and which gave designers an ample margin for useful payload. The main armament, eight 38cm (15in) guns in twin turrets, was not exceptional by the standards of the day. The choice reflected the continuing influence of Versailles; the treaty had restricted the German Navy to an 11in maximum and time for further development had been short. Nevertheless, the new 38cm gun developed by Krupp of Essen was a state-of-the-art weapon with a muzzle velocity rather higher than that of its British equivalents. It had a maximum range of 36,000m and fired a shell weighing 798kg (1,760lb). The secondary battery consisted of twelve 15cm (5.9in) guns with a range of 23,000m. The anti-aircraft armament included sixteen 10.5cm (4in) guns and more than thirty quick-firing weapons. In terms of weight, this armament package was almost exactly the same as that installed in the *King George V*, although it represented a rather lower proportion of total displacement.

The main machinery, three steam turbines driving three shafts, was designed to produce 138,000 shaft horsepower, a figure exceeded during trials. Power requirements (and installation weights) were 15–20 per cent higher than those of equivalent British and American ships because of the unusually broad hull form adopted by the designers. Stability was one reason for their choice, internal layout another. The broad beam allowed optimum positioning of the two longitudinal or 'torpedo' bulkheads that protected the ship's main services from underwater attack. There seems to have been little penalty in terms of speed. The ship worked up to more than 30kts during trials, a speed approaching that of the best battlecruisers of the day. A fuel capacity of 8,700 tons gave a cruising range of 8,900 miles at 17kts, a shorter range than that of American battleships built with Pacific operations in mind but rather better than that of British ships of the period.[10]

If Ship 'F' led the field in any single respect, it was in the area of armour and protection. Here, Raeder's designers had followed established German practice. The ship's hull was protected by more than 17,500 tons of armour plate. This total represented nearly 39 per cent of displacement as compared to 34 per cent in the *Washington* and 30 per cent in the *King George V*. An additional 6,000 tons of armour protected turrets, fire control stations and conning positions. The main armoured belts covered 70 per cent of the ship's length and varied in thickness from 5½in at deck-edge level to nearly 13in at the waterline. Horizontal protection was provided by an armoured weather deck (designed to detonate or retard projectiles passing over the belt armour) and by a main armoured deck at waterline level. This had a thickness of 3½in at the centreline, increasing to 4in outboard of the torpedo bulkheads where it sloped downwards to meet the belt armour below the waterline. This was a well-proven (if conventional) scheme of armour protection designed with one prime purpose in mind – to give high probabilities of survival in a naval action with equivalent heavy ships.

On all major counts, Ship 'F' was designed to match anything under development elsewhere; she would be more than a match for the ageing capital ships which, following the 'building holidays' imposed under the Washington and London Treaties, made up the bulk of the world's battle fleets. She represented a leap into the premier league. Building contracts for Ship 'F' and for a sister-ship, 'G', were placed with Blohm und Voss of Hamburg and with the Navy Yard in Wilhelmshaven in the early months of 1936. The keel for Ship 'F' was laid on 1 July; work on Ship 'G' began in October as soon as the new *Scharnhorst* had left the slip. They would be launched in due course with that blend of pomp and arrogance peculiar to Nazi ceremonial, their names, *Bismarck* and *Tirpitz*, pregnant with historical meaning.

Had Raeder looked ahead to some still distant day when he could mount an open challenge to British naval supremacy? Some German historians suggest that he had, although the evidence is slim. For the immediate future – and for as far ahead as any prudent planner could look – the issue did not arise. A maritime war at this stage of the Navy's development could serve no rational purpose. Nor had such a war seemed likely. Weimar Germany's policies had been cautious. The governing élite had been determined above all else to avoid policy initiatives that might revive the Anglo-French alignment of 1914–18. And Hitler had been working for an accommodation with Britain.[11] The national consensus had seemed absolute and unshakable.

Raeder, therefore, had built his plans on the assumption of British neutrality. He had been strengthened in his convictions by Britain's willing-ness, in the summer of 1935, to accept German proposals on fleet ratios. (No one had needed reminding of the baleful influence of the Tirpitz programme in the first decade of the century: a sign of British acquiescence had been the key to progress.) He had seen the Anglo-German Naval Agreement as giving him the green light.[12] He had pressed ahead with his building programme despite growing signs – evident to other members of the German military élite though not, apparently, to him – that Hitler's policies were reawakening political and military alignments that were best left dormant. His answer to the developing crisis in European relations and to the simultaneous, though largely unrelated, breakdown in the naval conference system had been 'more of the same'. During the course of 1937, and despite the inability of German industry to meet existing demands, he had added six more super-battleships to his forward projections. A decade of peaceful development would give him a fleet to rival that of his great predecessor.

However, by summer 1938 the storm clouds on the horizon had become too threatening to ignore. With Hitler declaring his intention to 'settle the German [minorities] question by force' and warning that the hostility of 'hate-inspired antagonists' in the West was bringing the outbreak of a general European war sensibly closer, it was time to think the unthinkable.[13] As the Sudetenland crisis approached flash point, Raeder ordered his operations staff to prepare a memorandum on the conduct of a naval war with Britain and on what such a war would mean for the Navy's strategic objectives and building plans.

* * *

The Heye Memorandum[14] (named after its author Commander Helmuth Heye) was typical of those 'straw man' papers often used in large bureaucracies to focus people's minds in times of difficulty: it was strong on principle but weak on detail and it marched boldly into a number of specialist areas that the author knew little about. But it helped to forge a new consensus and it reveals a good deal about the thinking of the German naval hierarchy on the eve of war. Raeder's personal role in shaping it should not be underestimated.

The basic conclusion of the Heye review was that British sea power rested on such solid geo-strategic and industrial foundations that a continental state, preoccupied with questions of land warfare, could never hope to match it. Conventional naval strategies based on 'decisive battle' and 'command of the sea' had therefore to be ruled out. Instead, Germany would have to exploit Britain's unique dependence on maritime lines of supply and adjust its thinking and its building plans accordingly.[15] Heye gave his strategy its traditional title 'cruiser warfare'. The terminology was significant; although he took care to present his campaign as a comprehensive one, employing submarines, mines and aircraft as well as a spectrum of different ship types, he left his readers in no doubt as to where the main emphasis should lie.

Heye's preferences (or preconceptions) were based on an analysis of British strengths and weaknesses which owed more to academic theory than to the lessons of history. According to this, Britain's maritime structure rested on the concentrated strength of a battle fleet stationed (as in 1914–18) to contain the German Navy and control access to the high seas. A direct challenge to this fleet was out of the question; it would play into the enemy's hands. But the vast network of ocean communications which lay beyond it – and which was shielded by it – was inherently vulnerable. Mobile forces, loose on the high seas and free to switch their point of attack from one ocean area to another, would leave the enemy confused and disorganised. To counter German raiding forces, Britain would have to escort her shipping or form hunting groups; it mattered little which. She could meet the threat only by adopting a general policy of dispersal. She would have to loosen her grip on home waters (the basis of her strategy) and she might even expose her naval forces, or important elements of them, to defeat in detail. Heye stopped short of the claim that a succession of local victories could tilt the balance of naval power in Germany's favour (some of his seniors were far less reticent); he presented cruiser warfare as the strategy best calculated to place dispro-portionate burdens on the defence and as the route to the strategic initiative.

In the light of First War precedents and of decisions taken only a year later, it is perhaps surprising that Heye should have rejected a campaign based primarily on the U-boat as 'unlikely to produce decisive results'.[16] His thinking was influenced by the prevailing belief that technical developments ('sophisticated means of location') had reduced the submarine's former effectiveness and by fears that the political authorities might withhold permission for an unrestricted U-boat campaign as they had done in the period 1914–16. But his reservations went much further: he saw the submarine as a solitary and static weapon, useful off enemy coasts and harbours where the strength of the defence would preclude surface opera-tions but lacking the mobility and power of concentration that his concept for ocean warfare seemed to demand.[17] If he took his inspiration from any episode in German naval history, he took it from the events of November 1914 when von Spee's cruisers, working off the Chilean coast, had defeated the weak and isolated British squadron sent to intercept them. Raeder had studied von Spee's campaign in depth and had grasped the forces that had shaped it. He would make this mode of warfare his own.[18]

In the spring of 1939 the principles of cruiser warfare were incorporated into the Navy's Battle Instructions, the formal statement governing its conduct in war. The new edition, the first to point to a general European war, invited the fleet to adjust itself to the possibility of war on two fronts (Russia or Poland in the east and Britain and France in the west) and warned that the struggle had already begun, 'so far without recourse to arms'. The broad approach would be this. The Navy would adopt a strictly defensive posture in the Baltic and open an offensive in the West, where the aim would be 'to cripple British and French imports by water'. The U-boat flotilla would concentrate in British waters but a successful offensive would be possible 'only on the oceans'. The ocean campaign would be the linchpin of German strategy: ships at home would engage in 'constant harassing action' to tie down units of the British fleet and relieve pressure on the high seas. From time to time, the Navy would mount larger operations to cover the movement of raiding forces to and from the Atlantic.[19]

* * *

So much for the theory. Could it be put into effect? The naval leadership seems to have recognised, clearly enough, that the gulf between concept and execution remained wide. It was easy to postulate a war of manoeuvre in the enemy's sensitive strategic rear, far more difficult to see how an ocean campaign could be kept going when Germany had no overseas bases and when access to German waters was controlled by the British fleet. Heye had done much to highlight these problems and to propose solutions. He had called for the covert deployment of cruisers before the start of hostilities.[20] He had stressed the need for a comprehensive system of seaborne support and for access to the bases of potential allies. Germany, he had suggested, needed to develop her ties with Spain, Italy and Japan, although he had recognised, almost in the same breath, that Japan was too remote, that Spain was 'militarily impotent' and that Italian bases were of little use while Britain controlled the approaches to the Mediterranean.[21] Like many of his contemporaries, he had been preoccupied with the disadvantages of Germany's 'military-geographical position'; he had pointed to the benefits of territorial expansion, northwards into Scandinavia and westwards to the Channel coast, to turn the flank of the British blockade.[22] But matters like these had been beyond the scope of naval policy-making: they had implied decisions at the highest level. Heye's message for Raeder had been this: that the Navy's material preparations for war with Britain would have to be backed by a range of political, diplomatic and perhaps even military initiatives. It was for the leadership to work towards these ends in a deliberate and systematic way.

Heye's proposals on the future shape of the fleet were equally far-reaching. His recommendations on ship design came partly from the nature of ocean warfare itself – he put speed and radius of action at the top of his priorities and was ready to compromise on armament and protection – and partly from the conviction that the class standards adopted by established navies worked to Germany's disadvantage.[23] He advocated a range of intermediate ship types that would either outrun or outfight their nearest enemy equivalents. He predicted a 'short life expectancy' for the (slow) pocket-battleships of the *Deutschland* class and condemned their successors (the battlecruisers and battleships that Raeder was building) as relying too heavily on base support. He saw the burden of his campaign as falling on a new class of pocket-battleships, larger and faster than those already in service but with a comparable (28cm) main armament. Their purpose, as he saw it, was not to do battle with enemy capital ships but to make the 10,000-ton Washington Treaty cruiser, workhorse of established navies, obsolete.[24]

The role of Raeder's battle fleet in the larger scheme of things was by now a little uncertain. Heavy ships would still have a part to play in a war against France alone, but it was less easy to determine their function in a war with Britain. For Heye, the prospects for an inferior battle fleet working from the German Bight were 'absolutely hopeless'.[25] A few capital ships would be needed for defensive tasks in the North Sea and the Baltic and for diversionary action in support of the ocean campaign. They might even have a role in ocean warfare itself if the leadership was ready to take the risk. But Heye left his readers in no doubt that, in his view, the battle fleet had lost a good deal of its former significance and that the continued building of vast and expensive capital ships could only divert resources from the kind of vessels that Germany really needed. He proposed therefore to terminate the capital ship programme at hulls 'H' and 'J' (the immediate successors to the*Bismarck* and *Tirpitz*) and to use the spare capacity for his new *Panzerschiff* class.[26]

The high-level committees set up to examine Heye's proposals looked on the notion of an emasculated battle fleet with considerable distaste. They had continued to debate the proper balance between battleships and pocket-battleships in the future Navy well into the autumn. But, by the end of October 1938, Raeder had accepted recommendations that would produce four new pocket-battleships by December 1943 and the two leviathans ('H' and 'J') by the end of the following year. It is clear, therefore, that Raeder – usually presented as the model of naval orthodoxy – had accepted the case for Heye's strategy and for a corresponding shift in Germany's shipbuilding priorities. Hitler was less easily convinced. There is no written record of the meeting (1 November) at which Raeder attempted to get the *Führer's* agreement to this change of direction. But the gist of the discussion seems plain enough. Hitler was prepared to accept the new *Panzerschiff* class, but not at the expense of a battleship programme that had promised to give him political leverage in his dealings with the Western Powers.[27]

In the weeks that followed, the Naval Staff struggled manfully to reconcile Hitler's wishes with its own sense of strategic priorities. It failed. The next meeting was bitter. Hitler's harsh criticism of the Navy's plans brought Raeder to the brink of resignation. Through the winter of 1938/39, the Navy's Construction Department reworked its figures. By mid-January it had identified a schedule that appeared to promise four new pocket-battleships by 1943, six super-battleships by 1944 and a further batch of pocket-battleships by 1945, as well as cruisers, destroyers and submarines in large numbers. It was a 'compromise' which satisfied both parties. Hitler approved the 'Z Plan' ('X' and 'Y' having been scrapped along the way) at the end of January 1939; and Raeder began, without further ado, to put it into effect.

The startling contradiction between naval policies geared to the longer term and the ominous developments of spring 1939 have continued to baffle historians.[28] For, as Hitler finished his destruction of the Czech state, denounced the Anglo-German Naval Agreement and issued his preliminary directives for operations against Poland (*Fall 'Weiss'*), Raeder placed contracts for Ships 'H' and 'J'. And, as he issued his own directives covering the Navy's part in *Fall 'Weiss'*, he placed contracts for 'K', 'L', 'M' and 'N', cautioning a Staff, confused by the odd juxtaposition of events, that they must draw a clear distinction between the Polish question, a local problem which would be contained by swift and decisive action on the ground, and the more distant general conflict which was shaping his plans.[29]

It is hard to believe that this archetypal military mandarin, the servant of three regimes, cannot sometimes have wondered where the events of spring 1939 were leading. The answer to the riddle seems to lie in the convictions of a patriot (if, perhaps, a narrow one) who had lived through the turmoil of the Weimar period and who had witnessed the corrosive effects of political factionalism at first hand. He had created his navy as the apolitical agent of the state. It could advise and warn, but, in the end, it had to act within the framework laid down by the (lawful) civil power. Anything else meant chaos, or, in the well-worn phrase of the time, *finis Germaniae*. There is, perhaps, another factor in the equation. An early war threatened the emotional and material investment of decades. The idea was too painful to contemplate.

* * *

The events of 3 September came 'like a bombshell'.[30] Raeder had no choice but to put his great project on hold and switch resources to ships that would reach the front line in months rather than years. He began a review of mobilisation plans at once. He ordered savage cuts in the surface ship programme and doubled the U-boat building rate. It soon became clear that production would barely keep pace with losses. In early October he submitted an accelerated U-boat programme based on the full resources of the 'Z Plan'.[31] Beyond the *Bismarck*, the *Tirpitz* and the heavy cruiser *Prinz Eugen*, all well advanced and offering little by way of savings, no other large building project would survive.

Raeder's prognosis for the coming war was deeply pessimistic. In a naive and emotional defence of his former policies, written in the hushed silence that followed news of Britain's declaration, he had reflected on how things might have been if political developments in Europe had followed Hitler's projections. He had painted a picture of cruisers on the rampage and of powerful task forces loose on the high seas, each strong enough to deal with anything that a confused and distracted enemy might send against them. With a well-timed diversionary campaign in home waters and with the help of Italy and Japan, he would have had some chance of 'settling the British question conclusively'. As things were, his fleet was far too weak to have a decisive influence on the course of events. Indeed, there had seemed little that his heavy ships could do bar show that they knew 'how to die gallantly' and 'create the foundations for later reconstruction'.[32]

Yet the strategy of cruiser warfare had remained the logical course to follow. Raeder had sailed his pocket-battleships and their tankers during the third week of August, their deployment having been one of the Navy's main precautionary moves in the prelude to *Fall 'Weiss'*. They were now in position. If they were handled adroitly, there was no reason why they should not remain at sea for several months. They would have to avoid action with enemy naval forces; that was clear.[33] Even minor action damage might bring operations to a premature end. They might have to lie low in remote and unfrequented areas if the pressures became too great. But their presence on the high seas would have important psychological effects. They would force Britain to introduce convoy on her more important oceanic routes. (The cost, particularly in terms of port congestion, would be high.) Elsewhere, the enemy would divert shipping; sometimes he might have to suspend sailings altogether. And neutral ship-owners would think twice about the risks and benefits of trading with the enemy. The pocket-battleships would exert an influence out of all proportion to their numbers. They would act as a powerful brake on maritime traffic flows at a time when the Western Powers were seeking urgently to raise the output of their war industries.

As hopes for an early settlement faded, Raeder released the *Deutschland* and the *Graf Spee*[34] from their holding areas to begin operations against shipping on the North and South Atlantic routes. He applied his Battle Instructions to the letter. When survivors from the *Graf Spee*'s first victim reached Pernambuco on the South American coast bringing news of a powerful raider loose in equatorial waters, he sailed the *Gneisenau* to make a demonstration off the Norwegian coast.[35] The enemy had responded in the expected way. Home Fleet capital ships had sailed for an intercept position off Bergen and a cruiser force had moved on the Skagerrak in an apparent attempt to cut the line of retreat.

But the diversionary effects produced by the *Gneisenau*'s brief sortie proved short-lived. By the third week of October, enemy strength in the South Atlantic was reaching danger levels. Raeder encouraged the *Graf Spee* to make a sweep into the Indian Ocean in the hope of putting the enemy off the scent. As the full scope of the enemy's operations became clearer,

Raeder's difficulties mounted. The *Graf Spee* was safe for the moment, but the *Deutschland*, slower to make her presence felt, was now coming under pressure too. Worryingly, some in High Command circles seemed to be losing their nerve. Hitler was beginning to complain that the loss of the *Deutschland* might be taken as a 'bad omen' by the people.[36]

Raeder resisted Hitler's demands for the recall of the *Deutschland* as long as he could. Her return to German waters would complicate plans for diversionary action at home and leave her consort dangerously exposed. Eventually, he could resist no longer. On 1 November he decided to bring her back. She was to make her passage through British lines at the next new moon (15 November), when nights would be at their darkest.

With the *Deutschland* (soon to be renamed *Lützow*) safely recovered, Raeder returned to the diversionary strategy that his Battle Instructions prescribed. A new move in home waters was urgent. The *Graf Spee* was already returning to the South Atlantic to take fuel from her oiler (the *Altmark*) and to resume operations north-west of the Cape. Raeder's new plan was more ambitious than the last. This time, his battlecruisers would raid British patrol lines in the Iceland–Faeroes passage and make a feint towards the Atlantic. If they could demonstrate the fragility of British blockading arrangements and threaten the shipping routes that lay beyond them, they might begin to exert some permanent influence on British dispositions.

The *Gneisenau* and *Scharnhorst* left Wilhelmshaven during the afternoon of 21 November and set course for the Faeroes. They reached the objective area undetected and, at dawn on the 23rd, began to search north-west towards the coast of Iceland. For some hours they found nothing, but towards evening they sighted the *Rawalpindi*, an armed merchant cruiser of the Northern Patrol. After a brief chase and a brief exchange of fire they sank her. It was now dusk and time for the Fleet Commander, Admiral Marschall, to consider his next moves. Judging that the *Rawalpindi*'s enemy report would bring the whole strength of the Home Fleet against him, and worried by the approach of an unidentified warship that he (rightly) believed would try to shadow him, Marschall cut short his operations in the Iceland–Faeroes passage and withdrew eastward at high speed. When satisfied that he had outrun the pursuit, he turned north-east and made for open waters between Iceland and the coast of Norway. Here he loitered, monitoring developments closely, until it was safe to make a break for home. Taking advantage of foul weather and helped by air reconnaissance, he picked his way through British lines and reached German waters undetected and unscathed.

If Marschall's achievements during the period 21–27 November fell a little short of what the Naval Staff had hoped for, there were solid grounds for believing that the main purpose behind his operation had been achieved. The Royal Navy had suspended all routine activities. Convoys had been diverted or held back. Planned deployments had been cancelled. Reliefs for ships of the Northern Patrol had been diverted to other tasks. The entire strength of the Home Fleet, capital ships, cruisers and destroyers, as well as elements of the French Navy, had been drawn into a massive and ultimately fruitless search operation that had lasted for the best part of a week.[37] In a review of the operation ten days after the event, Raeder had been able to tell Hitler that the situation in the South Atlantic had 'eased'.[38] However, at dawn on 13 December a British cruiser force had caught the *Graf Spee* off the River Plate. They had forced her to seek refuge in the neutral port of Montevideo. Urgent attempts to extend the legal deadline and effect repairs had failed, and in the end Captain Langsdorff had been forced to scuttle his ship.

* * *

Raeder's first and tentative experiment in ocean warfare had lasted little more than two months. While errors of judgment by the man on the spot had contributed to the recent humiliation, it was clear that far broader factors had been at work. The recall of the *Deutschland* had left the *Graf Spee* exposed to the undivided attention of two powerful navies, and Germany, acting alone, had been unable to redress the balance. The campaign in home waters had fallen flat. The Naval Staff had tried hard to inject some life into it, but the availability of the new battlecruisers, the *Scharnhorst* and *Gneisenau*, had been lamentable and the operational commands had seemed half-hearted at best. Through the winter of 1939/40 the Naval Staff had urged faint hearts in Kiel and Wilhelmshaven to understand what was at stake. Defence was not an option. This had to be a war of calculated risk; the Navy could not allow itself to be intimidated by the 'psychological pressures of a much superior enemy'.[39]

Despite the lessons of December 1939, a return to ocean warfare had remained at the top of the Naval Staff's agenda. When plans for the invasion of Norway had come up for discussion, the ocean deployment of the *Lützow* (ex-*Deutschland*) had been the item in the forward programme that the Staff had fought hardest to protect. They had failed. The Supreme Command's insistence on using this ship in '*Weserübung*' had been a '*definite strategic error*'.[40]

For Raeder and his operational planners, a return to the strategy of ocean warfare required only the right opportunity. The shelving of Operation '*Seelöwe*' opened that opportunity and, in the minds of navalists at least, raised the maritime campaign to the forefront of Germany's strategic priorities.

As they put the finishing touches to their campaign plans in the final months of 1940, Raeder and his staff looked out on a strategic landscape that had changed beyond recognition. Mussolini's declaration of war on the one hand and the neutralisation of the French fleet on the other had produced an appreciable shift in the balance of naval advantage. A large proportion of Britain's battle fleet was now committed to the Mediterranean.[41] The Royal Navy was under unprecedented strain. The war situation as a whole was close to the one which cruiser warfare theorists had postulated.

The strategic bases on the Atlantic coast of France, ceded to Germany under the terms of the Armistice, were a second and vitally important factor in the equation. Raeder had made much of them in his mid-October meeting with Hitler.[42] If these and other bases in Spain and French West Africa could be opened up (didn't political influence follow military dominance as night follows day?), Germany would have solved the elemental problem of British containment that theorists had seen as one of the main obstacles to a protracted ocean campaign. There would be tankers and stores ships aplenty. It was becoming possible to think in terms of a full concentration of the German fleet in the Atlantic, something that the Imperial Navy had barely dreamed of and scarcely seen the need for.

The numerical weakness of the German surface fleet was, and would remain, a matter of concern. But winter 1940/'41 was not to be compared with autumn 1939. The global deployment of auxiliary cruisers was already exerting a distractive effect. The movement of the *Admiral Scheer* towards the South Atlantic would add to it. The heavy cruiser *Hipper*, damaged during '*Weserübung*' and since delayed by mechanical defects, would follow in late November. The *Gneisenau* and *Scharnhorst* (also damaged during the course of the Norwegian campaign) would be ready by the end of the year. After them would come the *Bismarck*, the *Prince Eugen* and, later still, the *Tirpitz*.

These would be enough, if handled with skill and caution, to provide the basis for a sustained offensive against British supplies. And, unlike their predecessors, these new ships would have the speed, agility and combat strength to survive in the dangerous (but vital) North Atlantic zone of operations where British supply lines converged.

With 'Seelöwe' on the shelf and gathering dust, the imperative for the coming winter was to bring about the progressive concentration of the surface fleet in the northern Atlantic and begin an extended campaign of maritime disruption. The risks had been weighed; the doctrines were in place. The future was full of uncertainty and challenge; a host of practical problems had yet to be resolved. But Britain's military and economic position was as fragile now as at any time since the spring of 1917 (far more fragile than any pre-war theorist could have dared to predict).

It was a historic moment – one of those times when military men have to put qualms aside and seize the opportunities before them.

Notes to Chapter 1

1   Conference report, 26 January 1940, *Führer Conferences*, p. 77.
2   Report dated 11 July 1940, *Führer Conferences*, pp. 113-115.
3   *Führer Conferences*, pp. 119–20.
4   Conference report, 31 July 1940, *Führer Conferences*, p. 125.
5   Report of 6 September 40, *Führer Conferences*, pp. 132–6. In the light of later events, this naval staff analysis appears perceptive. It was influenced by a number of recent developments, notably the ratification by the US Congress of the 'destroyers for bases' deal on 2 September. It seems also to have been driven by Hitler's apparent (and, to naval eyes, dangerous) preoccupation with the Russian problem.
6   Conference report, 26 September 1940, *Führer Conferences*, pp. 141–3.
7   Conference report, 14 October 1940, *Führer Conferences*, pp. 143–5.
8   I have followed British convention in calling these ships 'battlecruisers'. The German Navy classed them as battleships.
9   This assessment is based on data published in Friedman, Norman, *Battleship Design and Development, 1905–1945* (Greenwich: Conway Maritime Press, 1978). See also, Lenton H. T., *German Warships of the Second World War* (London: Macdonald and Jane's, 1975) and Schmalenbach, Paul, *Kriegsmarine Bismarck*, Warship Profile 18 (Windsor: Profile Books, 1971).

10 Range at full power would, of course, have been substantially less than the figure quoted. On the basis of the commonly cited cube law, range at 25kts would have been about 3,000 miles.

11 Hitler had seen no conflict between British interests (primarily commercial and imperial) and his own continental ambitions. He had hoped for an accommodation on that basis. For an analysis of Hitler's foreign policy at the time see Messerschmidt, 'Foreign Policy and Preparation for War', in *Germany and the Second World War*, Vol. 1. p. 549; and Hillgruber, pp. 50–2.

12 The Anglo-German Naval Agreement of June 1935 signalled that the naval provisions of the Treaty of Versailles had become a dead letter. The agreement set the German building limit at 35 per cent of British tonnage in each surface ship category. An exception was made in the case of submarines; here the limit was set at 45 per cent, although the agreement conceded Germany's right to match British figures after giving notice.

13 For an analysis of naval policy developments at this critical time, see Deist, pp. 472–3; and Thomas, pp. 175–7.

14 The text of the Heye Memorandum is given in Salewski,*Die deutsche Seekriegsleitung, Band III; Denksschriften und Lagebetrachtungen 1938–44* (Neustadt: 1973). This summary is based on that text.

15 Heye Memorandum, pp. 32–3.

16 *Ibid.*, p. 37.

17 *Ibid.*, p. 40.

18 Vice-Admiral Maximilian Graf von Spee, commanding the Imperial Navy's East Asiatic Squadron, had defeated Rear-Admiral Cradock's armoured cruisers off Coronel on 1 November 1914. Admiral Fisher's response had been to detach a Grand Fleet battlecruiser squadron under Vice-Admiral Sir Doveton Sturdee to hunt him down. By mischance, von Spee had approached the Falklands on 8 December, where Sturdee, newly arrived, was coaling his ships. The East Asiatic Squadron had been annihilated. Raeder had written the volume of the official history covering von Spee's campaign. Raeder, p.113.

19 *Führer Directives and Other Top Level Directives*, pp. 25–30.

20 Later adopted in the orders for *Fall 'Weiss'*.

21 Heye Memorandum, p. 43. Talks with the Italian Naval Staff on a common approach to cruiser warfare started in June 1939.

22 *Ibid.*, p. 44. Here he was drawing on the ideas of Vice-Admiral Wolfgang Wegener, whose influential book *The Naval Strategy of the World War* had been published in 1929.

23 *Ibid.*, pp. 45–6. According to Salewski, this view was widely held in German naval circles. Established class standards were seen as a device for perpetuating German naval inferiority.

24 *Ibid.*, p. 49. The 10,000-ton cruiser had been an unintended by-product of the

1922 Washington Naval Treaty. Britain had generally favoured smaller ships which could be built in larger numbers.

25 *Ibid.*, p. 39.

26 *Ibid.*, pp. 39, 61.

27 Deist, pp. 476–7. This seems to support Raeder's view (Raeder, p. 271) that Hitler was 'concerned with warships – particularly battleships – purely as symbols of power and showed little interest in their deployment and use in actual operation'.

28 Deist remarks (p. 479), 'One searches in vain for any guiding principle in the German naval construction programme at this time.'

29 Memorandum for Naval Staff, 16 May 1939, *Führer Directives and Other Top Level Directives*, p. 6.

30 Raeder, p. 278.

31 For early decisions on the U-boat programme see Rössler, 'U-Boat Development and Building', in Howarth (ed.), *The Battle of the Atlantic*, pp. 126–9.

32 'Reflections of the CinC Navy on the Outbreak of War', *Führer Conferences*, pp. 37–8.

33 Combat action was 'not an end in itself' and was therefore 'not to be sought'. This and the other operational principles described here had been set out in Battle Instructions. *Führer Directives and Other Top Level Directives*, pp. 25–30.

34 The third pocket-battleship, *Admiral Scheer*, was refitting.

35 This seems to have been a conscious attempt on Raeder's part to hold British battlecruisers in home waters and thus to prevent a repetition of the events of December 1914. See note 18.

36 Report, 23 October 1939, *Führer Conferences*, p. 53.

37 For an account of Home Fleet operations following the sinking of the *Rawalpindi*, see Roskill, *The War at Sea*, Vol. 1, pp. 83–7.

38 Report, 8 December 1939, *Führer Conferences*, p. 62.

39 Rear-Admiral Kurt Fricke, Head of Naval Staff Operations Division, summarising difficult discussions with Deputy Commander Group West on the employment of heavy ships in home waters. Naval Staff War Diary, Part A, Vol. 7, p. 10.

40 Naval Staff War Diary, Part A, Vol. 8, p. 62 (original emphasis). The *Lützow* had been crippled by the British submarine *Spearfish* while hurrying back from Oslo.

41 According to German intelligence, eight of her thirteen capital ships were stationed there.

42 *Führer Conferences*, pp. 144–5.

2

Operation 'Berlin':
The Experiment Begins

In a generation of German officers starved of command experience, Günther Lütjens stood out as something of an exception. He had risen to command a torpedo-boat half-flotilla during the Great War and he had continued his association with small ships in the post-war German Navy. A cruiser command had followed. The opening of the Second World War had found him as Rear-Admiral Torpedo-Boats and soon as Commander Scouting Forces North Sea. But the invasion of Norway in April 1940 had brought him to national prominence. In the absence of Admiral Marschall, the Fleet Commander, he had commanded the battle force covering the northern invasion groups. He had delivered the Trondheim and Narvik groups to their objectives, encountered and evaded a superior British force off the Lofotens and brought his ships home safely in the face of a fully alerted British fleet. His actions had been cautious by conventional standards and certainly unheroic; but that was what nervous admirals in Berlin had most wanted at a time when the future of the German fleet had been hanging in the balance. Now, nine months on and Fleet Commander in his own right, he was being called on again, this time to provide the main impetus behind Admiral Raeder's Atlantic campaign.

Lütjens was a tall, sparely built man in his early fifties. Subordinates saw him as something of an ascetic. They described him as 'serious', 'undemonstrative' and 'taciturn', though they recognised an incisive mind and they knew that little escaped his notice.[1] He was not the kind of leader who stamps his personality on a fleet or who attracts a retinue of loyal (and uncritical) followers. His qualities were different. He was disciplined, methodical and analytical, and he expected other people to think and act with his own brand of precision. (They seldom did, and their wayward and unpredictable habits were not an easy cross to bear.) People saw him as a man of action, though the description needs qualification. His actions were never impulsive; he was a thinker and a planner and he had learned the benefit of keeping his options open until the point of decision had come. He was not untypical of his kind. Men of a similar stamp had risen to high rank in the Royal Navy. They were sometimes dismissed as 'book keepers' but they satisfied some primordial need.

The third week of January 1941 found Lütjens dealing with an unfortunate though unavoidable change of plan. A first attempt to reach the Atlantic had ended in failure. On the last day of December the battlecruisers *Gneisenau* and *Scharnhorst* had run into a storm off the coast of Norway and Lütjens had been forced to return to Kiel for repairs. The resumption of 'Berlin' (code-name for his Atlantic sortie) was now being threatened by the approach of winter and the Naval High Command was becoming seriously concerned about the implications of further delay.

Getting clear of the Baltic without alerting enemy intelligence or running foul of air patrols off the south-western coast of Norway depended above all on careful timing. The passage of the Great Belt (the narrow waterway leading north from Kiel) was best done under cover of darkness to minimise the risk of observation from the shore. Ships would reach the northern tip of Jutland (the Skaw) at daybreak, negotiate the defensive minefields, pick up an anti-submarine escort and be far enough to the west by nightfall to ensure that they were clear through the area of maximum patrol activity by dawn. This had been the basis of the December plan, but, with the Baltic winter setting in, progress would be much less predictable.

On 21 January, reports that ice in the Great Belt was already 30cm thick and that offshore navigation marks could no longer be relied on forced Lütjens to change his timetable. He decided that the Great Belt, or at least its trickier northern section, would have to be tackled in daylight. It was a risk that he would have to take. He would then wait overnight at the Skaw before resuming his established timetable. But in winter almost anything could happen. As an additional precaution against accidents of timing that might leave him exposed to British reconnaissance off the Norwegian coast, Lütjens made contingency plans to lie up during daylight hours in the fjords near Bergen. Here, if need be, fighter cover could be relied on to keep snoopers at arm's length.

Lütjens had been prepared for most things, but not for the extraordinary lapses of the shore command. The battlecruisers had left Kiel in darkness and had cleared the Great Belt during the morning of 23 January. Then, in late evening, they had anchored off the Skaw (just short of the defensive minefield) to wait for daylight and the arrival of their escort. Dawn had come but not the escort. By noon Lütjens had established that the First Torpedo-Boat Flotilla was still in harbour; it had been told to stay there because of the weather. With movement that day out of the question, he sent a staff officer ashore to fix a new rendezvous for 1000 next morning. A twenty-four hour delay had become inevitable.

The afternoon brought further complications and further evidence of muddle ashore. At 1500, Lütjens received reports of two British cruisers and several merchant ships close off the Norwegian coast. It was puzzling that the enemy should be so far forward in daylight; everything pointed to a minelaying operation and one that seemed to be perilously close to his planned route. As he pondered the implications of this new development, Lütjens was amazed to receive a signal from the shore authorities saying, 'Turn back due enemy situation. More later. Lights for Kristiansand ordered.' Group Command appeared to think that he was already far advanced on his passage westward in spite of the absence of a screen. This was against everything that had been agreed. During his briefings in Berlin, Raeder had told him to 'insist on torpedo boats no matter what'. Now, apparently, the authorities thought it safe for him to proceed unescorted. At 1900 on 24 January Lütjens broke radio silence to inform Group North, 'Anchored [off Skaw] awaiting screen. Will move as planned on 25th'.[2]

Lütjens sailed at sunrise on 25 January, though not without misgivings. He had been grieved to find his escort reduced in numbers. Half the ships of the 1st Flotilla had been sent ahead to check his route for mines. (Half an escort and a skimpy search of the mined area – it had looked like the worst of both worlds!) In the late afternoon he told Group North that he could not accept responsibility for entering the mined area. At 1847 he received the Group Commander's reply: 'Probability of mines on route is low. Advanced sweep is investigating route. If mines found, intention is to break off *"Berlin"*. Because of operation's urgency, continue until then. CinC Navy agrees.'[3]

Reassured that the authorities were beginning to appreciate his predicament, Lütjens decided to continue. 'With this order and its endorsement,' he noted, 'the situation becomes completely clear to me. I would have been

35

spared much aggravation if I had received it sooner.' At least it was now clear where responsibility for any mishap would lie.

* * *

By dawn on 26 January Lütjens had crossed the Shetlands–Norway line. Leaving the Baltic had been a protracted affair, marked by incompetence and unnecessary delay. A passage that, in normal times, should have taken 36 hours had extended to more than three days. But he could now discount the risk of detection by enemy air patrols and consider his next moves.

The main question occupying his mind was whether he should make an immediate break for the Atlantic or whether he should refuel from the tanker *Adria*, positioned off Jan Mayen in case of need. His first inclination was to fuel. He was under no pressure to reach the Atlantic early. His orders required him to co-ordinate his actions with those of the *Hipper* – Group Command West had insisted on this, despite his protests – and it had become clear in recent hours that the cruiser would not be ready to resume operations until the end of the month. Lütjens had time in hand. He could usefully spend it refuelling in the Arctic Ocean and make his appearance on the convoy routes on or about 2 February. He turned north accordingly.

But towards evening on 26 January the Staff meteorologist forecast low visibility and flurries of snow in the area south of Iceland, conditions that would be ideal for a break-out. The need to fuel was not pressing. Lütjens kept to his northerly course for the moment but decided that, if the forecasts were confirmed, he would seize his opportunity. The meteorologist stood by his predictions and, in the early hours of 27 January, Lütjens turned his squadron to the south-west.

He moved with caution for intelligence was sparse. A German aircraft had looked into the Firth of Forth 36 hours earlier, but there had been no reconnaissance over the enemy's main fleet base at Scapa Flow for six days. There had been nothing in the air waves, on the other hand, to suggest that the enemy had got wind of his movements or that the Home Fleet was at sea. Yet Lütjens was uneasy. His *B-Dienst* (radio intelligence) team had heard several merchant ships reporting unidentified warships in the area south of Iceland, and Reykjavik radio had reported the sighting of what was thought to be a submarine. 'These repeated false reports,' Lütjens recorded, 'show a marked confusion in this area and lead to the conclusion that the area is being watched more closely than before.'[4]

By 6 o'clock in the morning of 28 January Lütjens was approaching the area of greatest danger. Twilight of an Arctic morning was just beginning to show. Visibility was poor. The *Gneisenau's* radar was defective, but the technicians were promising that all would be well in a few minutes. Lütjens continued to lead his formation.

Just after 6 o'clock a look-out reported a dim shadow on the starboard beam. Lütjens wheeled briefly to port to give the shadow a wider berth and resumed his course to the south-west. Twenty minutes later another shadow appeared, this time on the port bow. The alarm was given and the battlecruisers wheeled sharply to starboard. It had been difficult to determine the vessel's type: it was possibly a destroyer, perhaps even a small cruiser. The distance was estimated at between four and five miles.

Lütjens was preparing to swing back to the south-west when a new shape appeared on the port bow, this time at close range. A turn to port was out of the question. Lütjens again wheeled sharply to starboard, increasing to 28kts as he did so. His course was now north-east. The ship had been a cruiser with two funnels; it had been signalling to another unit somewhere to the north-west. The range had been about two miles.

By 0635 the latest enemy was dropping rapidly astern and it was now that the flagship's radar first began to present Lütjens with a clearer picture of the situation. At some 7,000yds on his starboard beam there appeared to be one large contact and four or five smaller ones. The position matched the first contact that he had stumbled on. It now seemed to be a cruiser with a flotilla of destroyers in company. The risk of torpedo attack seemed slight, but, to be on the safe side, Lütjens ordered flank speed.

As he drew away from this formation Lütjens began to adjust his course to port, hoping to work his way to the north and west of the enemy, but at 0656 his radar reported a new contact on his port side. The patrol line seemed to extend north-westward indefinitely, conceivably as far as Iceland itself. Should he attempt to outflank the enemy to the south instead? Lütjens decided against it. It would be light in an hour and the cruisers astern of him were probably in contact. He had no definite knowledge of the situation in Scapa Flow, but, given the unusual strength of the enemy in the area, he had to assume that a major fleet operation was in progress and that there would be one or more battle groups to the south-west. If he continued in his break-out attempt he might easily meet them in daylight. It seemed better, all things considered, to wait for a more favourable opportunity, to retire at high speed to the eastward hoping to shake off the cruisers before full daylight. He could then set a refuelling rendezvous for the *Adria* and, in due course, make his break-out under less hazardous conditions.

By 0740 radar observations showed that the two cruisers were still dropping astern. Unaccountably, they seemed not to be giving chase. But at 0748 a new target was detected to the north-west and it seemed to be closing rapidly. Almost immediately the radio monitoring team intercepted an urgent signal from this unit, apparently an enemy report. Lütjens altered to starboard. Almost imperceptibly the range began to open and the bearing of the contact to drift slowly astern. The enemy seemed to be steering to the north-east and had not, apparently, detected the battlecruisers' change of course. At 0830 Lütjens adjusted his course still further to starboard to put more distance between himself and the enemy so that, when full daylight came, there would be no chance that he would be seen.

When the sun came up the horizon was empty. There were no contacts on radar. The enemy, the Admiral recorded, 'appears to be completely confused by the events of this morning. At least, his signal traffic has not been affected by them in any way.'[5]

* * *

The Admiralty had received first tentative intelligence that a break-out might be in the offing more than a week earlier. The new Commander-in-Chief Home Fleet, Admiral Sir John Tovey, had at once reinforced his cruiser patrols in the Iceland–Faeroes passage. Then, during the evening of 25 January, he had been informed that two heavy ships had been seen leaving the Great Belt during the morning of the 23rd.[6] He had sailed at once with the *Nelson*, *Rodney* and *Repulse* and a force of eight cruisers and eleven destroyers and taken up a position some 120 miles south of Iceland from which he would be able to cover all likely routes to the Atlantic. He had arranged for intensive air patrols in the sector Iceland–Faeroes. If a break-out were intended (there could be no certainty), it would come during the nights 25/26 or, perhaps, 26/27 January.

By morning on 28 January nearly five days had elapsed since the sighting in the Great Belt and Tovey had begun to question the assumptions that he was acting on. He had certainly come to recognise that his decision to bring the whole fleet with him had been precipitate, and, to prolong his operations, he had sent the *Rodney* and a handful of cruisers and destroyers back to Scapa to refuel. He meanwhile had kept his remaining ships within easy range of Hvalfjord, where he could refuel his destroyers. During the early hours of 28 January he had been steering an easterly course with his cruisers spread out in a broad arc around him.

At 0640 the *Naiad*, stationed on the port bow of the flagship, saw what appeared to be two large ships to the south-east. They were on a converging course. At 0649 she reported them as 'two unknown ships' on a bearing of 110°. Ten minutes later she added that they were steering north-east and that she was giving chase. Tovey turned the fleet in the same direction and ordered the *Repulse* forward to provide support.

But the two shadows, half-glimpsed against the eastern horizon, had quickly disappeared. At 0700 the *Naiad*'s look-outs had been able to make out just one; it was later suggested that the ships might have separated. By 0715 nothing could be seen at all, a fleeting radar contact providing the only additional clue that something tangible had been there. The cruisers swept north-eastward at their best speed for several hours, but nothing further was seen. By early afternoon Tovey had concluded that it was pointless to continue and had told the Admiralty that he was returning to Scapa. It had been hard to make sense of the incident. It was puzzling, given the direction of the *Naiad*'s first sighting, that no other ship in the screen had seen anything. The course of the supposed enemy defied explanation and the *Naiad* had been notably vague about identity. The weather had been deceptive. The evidence, Tovey later told the Admiralty, had been 'far from conclusive'. Visibility had been patchy; snow squalls had made radar reception 'misleading'. There was a small possibility that a fast ship might have worked round to the north of the formation and escaped to the westward, but he thought it unlikely that an enemy ship had been present.[7]

* * *

What had given Lütjens the critical edge? It was not, as some have assumed, the superiority of German surface warning radar. The Fleet Commander's war diaries make it clear that alert look-outs played the more important part in the crucial early minutes of the encounter. In the weather conditions prevailing, radar was a source of confusion, a hindrance to both sides. The difference seems to lie in speed of reaction. German evasion was prompt and immediate; the British pursuit lethargic in comparison. The delays that had attended Lütjens' departure from the Baltic seem certainly to have contributed to this. Towards the end of their third consecutive night in Arctic waters, some, it seems, had lost faith in what they were doing.

That said, Lütjens had handled his squadron with considerable skill. As the situation unfolded, he had reacted with the instinctive assurance of a man who has rehearsed his moves beforehand. His command system had served him well, and he had been able to integrate information from a variety of sources –the human eye, radar and radio surveillance. Despite the pressure of events, he had preserved his capacity for rigorous analysis and logical decision-making. It was a performance very much in the tradition of those old masters, Hipper and Scheer, who had turned disengagement and evasion into a fine art.

As the battlecruisers continued their withdrawal during the daylight hours of 28 January, little happened to disturb the Fleet Commander's peace of mind. The masts of what appeared to be a cruiser of the *Dido* class were sighted to the south-west shortly before midday and Lütjens made a brief alteration to port, judging that he would not be seen against the darkening eastern horizon. In the afternoon he sent two short coded signals[8] to Group North reporting his encounter with the enemy and his decision to withdraw. He then ran east at 24kts, intending to launch an aircraft for Trondheim with a full account of what had occurred.[9]

At 1040 in the morning of 29 January Lütjens told Group North that he intended to break out through the Denmark Strait and, shortly afterwards, sent his aircraft ashore. He then turned north to rendezvous with his tanker in the Arctic Ocean.

* * *

Lütjens had expected that fuelling would take two days. In the event, the numbing cold on the decks of the battlecruisers and the need to break off the operation from time to time to search for water that was clear of ice made it longer still, and it was not until late on 1 February that the task force, tanks now full, was ready to proceed. The interval had been one of frustration for the Admiral. He suspected now that the *Hipper* would reach the convoy routes before him and, no doubt, set off a chain of precautionary moves that would greatly complicate his task. But the long interval had given him time to review what had happened during that early dawn south of Iceland and to weigh up the choices open to him.

The events of 28 January, he now thought, had a number of unexplained features. The spacing of the British cruisers was the first problem. With a spacing of five miles, the enemy could not possibly have hoped to cover more than a small part of the area concerned. Then there was the extraordinary lethargy of the enemy reaction. The British cruiser had been in no hurry to report his presence, and even then had mentioned only 'two unknown ships' on a north-easterly course. After that, there had been little sign of an increase in air patrols. It had been too easy, perhaps, to leap to the conclusion that the enemy had been warned of his departure and was lying in wait for him. It seemed more likely that this had been a random encounter with the cruiser screen either of some important convoy or of the Home Fleet deployed for reasons unconnected with his movement. 'I therefore assume,' he wrote, 'that, so far, the enemy has had no report of the battleships being at sea.'[10]

Yet he had to reconcile this conclusion with indications from radio intelligence of 'a marked turbulence' in enemy activity throughout the Atlantic. To the west of Iceland and in the north-west approaches to the United Kingdom, a zone which Lütjens referred to as the 'convoy reception area', merchant ships, all sailing independently, were receiving a stream of routing amendments. Naval units, it seemed , were also being redeployed. And the same thing seemed to be happening off Bermuda, Freetown and the Falklands. Did this restless activity suggest that the enemy was making precautionary moves throughout the Atlantic in anticipation of his arrival? Lütjens concluded that it did not. The patterns were consistent with the activities of U-boats and, further afield, of the *Admiral Scheer* and the auxiliary cruisers. It was consistent, too, with the increase in independent sailings that was being reported by German agents in the United States.

Having satisfied himself that the prospects for successful operations in the Atlantic remained relatively favourable, Lütjens turned to the question of his break-out plan. Although he acknowledged that the enemy's strength south

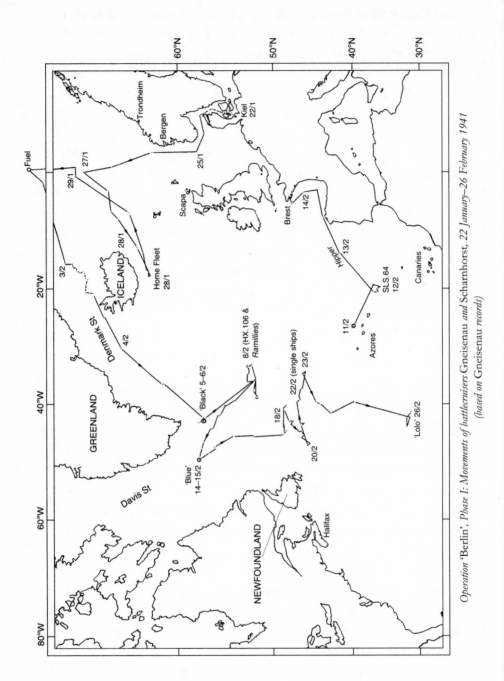

Operation 'Berlin', Phase I: Movements of battlecruisers Gneisenau and Scharnhorst, 22 January–26 February 1941 (based on Gneisenau records)

of Iceland had been unusual and that it was probably unsustainable over the long term, his mind was turning increasingly to the advantages of the Denmark Strait. Admiral Carls (Group North), he recalled, had advised against it because of the lack of sea room between the ice edge and the land; and there had been no reconnaissance of the area since the*Hipper*'s departure nearly two months before. But there were many factors in its favour. Enemy air reconnaissance would be weak, perhaps non-existent, and there was the virtual certainty of low visibility along the ice edge. The Strait was undoubtedly narrow and the room for evasive manoeuvre limited. On the other hand, the British would not be able to use thin-skinned ships such as destroyers close to the ice boundary and the risk of torpedo attack would be relatively low. Above all, perhaps, his squadron would bypass the convoy reception area and minimise the risk of random encounters with powerful British forces. On the strength of these considerations, Lütjens decided in favour of the Denmark Strait. If the passage proved impracticable, he would reverse course and make another attempt at the southern route, aiming, this time, to keep rather further from the coast of Iceland.

* * *

The battlecruisers left their refuelling area off Jan Mayen in the early hours of 2 February and steamed rapidly south-westward until, some twenty-four hours later, they met the ice edge in longitude 15°W – the longitude, roughly, of the east coast of Iceland. Here they began to work their way westward, skirting the edges of the icefields, until, at 1800 on 3 February, they began to feel the effects of the Irminger current. Sea water temperature rose rapidly and the icefields receded northwards. Lütjens ordered full speed and steered to pass ten miles off the North Cape.

The squadron was now approaching the narrowest part of the passage, the area that was most likely to be patrolled by the enemy. Lütjens brought his ships to the action state. The narrows themselves were unguarded and ice-free but, at 0335 in the morning of 4 February, the*Gneisenau*'s radar operators reported a surface contact fine on the port bow at a range of seven miles. The vessel appeared to be steering north-west at 12kts. It was clearly a patrol vessel, probably an auxiliary cruiser; no merchant vessel making a passage of the Strait would be on such a course. The range closed slowly to five, four and finally three and a half miles and then began to open. There was no reaction on the part of the enemy.

At 0800 in the morning of 4 February Lütjens noted in his war diary, 'For all practical purposes I have reached the open Atlantic and remained undetected.' It was a moment for celebration. 'For the first time in military history,' he said in a signal to the *Gneisenau* and *Scharnhorst*, 'German battleships have succeeded in breaking out into the Atlantic. Now go to it!'[11]

* * *

On clearing the Denmark Strait Lütjens set course for point 'Black', a position some one hundred miles south of Cape Farewell, where he planned to meet the tanker *Schlettstadt*. He told Group West (his command authority from now on) that he would enter the operational zone on 10 February at the earliest. This, he recorded, was to 'prevent premature activities by the *Hipper*'. If fuelling went according to plan, he would get there a good deal earlier, but this, he reasoned, would not matter. You could not predict exactly when you might run into a convoy.

Lütjens could now consider his plans in detail. His best target, he decided, would be a convoy reported as leaving Halifax on 30 January and which would now be approaching mid-Atlantic. From his knowledge of the British convoy cycle he assumed it to be HX.108.[12]

If he were to find this convoy at its most vulnerable, he would need, he decided, to carry out his attack eastwards of 38°. He knew that two British capital ships, the *Ramillies* and the *Revenge*, were stationed in Canada and assumed, given the volume of traffic requiring their protection, that they could provide cover for the first thousand miles of the passage only. They would then retire westwards to refuel and pick up the next convoy. He would set his trap to the east of the battleship limit.

Eastbound convoys, he believed, ran north-eastward from Halifax, along the coast of Newfoundland, and onwards to the northern approaches to the United Kingdom in a broad swathe which, in mid-Atlantic, might be more than 200 miles wide. Lütjens felt that he could predict a convoy's easterly progress fairly accurately; the challenge would lie in achieving a sufficiently broad search front. He would, he decided, tackle the problem in stages. He would start at the northern limit of the convoy routes and, with his ships well spread, patrol to and fro across the enemy's line of advance, aiming to cover a sixty-mile strip by the evening of the first day. His ships would then join up, steam eastwards overnight to allow for convoy movement and begin the second sixty-mile strip at dawn next morning. He would thus cover the complete frontal width over four successive days.[13]

He did not expect to encounter westbound convoys in this area. Intelligence suggested that these kept well to the southward, ships dispersing to their various destinations on reaching longitude 45°W. He might well, on the other hand, meet ships sailing independently. They would be a threat to the security of his operations. They were to be evaded if possible; if not, their radio transmissions were to be jammed and the ships sunk.

The battlecruisers left their refuelling rendezvous at 1000 on 6 February and set course for the operational area. Lütjens took the opportunity to test the seakeeping qualities of his ships under Atlantic conditions. Head to sea, they appeared to behave well, but with the sea abeam they rolled abominably. The intelligence picture was becoming clearer. A new convoy was forming off Halifax, evidently HX.109 leaving on schedule. A slow convoy of up to 38 ships, probably SC.22, had just left Cape Breton; an auxiliary cruiser with 1,500 Canadian soldiers on board was due to join it. Force H had sailed from Gibraltar, probably to cover a southbound convoy.[14] Prospects seemed favourable.

The search began at dawn on 7 February. Nothing was sighted that day, and at dusk the ships joined up and set out for a new search line a hundred miles to the eastward. By dawn on 8 February they were in position, the *Scharnhorst* on the northern flank and the *Gneisenau* forty miles to the south and east. Visibility was good.

At 0835 look-outs on board the *Gneisenau* spotted a mast on the western horizon. It seemed suspiciously large – possibly a warship's fighting top. Soon other masts could be made out beyond it. Lütjens decided that the target must be approached with caution until the identity of the escort could be established. He turned away to the eastward to prevent the enemy from sighting him in turn, passed the target position to the *Scharnhorst* and gave his orders for a coordinated attack. 'Enemy steers north-east,' he signalled, 'intend attack from south; expect your attack from north at 1030.'[15]

Towards 1000 Lütjens turned back to the south-west to approach the target from its starboard bow. He was now virtually certain that the mast sighted by his look-outs was that of a warship but he was not yet ready to exclude the possibility that it belonged to the cruiser *Emerald*.[16] If this were so, the attack could safely continue. But at 0959 the *Scharnhorst* reported a battleship close to the convoy. Lütjens turned away and told the *Scharnhorst* to do the same. 'With a heavy heart,' he wrote in his diary, 'I must break off the attack.' He would turn his attention to the SC convoy that would soon be approaching his position. The outcome was clearly disappointing, but at least his search plan had proved itself and he had avoided disclosing his position. The element of surprise remained with him.[17]

It was worrying, nevertheless, to have found a battleship so far to the eastward. As he repositioned his squadron to search for the second convoy, Lütjens reconsidered his earlier assumptions. Was it possible that the enemy could be providing heavy cover over the central section of the Atlantic route, leaving the eastern and western extremities to be patrolled by light forces and aircraft? It seemed on reflection all too possible, and, worse still, a quick calculation suggested that the British would be able to cover two out of every three convoys in this way. The chances of finding the one convoy in three covered by a cruiser or auxiliary cruiser seemed remote; his search capability in this vast sea area was limited at best. The lack of scouting cruisers, the Admiral recorded a little ruefully, 'becomes daily more aggravating'. With four of them he could cover the entire width of the convoy route simultaneously. Their torpedo armament would be invaluable. Even destroyers would be better than nothing. 'If they were more seaworthy,' he recorded, 'I would accept the difficulty of refuelling them and use them in concert with the battlecruisers until something better came along.'[18]

The Fleet Commander's mood was already gloomy when he met the *Scharnhorst* at dusk that evening. When he received Captain Hoffmann's report on the day's events, gloom turned to anger. He learned that the *Scharnhorst* had closed to within twelve miles of the convoy in an attempt to draw the escort away to the northward. Hoffmann had identified the enemy as the *Ramillies* and had only turned away on receiving the order to break off the attack. From the Admiral's perspective, the *Scharnhorst*'s captain had erred on two counts. He had disobeyed explicit instructions to avoid opponents of equal strength. More seriously still, he had disclosed his presence to the enemy; the British would now bring in a range of counter-measures that would make operations in mid-Atlantic difficult if not impossible. Hoffmann's actions had been 'completely incomprehensible'. He had failed to show the 'tactical grasp' expected of a battlecruiser captain. Lütjens expressed his 'strongest disapproval' in a personal radio telephone call and then sent the signal, 'Urgently request strictest obedience to my orders in future.'[19]

* * *

As the ships took up their search positions for the morning of 9 February, Lütjens remained convinced that the *Scharnhorst*'s folly had seriously damaged his chances of success. Towards 1000 his fears were confirmed. A signal from Group West showed that, between noon and midnight the day before, a British unit in mid-Atlantic had briefly sighted one or more ships, possibly enemy.[20] Surprise had been lost. In all probability the British Admiralty was already preparing task forces for dispatch to the central Atlantic and issuing routing amendments to its convoys. The chances of finding a weakly defended target on the Halifax route over the next few days seemed remote. There was one possibility. There was a slim chance that the *Ramillies* might have mistaken the *Scharnhorst* for the *Hipper*. If the latter was now to make an appearance on the north–south convoy route, the enemy might be deceived into thinking that he was dealing with a single adversary and shift the focus of his attention to the south-eastward.

Lütjens was convinced that Group West would see things in the same light and waited on tenterhooks for the shore authority to act. By evening, he could wait no longer. At 2156 he signalled 'Operation has been detected by the enemy.' Group West took the hint and in the early hours of 10 February gave the *Hipper* freedom to begin operations.

Lütjens had decided by now that it would be unwise to remain in his present area beyond nightfall. But where should he go instead? He rejected the option of joining the *Hipper* on the southern route for the sound, if obvious, reason that by the time he arrived the alarm would have been raised there too. He rejected the option of searching for the single ships that he believed were routed to the north of his position since he had not given up hope of starting his campaign with an attack on a weakly defended convoy. The best course, he decided, was to lie low for a while. If *Hipper*'s operations in the south provided a successful diversion, he could return to the Halifax route in a few days time and again find it 'virgin territory'. This course of action, he thought, came closest to meeting Group West's broad concept for the campaign – the dislocation of British defensive arrangements by alternating attacks on the Halifax and southern routes. On the evening of 10 February, therefore, Lütjens set course for point 'Blue', a prearranged rendezvous in the Davis Strait, where he would take on fuel from the *Schlettstadt* and the *Esso Hamburg* and await developments.

As the battlecruisers withdrew northwards overnight, the air waves remained deceptively quiet. It was clear that the Home Fleet was missing from its base in Scapa Flow, but such evidence as there was pointed to an operation in the convoy reception area. Force H, which, it was now clear, had been operating off the Italian coast, was returning to Gibraltar. There was nothing in Group West's intelligence summaries to suggest any unusual activity on the part of the enemy or that a task force might be on its way to the central Atlantic. To the south-eastward, things seemed to be shaping up nicely. *U-37* had been shadowing a convoy northbound from Gibraltar for some days and was acting as a beacon for the *Hipper*. A meeting seemed likely from noon 11 February onwards. By the morning of 12 February it was clear that the meeting had taken place. The *Hipper* was claiming a spectacular success, but for some unaccountable reason she seemed, now, to be returning to Brest. Group West's disappointment had been obvious. 'Assume compelling reasons for [your] return;' he had signalled to the cruiser, 'otherwise fuel and ammunition from *Brehme* and stay at sea for diversionary effect.'[21]

But by now Lütjens was preoccupied with other things. As he made for his rendezvous off Greenland he had run into an Arctic storm that had tested the sea-keeping qualities of his ships to the limit. Head to sea, the battlecruisers had slammed and shuddered so badly that their captains had feared structural damage. Beam to sea, their behaviour had been even worse. During the evening of 12 February the *Scharnhorst* reported that severe rolling had unseated a turret. Later, incoming water had damaged an electrical switchboard. At midnight she had reported all but three of her anti-aircraft guns non-operational and the fire control directors of her main and secondary batteries out of alignment. He would need, so Captain Hoffmann reported, a three-day breathing space to bring his ship back to operational readiness.

* * *

It was not until 16 February, eight days after his meeting with the *Ramillies*, that Lütjens could begin to consider his options once again. The intelligence picture was less than clear. Force H had sailed from Gibraltar, evidently in response to actions by the *Hipper*, and was still at sea. Its position could only be guessed at. There were several indications that a major fleet operation had been under way in the general area of the Azores and Canaries at the time of the *Hipper*'s appearance on the southern route.[22] If so, this could only have involved units of the Home Fleet. British communiqués had hinted at Home Fleet actions over a vast front, but the purpose of those actions and the position of the major units had remained obscure. There was little, however, to suggest an immediate threat to a renewal of German operations on the Halifax route.

As Lütjens came south to renew operations his plans were again directed towards specific targets. Although there were indications that the British had changed the departure dates for SC convoys, HX convoys seemed to be forming and sailing according to plan. There were signs, too, that a number of unscheduled convoys were being prepared. There were reports that the 3rd Canadian Division was embarking and that their movement was to be covered by the battlecruiser *Repulse*. The German Naval Attaché in Washington had reported that a special convoy made up of ships from American ports had been assembling east of Halifax on the 15th. It would have left by now. Lütjens decided that his first target would be HX.111. Following the lessons learned earlier in the month, he would begin his search well to the westward, where convoy escort would, as he thought, be limited to light forces only.

He began his operations at dawn on 17 February. Two days of searching produced no result and, by evening on the 19th he had concluded that HX.111 and the special convoy reported by the Naval Attaché must have eluded him. Monitoring of merchant ship wavelengths suggested that what little movement there was remained well to the south-west. Lütjens decided to turn his attention to the next Halifax convoy, HX.112, and to move his search operation still further to the westward in the hope of intercepting the convoy in 48°W, four days after its scheduled departure. Given moderate weather, he would use his aircraft to help in the search.

The evening signals brought gentle hints that the shore authorities were becoming impatient with the lengthy silence on the Atlantic sea lanes. '[It] remains unclear,' signalled Group West, 'whether enemy is expecting heavy cruisers in [the] North Atlantic. If appearance of task force is delayed by decision based on enemy situation, we approve.' But the enemy situation was not the problem: the source of his difficulties, Lütjens reflected, lay in an inadequate search capability. 'The difficulties of locating a convoy without any reconnaissance at all,' he recorded, 'are far greater than was generally assumed.'[23]

During 20 February the task force steamed south-westward to take up its new search position. Aircraft from both ships would search up to 100 miles ahead; they were to keep radio silence and were to remain undetected at all costs. But as the ships drew closer to the Labrador current the visibility began to close in. Flying was cancelled. By evening the visibility was 1,500m or less. Lütjens turned his squadron to the eastward, hoping to find better conditions the next day.

The search for convoy HX.112 continued through 21 February. Frustration increased. Towards noon the *Scharnhorst* asked permission to close the flagship to send a message by signal lamp. Captain Hoffmann reported a close encounter with a merchant ship that had emerged suddenly from a fog bank. He had been seen for certain, although there had been no sign that the ship had made a report. He believed that the search had now extended too far towards the routes used by single ships sailing westbound and recommended a 'change in the whole search plan'. The Admiral's response was abrupt. 'Resume previous positions,' he signalled to his ships, 'prepare one aircraft each for Search Plan C, direction south-west. Be ready to launch by 1400.'[24] The presence of single ships did not exclude the possibility that convoys might use the area as well. It was even possible, Lütjens reflected, that the enemy might be using single ships as advanced scouts for the protection of convoys.

The long fallow period was now coming to an end. More by accident than by design, Lütjens had stumbled on an area where ships released from westbound convoys made their way singly to their various destinations. During the night of 21/22 February several ships, all steering south-west, passed within range of German radar. As dawn broke on a bright clear morning, look-outs in the *Gneisenau* could see one large vessel on the eastern horizon, two ships to the north, the nearest a tanker at about twenty miles, and the smoke of a fourth ship away to the south-east. Lütjens felt himself 'surrounded by ships'. It would be hard for him to remain unseen. He could see four potential targets, and, with visibility good and seas calm, he could reasonably hope to take them all. Lütjens decided that he had better seize his opportunity. He cancelled plans for flying operations, assigned the two northerly ships to the *Scharnhorst* and set off to close the ship on the eastern horizon.

As the range closed, watchers in the *Gneisenau* could begin to make out the characteristics of the ship ahead. She seemed to be a cargo vessel of some size. There was a gun on the foredeck. At twelve miles, the ship turned away abruptly. Monitoring teams listened for any sign of a raider report; soon after 10 o'clock they heard the start of a transmission and at once began to jam the frequency. Lütjens ordered a shot across the bow. Five minutes later, with no sign of compliance on the part of the enemy, he brought his secondary batteries into action. The ship began to heave to. At 1024 she started to transmit again; Lütjens brought his main battery into play at a range of 9,000m. The target was soon burning fiercely. She was the *Kantara*, 3,273 tons, carrying general cargo and three aircraft. She sank at 1055, the *Gneisenau* taking her crew of 37 on board.

Lütjens now set off to the southward in pursuit of the second ship and by midday he had caught up with her. She, too, had tried to make a run for it and to broadcast a warning. She was the *Trelawny*, 4,689 tons, sailing in ballast. Lütjens dealt with her in the same way.

By mid-afternoon he had added a third ship to his tally, while, forty miles to the northward, the *Scharnhorst* had caught and sunk the tanker *Lustrous*. Jamming procedures had been working well: none of the victims so far had succeeded in clearing a raider report. But this was about to change. While disposing of his most recent victim, Lütjens had launched an aircraft to maintain contact with a further target that had appeared on the eastern horizon. The pilot's orders had been specific: he was to locate and shadow the enemy. Yet the ship concerned had broadcast a warning that she was being attacked by aircraft. The reasons behind this unauthorised initiative became clear when the aircraft returned. The pilot had found the ship 30 miles to the north-east of the *Gneisenau* and had identified her as the SS *Harlesden*; he had ordered her to close the battlecruiser. When she had failed to comply, he had attacked with bombs and raked her decks with machine-gun fire.

Lütjens was indignant. The pilot's action had been foolish in the extreme. He had undermined the careful precautions taken to keep the enemy in ignorance of the day's events. And it was hardly credible that the ship would keep to its ordered course once the aircraft had left the scene. The chances of finding the ship in the few hours of daylight remaining appeared very low indeed. But soon after 9 o'clock that night, in full darkness, the *Gneisenau*'s radar operators detected a contact on the starboard bow at nine miles. The flagship turned to close, and, with the range at little more than a mile, put her searchlights on the target and opened fire. It was the same ship. She sank at 2308, 33 of her crew of 41 being picked up. This sinking brought the tally for the day to five ships totalling 25,784 tons.

* * *

A month after leaving German waters, Lütjens had finally opened his account. In some respects at least, the ideas of the cruiser warfare theorists had been vindicated. He had made his way through British lines and operated freely in the enemy's sensitive rear areas. He had retained the initiative; his freedom of action had never been put at risk. But he had been unable so far to turn that freedom of action into genuine military success. The source of his difficulties was obvious. The scheduling and routing of convoys remained a riddle; the shore authorities had little feel for the complexities of the problem. Group West had responded to Lütjens' brief report on the events of 22 February by listing the positions and routes of all Atlantic convoys believed to be at sea. 'These theoretically calculated positions,' Lütjens had recorded in his diary, 'add nothing new. They agree with my own calculations . . . and only confirm that there is no new information available ashore.'

With only two ships, finding convoys was largely a matter of luck. From now on, he would have to bring in the *Hipper* – or, failing that, at least two of the supply ships – and run a broader search along rather than across the convoy routes. 'This,' Lütjens wrote, 'will increase the likelihood of sighting a convoy by a vast amount, even if it is running several days late. The risk to the supply ships must be accepted.'[25]

Notes to Chapter 2

1 Müllenheim-Rechberg, p. 89.
2 PG34677, entries for 24 and 25 January 1941.
3 *Ibid.*, entry for 1847, 25 January 1941.
4 *Ibid.*, entry for 2140, 27 January 1941.
5 *Ibid.*, entry at 1000, 28 January 1941.
6 The initial warning had come from traffic analysis. The sighting in the Great Belt had been passed to London by the British Naval Attaché in Stockholm, Captain H. W. Denham, whose name will feature again. Tovey had acted on Admiralty Message 1751/25 January. PRO ADM 234-327, p. 276.
7 CinC signal 0027/31 January 1941, PRO ADM 234-327, p. 278.
8 *Kurzsignal*: a 'brevity code' providing alphanumeric groups for standard messages.
9 Lütjens would come to regret a decision which left the *Gneisenau* with a single Arado floatplane. He had been determined, it seems, to pre-empt criticism. We will meet this characteristic again.
10 PG34677, entry for 1600, 1 February 1941.
11 *Ibid.*, entries for 4 February 1941.
12 'HX' series convoys assembled in Halifax, Nova Scotia, and were for fast ships. The convoy referred to here was, in fact, HX.106. Slow ships assembled at Sydney, Cape Breton, and were prefixed 'SC'. For a list of British convoy designators see Roskill, Stephen, *The War at Sea*, Vol. 1 (London: HMSO, 1954), Appendix J.
13 The Fleet Commander's plans for intercepting convoys were rather more sophisticated than those of Admiral Dönitz at this period. See, for example, the very amateurish assessment of the problem set out in the BdU War Diary for 6 May 1941, PG30288, p. 65.
14 Here German intelligence was mistaken. Force H had sailed eastwards for the bombardment of Genoa (Operation 'Grog'). It did not leave the Mediterranean to support convoys on the north–south route until 12 February. See Admiral Somerville's ROPs for 5–11 February and 11–25 February 1941, *The Somerville Papers*, Navy Records Society, Aldershot (Scolar Press), 1995, pp. 244–7.
15 PG34677, entry for 0838, 8 February 1941.
16 German intelligence was at fault here. The *Emerald* was escorting a troop convoy off the Cape of Good Hope. She would shortly become involved in the search for the *Admiral Scheer* in the Indian Ocean.
17 The flagship's special intelligence section monitored enemy radio frequencies but in this instance detected nothing to suggest that a sighting had occurred. PG34677, 8 February 1941.

18   PG34677, entry for 1200, 8 January 1941.

19   *Ibid.*, 8 February 1941. The charge that Hoffmann had disobeyed Group West directives appears somewhat harsh. If he had risked an action at all, the risk was a small one. And Lütjens had himself given what could be construed as an order to attack. The second charge seems closer to the mark. Lütjens's conduct of the sortie so far betrays a total preoccupation with secrecy and surprise. Hoffmann's action shows he was not well tuned to his Admiral's thinking on the subject.

20   Group West's message appears to be a paraphrase of HMS *Ramillies'* signal of 1050/8 February reporting a 'brief glimpse of mast and top of warship, possibly German *Hipper* class'. The text is in Broome, p. 102.

21   PG34677, entry for 1100, 12 February 1941. By the time of the *Hipper*'s arrival the convoy from Gibraltar had dispersed, but during the night of 11/12 February the cruiser had encountered an unescorted convoy homebound from Sierra Leone (SLS.64). Unopposed, she had sunk seven ships and damaged two others severely. Her decision to return to Brest rather than replenish at sea appears to have been based on a shortage of ammunition and on the forecast of foul weather.

22   This assessment appears to have been based on reported sightings of battle-ships, carriers and cruisers by fishing boats. It is clear that too much reliance was placed on this information.

23   PG34677, 19 February 1941. Admiral Dönitz would learn the same lesson when he, too, began to move his forces westwards from May 1941 onwards.

24   *Ibid.*, entry for 1238, 21 February 1941.

25   *Ibid.*, entries for 23 and 25 February 1941.

3

Operation 'Berlin': The Experiment Continues

Before resuming active operations, Lütjens had to consider refuelling his squadron, replenishing food and ammunition and resting his men. His ships had been at sea for more than a month and, for most of that time, men had been tied to their action stations. Main armament crews had been allowed to relax by day in conditions of good visibility, but secondary batteries had been kept at full alert throughout. There was a need to relieve the tension and to catch up on routine maintenance that, in past weeks, had become sorely neglected. Lütjens decided that he would make for point 'Lolo', a rendezvous position in the unfrequented ocean wastes south-west of the Azores, replenish from the supply ships *Ermland* and *Uckermark*, transfer prisoners (their numbers had become something of an embarrassment) and give his men a two- or three-day break.

A glimpse of conditions on board the battlecruisers as well as of the Admiral's precise attention to detail is to be found in orders addressed to both ships on the evening of 24 February:

> *Intention.* During passage to point 'Lolo', during the wait there, and when returning to the area of operations, crews are to be relieved as much as possible.

> *Execution.* Today, sleep fully clothed in hammocks, tomorrow undressed.

> *Duration of stay.* Remain at 'Lolo' at least until 1 March. By day, surface and AA look-outs only. By night, half-crews only, depending on visibility.[1]

The task group arrived at point 'Lolo' during the afternoon of 26 February. It was too rough for fuelling and, while waiting for the seas to abate, Lütjens moved his force to the eastward. He had become worried about the security of 'Lolo'. Several Spanish and Portuguese ships seemed from their position reports to have passed uncomfortably close. The support ships had seen nothing but the Admiral knew from personal observation that their look-out was slack.

Prospects for a few carefree days in sparkling weather south-west of the Azores were already under threat. Lütjens was considering alternative plans; he had just heard that the *Hipper*'s departure from Brest had been delayed and he had begun to think in terms of a thrust towards the Sierra Leone convoy routes. If he could divert enemy attention towards the Canaries and Cape Verdes, he would create the conditions for a new and successful attack on the Halifax routes when the cruiser finally became available. Lütjens postponed a decision pending news of Force H. He did not have to wait for long. On the evening of 25 February Group West reported that the battlecruiser *Renown*, flagship of Vice-Admiral Sir John Somerville, and the aircraft carrier *Ark Royal* had entered Gibraltar from the west. The way was now open. Lütjens decided to move forward as soon as fuelling was finished and to leave the rest period and the resupply of food and ammunition until later.

Lütjens began to study the movements of Sierra Leone convoys at once. As far as he could see, northbound convoys left Freetown at intervals of nine days. On occasion, it seemed, additional convoys were added to the cycle. (German intelligence referred to them as 'SLS convoys'.) These appeared to sail a day earlier than their routine counterparts and to reach the United Kingdom a day later. If fuelling went according to plan, he would attempt to catch SL.67 as it crossed latitude 35°N, about 150 miles south-east of the Azores. Failing that, he would aim for a point further south and intercept the next convoys – SL.68 and its slower component SLS.68 – once they had passed north of the Cape Verde Islands. 'Besides good results,' he noted, 'I expect long-lasting strategic effects from [my] appearance in these waters. I will inform Group Command of my intention to operate in the U-boat zone when refuelling is complete.'[2]

But when Lütjens told Group West of his intentions, he received a new assessment of traffic patterns which suggested that convoys were leaving Freetown ahead of schedule and that the interval between fast and slow components had increased. The change, Group West suggested, had been introduced so that a single task force could cover both convoys in the area between the Canaries and the Azores, the most dangerous part of their passage. Though disturbed by this apparent disagreement between Group Command and the intelligence authorities in Berlin, Lütjens decided to act on the new information. He would forget about SL.67 and look for the next pair of convoys, which, he now calculated, would pass the latitude of the

Canaries on 4 and 6 March. His new search area, he persuaded himself, had several advantages. There would be less danger of meeting single ships and thus of losing surprise; calmer weather would favour the use of aircraft; and the area was further removed from Gibraltar and from Force H.

At midday on 28 February, fuelling and the transfer of prisoners safely completed, the task force set out for its new zone of operations. The passage was uneventful and Lütjens took the opportunity to instruct his captains on some of the finer points of cruiser warfare. They were warned about profligate waste of ammunition. Scout aircraft were to remain undetected at all costs; if they detected a warship, they were to determine the type and return immediately. Radio deception procedures were to improve; the *Scharnhorst* was told to be less stiff and military and to introduce some slang into her messages.

* * *

Lütjens reached the latitude of the Canaries early on 3 March and began his search. He set his start line well north to allow for uncertainties in convoy departure date and, during the hours of daylight, ran southward. At dusk he reversed course to ensure that his quarry could not slip past him in the dark.

Over the next days the aircraft which Lütjens had been counting on to extend the width of his search became a source of aggravation and disappointment. Flying had been abandoned on the first day because the sea had been too high for recovery. Then, on 4 March, the *Gneisenau*'s aircraft had been damaged while landing. (Lütjens put it down to carelessness on the part of the pilot.) The machine would, it seemed, be out of action during the two critical days when the convoys could be expected 'with *some degree of certainty*'.[3] Restricting the *Gneisenau* to a single aircraft, the Admiral reflected, had been a grave mistake. The lack of a hangar was having 'serious negative effects'. He would demand a hangar for two aircraft as soon as he got back.[4]

Worse was to come. That same afternoon (4 March) one of the *Scharnhorst*'s aircraft lost its way and made a forced landing. The battlecruiser left the search area to recover it. Lütjens gave Captain Hoffmann a sharp reminder of his responsibilities. A few short directional transmissions would have helped the aircraft find its way back. As it was, the search that afternoon had

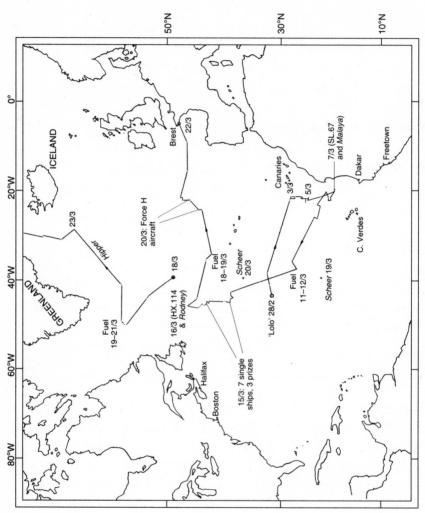

Operation 'Berlin', Phase II: Movements of battlecruisers Gneisenau and Scharnhorst, 28 February–22 March 1941 (based on Gneisenau records)

been a total loss. 'Breaking radio silence in this situation,' the Admiral recorded, 'is less serious than the tactical repercussions.'[5]

Lütjens was now certain that 5 March would be the critical day. Radio intelligence teams were reporting that Force H, or parts of it, were operating west of Gibraltar – a sure sign that the convoys must be approaching. For Lütjens, it was 'certain confirmation' that the convoy departure dates calculated by Group West were correct. There was every prospect of a successful action given only that aircraft were serviceable, that visibility was reasonable and that convoys were routed between the longitudes of 20° and 23°W.

But the day passed like the ones before it. The *Gneisenau*'s technicians had risen to the occasion and got their aircraft ready for the morning. By late afternoon it had completed two full sorties but had seen nothing. And it had now become clear that Force H was back in Gibraltar. As darkness came, Lütjens calculated that he had searched an area of nearly 30,000 square miles. His failure to find anything could only mean that convoys were following a different route or working to a different timetable. Of the two, the second seemed the most likely. He decided to ignore Group West's advice and to base his future plans on the original convoy schedule given him by the authorities in Berlin. That night he ran south, intending to begin his search again in latitude 24°N, roughly mid-way between the Canaries and the Cape Verde Islands.

Plans were now disrupted by developments of a different kind. Shortly before midnight the *Gneisenau* intercepted a U-boat signal reporting two 'heavy ships' and giving the exact position of the task force. The danger of mistaken identity seemed very real. Lütjens increased speed and cleared his force to the westward. To his intense annoyance, there appeared to be no way of resolving the problem quickly. A key code for the transmission of short signals between ships and submarines had not been issued. The only option was to inform the shore authorities and hope that they would sort things out. Lütjens told his ships that he would keep well clear of the search area until all doubts were dispelled.

As dawn approached, Lütjens turned back towards his search area. He remained less than satisfied with U-boat headquarters' attempts to clarify the situation, but he needed to get on with his search. At 10 o'clock he made contact with *U-124* and satisfied himself that all U-boats making for the zone

59

of operations off Freetown were aware of his presence. But the late start and further problems with aircraft restricted his coverage; by evening, he had concluded that both convoys must have passed his patrol line, whatever schedule they were working to.

Time was now running short. Lütjens calculated that the next northbound convoys, SLS.69 and SL.69, would reach the line of the Cape Verde Islands between 8 and 12 March. (It depended on which version of the convoy timetable was to be believed.) He had fuel enough to reach the Cape Verdes and operate there for three days; he would then need to break off and make for his refuelling rendezvous. It was worth a try. The aircraft situation remained 'highly unsatisfactory' – two of his three aircraft were beyond repair and the third an uncertain quantity – but there would be a heavy concentration of traffic in the focal zone between the islands and the African mainland and the scope for diversionary routing would be strictly limited. That night Lütjens ran south to take up his new search line. Force H was reported as being in Gibraltar; signal traffic in that area was 'very lively'. Signal traffic in the Freetown area was reported as 'normal'.[6]

* * *

The first signs of a change of fortune reached Lütjens at 0954 in the morning of 7 March when the *Scharnhorst* reported, 'Enemy battleship in quadrant 9948; enemy steers west.'[7] He at once concluded that he was dealing with a northbound convoy, as yet unsighted, with a battleship stationed ahead of it. He decided to take a look for himself and, recalling the unfortunate events of the month before, ordered the *Scharnhorst* to join him well to the east of the position reported.

As he steered for the rendezvous, Lütjens made out the masts of a convoy on the northern horizon. His assessment of the situation had been correct; but the convoy – only the second in more than a month of searching – was again escorted by a battleship. Should he let it go in the hope of finding a weakly defended convoy further south? Or should he make the most of his present opportunity? The new factor in the situation was the presence of U-boats. He might be unable to attack the convoy himself but he could at least help the U-boats to make contact; they might even dispose of the battleship. Acting as a scout for U-boats was not the role that he would have chosen for himself and it would hardly appeal to his ships' companies; but the chance was too good to miss. Lütjens decided that he would shadow the target and direct the U-boats towards it.

But how could he put his ideas into effect without disclosing his position to enemy D/F stations? In the absence of a short signal format for use between surface ships and submarines, the best that he could do was to send a key code message to the shore authorities and hope that they would recognise the possibilities of the situation. At 1140 he sent the message, 'Very strongly protected convoy in quadrant 9919.'

There followed a tense period of waiting. Nearly an hour and a half went by and still no German signal station had acknowledged his message or passed it on to the operational authorities. At 1300 Lütjens sent the message again. 'I am beside myself with rage at the failure of the Communications Service,' he noted in his War Diary:

> [T]hey have done this twice already, this year and last, when important signals sent from Norwegian waters were treated in the same way. While operations are in progress, listening posts *must* be constantly manned . . . and it *must* be made certain that the significance of signals is recognised and that they are passed on immediately to Group Command. For future operations I will make sure that direct communications between ships and submarines are possible. It is absolutely unacceptable to have two navies making war, one on the surface and the other below it. It is already bad enough that the navy and the air force have to speak different languages.[8]

At 1324 Group West confirmed that both messages had been received and understood. By mid afternoon Lütjens knew that U-Boat Command had given directions to the submarines. He conceded, a little grudgingly, that the operation seemed to be working.

Throughout the afternoon of 7 March the task force held its position off the eastern flank of the convoy at the extreme limit of visibility. The enemy battleship was the *Malaya*; there was at least one other warship with the convoy and possibly two. It was hard to tell whether they had detected the German presence; when questioned on the matter, Captain Hoffmann had seemed a little uncertain.

As night approached, Lütjens dropped back to take up a position astern of the convoy. He had no wish to expose himself to a night torpedo attack by the convoy escort or to get in the way of the U-boats. He waited with growing impatience for the U-boats to make contact with the target; he could devote one more day to putting them in touch, then he would have to leave for his refuelling position.

* * *

Dawn on 8 March found the Fleet Commander still trailing astern of the convoy. Thanks to his reports, two U-boats (*U-124* and later *U-105*) had made contact with the enemy during the night and both had succeeded in pressing home their attacks. But both had since lost touch. Lütjens waited to see whether they would regain contact without further intervention on his part. He had been monitoring enemy wavelengths carefully. There had been a marked increase in the volume of signal traffic addressed to Force H, and Freetown radio had sent an 'immediate' signal to all merchant ships off the West African coast – a most unusual event. The patterns in enemy signal traffic were much the same as those which had followed the *Hipper*'s attack on SLS.64 nearly a month earlier. Everything pointed to the conclusion that the presence of the task force had been detected and that counter-measures were being prepared.

At midday the U-boats were still out of touch. Lütjens left his trailing position and moved forward to relocate the convoy himself. At 1330 his look-outs made out the enemy battleship on the eastern horizon. There was another warship, possibly a light cruiser close to it; beyond that, it was just possible to make out the masts of the convoy itself although it was hard to assess in what direction it was moving. Lütjens turned away, hoping to remain unseen and intending to press home his reconnaissance from a safer direction. But the 'cruiser' followed him, hovering at the extreme limit of gun range and running for it when he attempted to close. As evening approached, Lütjens decided on a final attempt to press in close to the convoy and get an accurate estimate of its line of advance. At 1730 he adjusted his course to the eastward.

He sighted the *Malaya* almost at once. The range was about sixteen miles. Lütjens held his course, hoping to catch a glimpse of what lay beyond the battleship, but at fourteen miles he was forced to turn away, his purposes frustrated. If he had continued, an engagement would have been certain. The enemy had tried to follow him but had soon dropped out of sight. At 1800 Lütjens set course for his fuelling rendezvous.

* * *

Since 22 February, when emergency reports from shipping off the American seaboard had first revealed that a new and powerful threat was loose on the sea lanes, the Admiralty had redoubled its efforts to provide heavy escort for Atlantic convoys and had resisted Admiral Somerville's proposals for further operations in the Mediterranean. Force H had thus been kept in readiness to counter this unexpected and elusive threat and to intervene against the *Hipper* should she reappear.[9]

Precautions, however, had been general rather than specific. Convoy SL.67, escorted by the *Malaya*, the destroyers *Faulknor* and *Forester* and the armed merchant cruiser *Cilicia*, had been warned of U-boats off the Canaries and had diverted from its planned route. The diversion had been unsuccessful, and during the night of 7/8 March the convoy had lost five ships. But by morning the attacks had been beaten off and the *Forester* had been detached to a position on the convoy's western flank to keep down U-boats that might be attempting to close from that direction.

At 1331 the *Forester* had sighted what appeared to be a warship and had been ordered to investigate. Her contact had been a large one with a fighting top and a single funnel; by 1442 she had reported it as 'possibly the *Gneisenau*', an identification that the British authorities, remote from the scene, had found wholly incredible. The *Malaya* and the *Faulknor* had turned to close the enemy, leaving the convoy evading to the north-east. By mid-afternoon the *Malaya*'s Swordfish aircraft had succeeded in identifying two ships of the *Scharnhorst* class, but by now the raiders had been opening to the west at high speed. Unable to close the range, the British ships had turned back to catch up with the convoy before dark.[10]

That night the *Renown*, *Ark Royal* and *Arethusa* left Gibraltar and set course for the Canaries with 'utmost dispatch'. The Admiralty placed the *Repulse* and the *Furious* at Admiral Somerville's disposal as well; but they were low on fuel and they could contribute little to his immediate plans. He sent them to Gibraltar and released his own destroyers, which were having difficulty in keeping up with him. At 1330 on 10 March Somerville launched a flight of six reconnaissance aircraft to locate the convoy. At 1720 he joined it, took command of the escort and sent the *Malaya* back to Freetown.[11] But, as had happened with the *Hipper* the previous month, the heavy cavalry had arrived too late.

* * *

During the evening of 8 March Group West agreed to Lütjens' withdrawal from the Sierra Leone route. But his approval seemed less than whole-hearted. He could not resist pointing out that the next convoy would already be northbound from Freetown and that it would probably be sailing without the protection of a heavy ship. His remarks irritated Lütjens. Experience had shown that Sierra Leone convoys were not conforming to any known schedule. There was not a 'shred of evidence' to support Group West's calculations, and, besides, the enemy would have begun to divert his shipping and to initiate all necessary counter-measures.[12] Lütjens decided to ignore what he called 'this highly dubious convoy' and to make for his tankers as planned.

As the German battlecruisers made their way towards their mid-Atlantic rendezvous, it became clear that the authorities in Berlin were beginning a major review of operational plans. In the early hours of 11 March Lütjens received word that the *Hipper* and the pocket-battleship *Admiral Scheer* were to be recovered to German waters towards the end of the month. His role in their recovery would be to make a diversion as far to the south as possible. Within hours new instructions reached him. He was to be clear of the Halifax route by 17 March and make his diversion between the Azores and the Canaries. Thereafter, he was to consider bringing his operations to an end since his ships would be needed for a new sortie at the end of April, this time, in cooperation with the *Bismarck* and the *Prinz Eugen*. Finally, it was suggested to him that a well-timed entry into a French west-coast port would be equally effective in creating the diversion needed for the recovery of the *Hipper* and the *Scheer*.[13]

'This order,' Lütjens noted, 'requires me to change my plans totally.' His first step was a thorough review of the battlecruisers' material state. Both by now required careful nursing. A number of auxiliary systems in the *Gneisenau* were being husbanded for use in an emergency only. The situation on board the *Scharnhorst* was more serious: steam lines had been damaged through repeated overheating and defective boiler superheaters were preventing the generation of full power, and, as far as Lütjens could see, there was not the least possibility that she could be got ready to meet the April deadline set by the authorities ashore. The installation of new pipework would take at least ten weeks. The *Gneisenau* could be made ready in four weeks. Lütjens informed Group West accordingly.

What should he do with the ten days remaining? He was badly in need of a success, not simply for the military benefits that it would bring but also in the interests of morale. Given the stringent time limit set for operations in the north – he would be hard pressed to achieve two days on station even if he cut his replenishment plans to the bone – there was much to be said for a return to the Sierra Leone routes. Lütjens rejected this option, primarily, it seems, because of the lack of independently routed shipping in the area. Following his withdrawal on 8 March he had encountered and sunk the SS *Marathon*, a Greek collier bound for Alexandria via the Cape, but he had found nothing to compare with the concentration of single ships that he had attacked off the American seaboard.

In spite of the critical time pressures that he knew he would face, Lütjens decided to return to the area of his earlier successes. His reappearance in the west, he reasoned, would shift the focus of enemy attention to a point well away from his recent zone of operations and give not the smallest clue that his return to Europe was imminent. The recovery of the *Hipper* and the *Scheer* would not be prejudiced in any way. When the time came to retire from the area, he would refuel for the last time and next show himself in Brest, drawing enemy attention away from the passages north and south of Iceland just as the cruiser and the pocket-battleship were approaching them. Of the two options, this was by far the more promising.[14]

Towards midday on 12 March Lütjens completed his replenishment programme and set off to the northward. He took his two tankers, the *Uckermark* and the *Ermland*, with him and stationed them on the wings of his formation to extend the width of his search. The enemy situation was less than clear. Attention seemed still to be centred on the Sierra Leone route: two fast task forces, both including carriers, seemed to be operating there. On the Halifax route he could expect to find single, slow battleships acting in the escort role and perhaps also a fast task force built from units of the Home Fleet. For the moment at least, the enemy would be acting on the defensive.[15]

Two days passed without incident as the German formation swept northwards in extended line abreast. But at dawn on 15 March the westerly ship, the *Uckermark*, reported two ships to the north-west, possibly tankers. The *Gneisenau* set off in pursuit and by 1000 had overtaken the Norwegian tanker *Bianca*. The ship obeyed the *Gneisenau*'s warning shot and made no attempt to send a raider report. Lütjens decided to take her as a prize. He waited with growing impatience as the prize crew made their way on board and slowly took possession of the vessel. At noon he sent her to the Gironde.

An hour later Lütjens overtook the second tanker. This victim was less amenable than the first, trying to make off and attempting to transmit a warning. She stopped, however, when the *Gneisenau* brought her main battery into action. She was the British tanker *San Casimiro*, 8,046 tons, and another valuable prize. Lütjens put a second prize crew on board, this time in a matter of minutes, and ordered her to a French port.

By now the *Uckermark* was reporting more tankers to the south-east. Lütjens turned back to investigate and quickly overhauled two. The first proved to be the *Polycarp*; she obeyed his warning shots and became the third prize of the day. She, too, was sent eastwards. The second was the British tanker *Simnia*. She persisted in her attempts to send a raider report and Lütjens silenced her with a salvo from his heavy guns. She was a wreck and not worth saving, so Lütjens sank her and picked up the crew.[16]

The action continued at a brisk pace into the night of 15/16 March, the battlecruisers quartering the area like hounds after a scent. There was little order and none of the central control that Lütjens had sought to impose on his earlier actions. Each ship went after its own targets, careless of where its consorts were and what they were doing. It was a free-running mêlée constrained only by the risk of firing on friendly ships. By morning each battlecruiser had added two more ships to the score.

An interrogation of survivors showed that the ships concerned had all been part of a westbound convoy that had left Liverpool on 6 March and dispersed three days later. So far, Lütjens had met only the faster ships; the slower vessels would reach his area during the next twenty-four or forty-eight hours. Several of his recent victims had succeeded in getting off raider reports, and it had to be assumed that the Admiralty had already issued new routing instructions. The slower ships would probably have diverted to the northward. During 16 March, therefore, Lütjens continued his search in that direction.

The pattern of recent events continued, the *Uckermark* providing regular reports of the ships that she could see and the *Gneisenau* running them down. By mid-afternoon on 16 March the flagship had accounted for three more vessels, one Norwegian and two British. It was clear that the *Scharnhorst*, some way to the eastward, was having similar success. But the time was now approaching when Lütjens would have to bring his operations to an end. As daylight began to fade, he detached the *Uckermark* with what were, by his standards, fulsome thanks for her assistance and prepared to withdraw.

Just at that moment another ship came into sight and Lütjens decided on one final action. But this ship seemed different from the others. When he fired his warning shot, this one fired back, made smoke and attempted to evade. Lütjens brought his main armament into action. The ship continued to fire back but was soon in flames. She proved to be the *Chilean Reefer*, a British vessel of 1,831 tons. Lütjens assessed her as an auxiliary cruiser acting, perhaps, in concert with a task force. It was time to make good his getaway.

Sunset was now approaching. Lütjens was still attempting to recover survivors from the *Chilean Reefer* when several masts were reported on the north-western horizon. One appeared unusually large – almost certainly the fighting top of a warship. It could not be friendly; the *Scharnhorst* was well to the eastward. Within minutes it was reported as a battleship of the *Nelson* class. The range was about ten miles. The ship signalled a challenge. Lütjens signalled back '*Emerald*', swung round to the south and left at high speed, sending a warning to the *Uckermark* as he did so. But darkness was descending, and by 2054 the enemy's silhouette had faded into the gloom.[17] In all, this latest phase of Operation '*Berlin*' had cost the enemy sixteen ships totalling 82,000 tons.

* * *

Before examining the closing phase of Operation '*Berlin*', it is necessary to give a brief account of British dispositions in the days following Lütjens' appearance off the Cape Verdes. The *Malaya* sighting in the early evening of 8 March had presented the Admiralty with an unexpected and disturbing situation. With existing convoy escorts already at full stretch, London had ordered two front-line battleships, the *Rodney* and the *King George V*, to Halifax to cover the next pair of eastbound convoys, HX.114 and HX.115. Admiral Tovey, meanwhile, had strengthened his watch on the Denmark Strait to guard against an attempted break-back and had himself taken up a position south of Iceland with the only capital ship left to him. Somerville had continued to provide cover for SL.67 as it made its way northward until he had been forced to break off for fuel. With little to show where the enemy might strike next, British dispositions had inevitably been defensive.

The first intimations that Lütjens had shifted his point of attack to the Western Atlantic reached London during the evening of 15 March. Early reports had been inconclusive; even the *Rodney* – the ship that had brought Lütjens's activities to a close at dusk on the 16th – had referred initially to an 'unknown vessel'. But towards midnight (local time) she had provided information which put the matter beyond doubt. She had signalled:

> Captain and Chief Officer of *Chilean Reefer* picked up with 24 survivors [are] both stating quite clearly enemy warship was *Gneisenau*. Also state she altered course to south-east after initial retirement to north-east. Ship observed by survivors signalling . . . to another vessel thought to be [a] tanker . . .[18]

The *King George V* had left Halifax with all dispatch to follow up the sighting but the Admiralty's options had been limited. It had just become clear that the *Hipper* was missing from her berth in Brest, and, with yet another raider loose, there was little choice but to extend and reinforce the defensive dispositions already in place. The presumption that one or other German force would attempt a break-back to home waters was now very strong. (There was speculation in London that the *Bismarck* might make an appearance to support the movement.) Naval and air patrols in the northern passages were strengthened and the *Hood* and the *Queen Elizabeth*, both newly released from dockyard hands and still running trials, were sent north to flesh out Admiral Tovey's depleted stock of capital ships. In the south, SL.67 was crossing the latitude of Cape Finisterre; Force H hurried north to cover it as it approached home waters.

The stage was now set for the final incidents of Operation 'Berlin'. By dawn on 20 March Lütjens, newly refuelled, was approaching the Bay of Biscay from the south-west and entering the coverage of Admiral Somerville's air patrols. (The *Hipper* was fuelling off the southern tip of Greenland; the *Scheer* was passing the Azores, northbound.) At 0926 Lütjens's look-outs sighted an aircraft on the eastern horizon; it was a wheeled biplane, most probably a carrier aircraft. Lütjens altered to the northward, hoping that he had not been seen. That afternoon Lütjens learned that one of his prizes, the *Polycarp*, had also seen a British aircraft, quite possibly the same one; it had passed close overhead and there had been an exchange of cheery waves. A comparison of times and positions showed that the *Polycarp* had been some eighty miles to the north of him at the time (about 1000); he might well, he now realised, have passed within a few miles of a British carrier during the forenoon. But he had seen nothing and no further aircraft had come to investigate him. There was little cause for concern; the danger was over, the weather was beginning to close in and it was only a few hours until sunset.

Towards 6 o'clock Lütjens was warned of a second aircraft in his vicinity, this one at close range. It had clearly seen him and it was taking an unhealthy interest in his force. Its type was difficult to determine; it was reported as a multi-engine aircraft with a retractable undercarriage. It was probably land-based. Lütjens turned north and increased speed to 27kts until the aircraft had left. The incident was a puzzling one. The aircraft had not investigated him from a beam position; it had possibly not identified him, and it had made no radio report. Lütjens wondered whether it had been a German aircraft, an FW 200 perhaps, and why no one had told him about it. At sunset he turned east for his destination. The way seemed clear. Group West had no information to suggest the presence of an enemy task force in the area. British signal traffic was 'normal'.

It had been a close run thing – closer than the Fleet Commander had realised. Somerville's dusk air patrol in the evening of 19 March had identified the *Bianca*, the first of the German prizes. Half-laden Norwegian tankers on a course for Bordeaux were natural objects of suspicion. Patrols during the morning of the 20th had identified the *San Casimiro* and the *Polycarp* as well, and Somerville had decided to board them. He had been attempting (unsuccessfully) to salvage the *San Casimiro* during the evening of 20 March when a Fulmar fighter returning from patrol had reported the two battlecruisers 110 miles to the north-west, steering north at 20kts. The report came late; the Fulmar's radio had failed and it had returned to make its report by signal lamp. The range would now be more like 130 miles – too far for an air strike – and, besides, night was approaching and the visibility was closing in. Concerned for the security of the convoy under his charge, Somerville positioned himself to cover SL.67 and warned the Admiralty that 'night shadowing and attack was impracticable'.[19]

Somerville's sense of an opportunity missed was sharpened when it later transpired that, on first sighting, the enemy course had been not north but north-east. This information had emerged during aircrew debriefing but its significance had not been appreciated and the *Ark Royal* had been slow to pass it on. That night the truth struck home: the enemy was making for the French coast. Air patrols for dawn 21 March were hastily replanned. A destroyer flotilla was dispatched from Plymouth. Tovey, with the *Nelson*, *Hood* and *Queen Elizabeth*, came south from Iceland with all the speed that he could muster. They were again too late. Lütjens was sighted just once more (by a Coastal Command Hudson) during the late evening of 21 March. He was within a night's steaming of his destination and approaching the limits of German air cover.

His timing could hardy have been better. His appearance in the Bay of Biscay drew British attention away from the northern passages just as the *Hipper* and the *Scheer* were approaching them. Both passed through the Denmark Strait safely in the days which followed. In this respect at least the German reading of the enemy mind had been masterly.

Lütjens met his escort in the approaches to Brest in the early morning of 22 March. He wrote:

> With this, the first operation by German battleships in the Atlantic is over. The ships have been at sea continuously for sixty days without serious mishap. They have taken 22 enemy ships totalling 116,000 tons and have gained rich experience for future actions.

Admiral Raeder was generous in his praise. His signal to the Task Force commander read as follows:

> On completion of the first occasion in German naval history in which a squadron of our battleships has operated successfully in the wide spaces of the Atlantic, I congratulate you and your subordinates on the fine resolution you have shown and the splendid results you have achieved. I appreciate the vital part played by supply ships and escorts which also receive my fullest praise. I hope before long to be able to put an even stronger force under your command for a similar operation on the high seas.[20]

Notes to Chapter 3

1   PG34677, entry for 1900, 24 February 1941.
2   *Ibid.*, 26 February 1941.
3   *Ibid.*, 1230, 4 March 1941; original emphasis.
4   There is no sign in his notes that Lütjens acknowledged his own contribution to the current situation. He had sent the second aircraft ashore to Trondheim on 29 January.
5   PG34677, message to the *Scharnhorst*, 0810 5 March 1941.
6   *Ibid.*, 6 March 1941.

7   As in most German reports, position was expressed in a standard lettered and numbered grid. *Scharnhorst*'s report indicated the south-east corner of Quadrant DT.

8   PG34677, 1300 7 March 1941.

9   The appearance of *Fliegerkorps X* in the Mediterranean and the Axis threat to Greece had placed the British Mediterranean Fleet under great pressure. To relieve this, Somerville had proposed further operations against the Italian coast. See his ROPs for 11–25 February and 25–28 February 1941, *Somerville Papers*, pp. 247–9.

10   British authorities, including Somerville, treated these reports with considerable scepticism. The *Malaya*'s Swordfish pilot, Lieutenant G. R. Brown, had ditched at the end of his sortie and had been rescued by a Spanish vessel. He got his very positive message out through the British Consul in Tenerife. PRO ADM 234-327, p. 288.

11   Force H ROP, 8–23 March 1941, *Somerville Papers*, p. 251.

12   PG34677, 8 March 1941.

13   *Ibid.*, 2100, 11 March 1941.

14   *Ibid.*, Task Force Commander's appreciation, 12 March 1941.

15   *Ibid.*, Intelligence Assessments, 10–12 March 1941.

16   The *Bianca* and the *San Casimiro* were intercepted by Force H on 20 March and scuttled by the prize crews. The *Polykarp* was sighted but not intercepted; Admiral Somerville had more important matters on his mind. See *Somerville Papers*, p. 252.

17   PG34677, 16 March 1941. Lütjens had long assumed that the cruiser *Emerald* was deployed in Canadian waters. His information was out of date.

18   HMS *Rodney* signal 2355, 16 March 1941.

19   Force H ROP, 20 March 1941, *Somerville Papers*, p. 253.

20   Signal from CinC German Navy to Admiral Lütjens dated 21 March 1941; cited in Broom, *Make a Signal!*, p. 105.

4

Planning for 'Exercise Rhine'

During the winter of 1940/41 German strategy continued to move in directions that Admiral Raeder found deeply disturbing. Mussolini's disastrous Balkan adventure appeared to have handed the initiative in the Eastern Mediterranean to the enemy. Italian expeditionary forces in Albania had been brought to a standstill. The British were giving active support to the Greek government and seemed about to re-establish a presence on the European mainland. If that were not enough, the Royal Navy had established a virtual stranglehold over Mussolini's Mediterranean supply lines and Italian armies in Tripolitania were facing eviction. There was every sign that Germany would have to postpone operations designed to establish Axis dominance of the Strait of Gibraltar and the North African Atlantic seaboard – plans much favoured by the Naval Staff – in order to bale out an injudicious ally. More seriously still, it was now quite clear that the main strategic priority for the summer of 1941 was to be Operation *'Barbarossa'*, the *Führer*'s titanic project to encircle and crush the armed forces of the Soviet Union and extend the eastern borders of the *Reich* to the line of the Volga river. This, it had been established in Hitler's directive of 18 December 1940, was to go ahead whether the war against England had been brought to an end or not.

Certain that control of the sea had, in the end, determined the outcome of World War I, Raeder tried hard to counter what he saw as this inexorable drift towards continental engagement. 'The greatest task of the hour,' he told Hitler on 27 December, 'is the concentration of all our power against Britain.' All competing demands, he went on, 'must be deliberately set aside. There are serious doubts as to the advisability of Operation *"Barbarossa"* before the overthrow of Britain.'[1]

Raeder went on to describe new dangers looming on the horizon. Unless higher priority were given to the maritime campaign, Germany would face a war not simply against Britain but against the 'Anglo-Americans', a protracted conflict which would be decided in the end by economic and industrial potential. The British war economy, he argued, had been damaged, but not yet fatally damaged, and was meanwhile being sustained by infusions of industrial and war material from the United States. It seemed that the entire armament industry, particularly aircraft and ship construction, was being moved to America. Britain's supply lines were 'undoubtedly the decisive factor for the outcome of the war'. Yet the importance of the maritime campaign, the Admiral went on, was not properly reflected in Germany's production plans; because of competing demands from the other services, the rate of submarine construction remained 'totally inadequate'.

Raeder was prepared to acknowledge that Italian blunders had created a very difficult situation in the eastern Mediterranean. But Germany should not become engaged in the Balkans or in Libya at the expense of essential projects in the West. He argued in particular that Operation 'Felix' or some similar plan designed to enhance the security of the south-western flank was now more important than ever. The occupation of Gibraltar and the control of the Straits was the best guarantee of Italian security. It would protect essential military and economic links between Europe and North Africa, guarantee German access to the vulnerable West African seaboard, complicate British operations throughout the Mediterranean and eliminate a vital link in the British Atlantic convoy system. 'The strategic reasons for the speedy execution of Operation "Felix",' the Admiral concluded, 'still hold good.'

Despite the force of these arguments, Raeder could do little to divert Hitler from his purposes. At a two-day conference for commanders-in-chief and their senior staff officers, held in the Obersalzberg in early January, the *Führer* declared that saving Italy from defeat had become a political and psychological imperative. *Fleigerkorps X*[2] would operate from Sicilian bases and force the British Mediterranean Fleet on to the defensive. An armoured regiment would be shipped to Libya to help counter the British land offensive. A mountain division would reinforce Mussolini's crumbling Albanian front, and, as a further measure to relieve pressure on the hard-pressed Italians, access would be opened through Bulgarian territory to the eastern frontiers of Greece.

In a wide-ranging and rambling discourse on strategic trends, Hitler put forward what he surely intended as a deliberate counter to the maritime case

73

so recently advanced by Raeder. He played down the significance of Anglo-American industrial potential, declaring that the prospects for Germany and occupied Europe were far greater. Britain was sustained in her struggle by the hope that she could involve Russia in the conflict. Her diplomatic overtures to Russia were apparent; Stalin was a cold-blooded blackmailer who would, if expedient, tear up solemn treaties at any time. He, Hitler, must act now to remove this potential threat before it developed.

Turning to the vexed question of Operation 'Felix', Hitler said that he fully shared the Naval Staff's views on the strategic value of Gibraltar, but, for the time being, he saw little prospect of enlisting the support of Franco, despite generous offers of economic aid. The essential political conditions for the operation did not yet exist. Meanwhile, the Staffs need not concern themselves unduly with unfavourable developments in Africa since Germany's European stronghold was essentially impregnable. Britain could only win the war by defeating Germany on the continent of Europe, and this was no longer possible.[3]

A month later Raeder tried once again to focus attention on the maritime campaign. The British war economy, he said, was as strong as ever. The Royal Air Force was striking at targets in northern Germany and operating in strength in the Mediterranean. American aircraft and air crews, he claimed, were taking part in these attacks. British naval strength was on the increase too. The Royal Navy had taken delivery of four new battleships, three aircraft carriers, twelve cruisers and countless smaller vessels. All of this demonstrated the continued vitality of enemy industry and the strength of transatlantic links.

The CinC went on to make his strongest plea yet for a properly coordinated air and sea campaign against British shipping and the infrastructure that supported it. He did not, on this occasion, admit that the U-boat arm was at its lowest strength ever, although he did concede that small numbers and winter weather set limits to its potential. His remarks were directed primarily against the Luftwaffe's strategic air campaign, which, in his opinion, lacked any true grasp of the priorities. There was no sign, he claimed, that recent attacks on armament industries had reduced output or that terror raids had damaged civilian morale. Britain's true weakness was to be found in her shipping, in her shipbuilding and repair yards and in her ports. Targets such as these had not been attacked effectively. The volume of supplies entering London had not noticeably declined and the enemy seemed to be opening up new port capacity in the north and west of the country. All this could change. Working in concert, the *Kriegsmarine* and the *Luftwaffe* could exert ' a decisive influence in the struggle against Britain and America'. The *Führer* was of 'precisely the same opinion'.[4]

Two days after this meeting Hitler issued his Directive No 23, entitled 'Basic Principles for the Prosecution of War against the British War Economy'. It provided an accurate summary of Raeder's case but fell short of his rigorous conclusions. It gave Göring *carte blanche* to continue as before.

The problem that Raeder faced during the early months of 1941 had become depressingly familiar. His instincts told him that he had to strike effectively at Britain's war economy, primarily through her shipping, while political opinion in the United States was still divided and while American industrial mobilisation was still in its infancy. This was indeed the 'task of the hour'; all available resources needed to be concentrated on this one object. His essential difficulty was this: how to attract priority to a strategy of economic attrition while the *Führer* and Supreme Commander of the *Wehrmacht* remained addicted to alternative solutions which seemed to promise a quick and decisive outcome.

What was to be done? Raeder's options were limited. Advocacy alone was not enough. Despite limited resources, he would have to press ahead with the maritime campaign with all the energy that he could muster. If he did not, the *Kriegsmarine* would be pushed to the margins of German strategy, its strength dissipated in secondary and supporting roles. If he were to bring about a change in strategic priorities and avoid relegation to the minor league, Raeder needed a success. He had to show that the Navy had the potential to alter the course of the war.

While his staffs prepared for a renewal of the Atlantic campaign, Raeder continued his efforts to capture Hitler's attention. In his conferences with the *Führer* he dwelt increasingly on the failure of the *Luftwaffe* to chose appropriate targets, pointing out that the Tyne with its important concentration of shipbuilding yards had not yet been attacked at all. And he provided evidence, entirely anecdotal, that Göring's indiscriminate bombing campaign was serving merely to strengthen the enemy will. But his main emphasis was on evidence of increasing American involvement in the Atlantic. The US Navy, he claimed, was now escorting convoys as far as

Iceland. British escorts then took over. There were signs that British warships might soon be repaired in American yards. The proper response, he suggested, would be an extension of the present danger zone and the abolition of existing rules governing attacks on US shipping. He called for German propaganda to make more capital out of breaches of neutrality by the United States. But the key to the future continued to lie in a concerted attack on British shipping. This was Britain's most vulnerable spot and she remained critically short of escorts. If sinking rates could be raised to the levels achieved in 1917, Britain would be done for in six months.[5]

* * *

On 2 April 1941 – some twelve days, that is, after Lütjens' arrival in Brest – the Naval War Staff issued a new directive for surface ship operations in the Atlantic. The document assessed what had been achieved so far, highlighted the main difficulties that had been encountered and proposed solutions to them. It represented a genuine attempt to draw lessons from Operation *Berlin'* and to establish a common basis for future planning.

There is little sign in this directive that the Naval Staff had reached an inflated view of the Fleet Commander's achievements.[6] Results had been modest enough. There had been no seismic event such as the destruction of some valuable convoy to cause political shock waves in London or to shake confidence in Washington. And the U-boat arm, despite its weakness, had sunk nearly three times the tonnage during the period in question.[7] The document looked, therefore, to future potential rather than past achievement.

The objective of the coming summer campaign was 'to strike an annihilating blow at British supplies'. The scene of operations would be the North Atlantic, for here Britain's global network of trade routes converged. A 'comprehensive solution' to the problem, the seizure of command of the sea in the North Atlantic, was not possible with the limited resources that would be available in the short term, but 'the aim would be to establish local and temporary command of the sea and to work towards it step by step in a deliberate and systematic way'. Prospects for success looked favourable. The Royal Navy was stretched to the limit; it could not extend its escort policies (a major factor in frustrating German aims so far) without weakening fleet strengths in areas vital to British strategy. The purpose now would be to force the enemy to disperse his forces still further and then to apply concentrated force against the resulting areas of weakness. The next operation would be more powerful than the last. As well as the *Gneisenau* (getting ready in Brest), it would include the *Bismarck* and the *Prinz Eugen* (both nearing the end of their training programmes in the Baltic). If all went according to plan, the operation would be launched to coincide with the moonless period at the end of the month. It would be code-named *'Rheinübung'* ('Exercise Rhine').

After this bombastic and rather visionary preamble, the authors addressed some of the more important points raised by Lütjens in the wake of *'Berlin'*. Their first priority was a review of the rules prohibiting action with forces of equal strength. The question proved a difficult one: there was no escaping the fact that an unlucky hit from a single heavy shell could bring operations to a premature end. The Naval Staff was in little doubt that when two ships of the *Bismarck* class became available it would be possible to engage enemy ocean escorts with every prospect of success. But what guidance should be given in the interim? They decided on a half-way measure. A single battleship such as the *Bismarck* could court action with an enemy heavy ship, tie her down and keep her occupied, but not to the extent of becoming fully engaged. Other ships in the formation would then be free to get at the convoy. As finally agreed, the new rules allowed the *Bismarck* to engage units of equal strength, but 'only insofar as it contributes to the main aim and can be done without incurring excessive risk'. She should commit herself fully and unreservedly to action only when she had no other choice.[8]

In setting out their revised policies, the Staff recognised the continuing need for secrecy and surprise. The enemy, they suggested, would have drawn the conclusion from recent experience that a single battleship acting as convoy escort was enough. It was important that he continued in that opinion and therefore that he got no early warning of the composition and movement of German raiding forces. But detection and identification alone would not, it was agreed, provide adequate grounds for calling off an operation.

The directive went on to consider the relative merits of independent and combined operations. While recognising the case for an opening move by the *Gneisenau* in the direction of the Azores or Cape Verdes to take pressure off the northern passages, the Staff concluded that, in general, the three ships should act as a single task force. Here they leaned heavily towards the opinions of the Fleet Commander. Keeping all three together would enhance search capability, help deal with lighter escorts and provide the best prospects of success in the event of an encounter with a strongly defended convoy. The short endurance of the *Prinz Eugen* would complicate planning – that was inescapable – but if tankers were positioned carefully few problems would arise. The price to pay for the many advantages of a fully integrated task force would be small. That said, it was impossible to foresee all eventualities. The decision on whether or not to detach the *Prinz Eugen* for independent operations was left to the judgment of the Fleet Commander and Group West.

Although this emphasis on concentration of effort tended to rule out the diversionary operations and the two-pronged attacks that had been so strong a feature of German thinking during Operation 'Berlin', the directive continued to put stress on keeping the enemy off balance by rapid changes in the point of attack. The Naval Staff seem to have reached no consensus on whether Lütjens' recent sally towards the Canaries and Cape Verdes had been useful or not – they asked the Fleet Commander and Group West for a further evaluation of lessons learned – but they did point to new and promising opportunities on the oceanic routes between North America and Central Africa.[9] For the moment, the option of carrying the fight into the central and even the southern Atlantic was left open. A decision would be made when a full assessment of the benefits and risks had been made.

They turned finally to the vexed question of finding convoys. Operation 'Berlin' had demonstrated one thing with absolute clarity: the information gathered by German intelligence on the sailing and routing of convoys could not be relied on. The answer lay in better tactical reconnaissance. But how was it to be provided? The staff recognised that U-boats had a part to play. They would not form part of the task force itself since they would restrict its mobility, but they could prove useful as independent scouts and shadowers provided that command relationships were properly settled and that the problems of ship-to-submarine communications could be resolved. It was decided that, for future operations, U-boats would remain subordinate to U-Boat Headquarters but that the Fleet Commander could assume tactical command if he saw an opportunity for collaboration. A supplement to the U-boat short signal book would be issued to surface ships. At least two U-boats would be kept in the Freetown area to cooperate with surface forces and, on the Halifax route, two or more would be stationed far enough to the westwards to meet the Fleet Commander's requirements.

The Naval Staff accepted that Lütjens' use of supply ships in the scouting role had been 'extraordinarily useful'. While agreeing to leave this option to the discretion of the force commander, they warned that this should be a tactic of last resort since the loss of these ships would bring the operation to a premature close and damage prospects for future and more ambitious operations. Instead, Berlin would attempt to provide special reconnaissance ships, preferably with the speed and range to work directly with the battle group, and, failing that, less capable vessels that could keep watch in remoter and safer areas. Prizes taken during the course of the operation might prove useful as well. But operational commanders were warned not to count on too much additional support. Heavy demands were being made on German sea-transport capacity; shipping space had become 'abnormally strained'.[10]

* * *

The ink was scarcely dry on this new directive when the plans received a set back. It had been assumed up to now that Brest, that strategic prize in which so many hopes had been invested, could be made secure against British attack. When he had first alluded to the possibility of basing heavy forces in the West, Raeder had assured Hitler that anti-aircraft defences would be adequate and that all necessary stocks of boom-defence equipment and anti-torpedo netting would be in place. Experience during January and February 1941 had done much to bear him out. During the period of the *Hipper*'s stay, the *Luftwaffe* had seen to it that daylight attacks were costly and ineffective. And the periodic night raids mounted by the RAF had left the cruiser unscathed.

But the arrival of the battlecruisers at the end of March had made Brest the focus of enemy attention. The Admiralty had done what it could to keep a fast task force on permanent watch in the Bay of Biscay and had called on the Air Staff to provide the heaviest possible scale of air attack. Raids mounted during the nights of 30/31 March and 3/4 April had been unsuccessful, but during a daylight raid on 6 April a Beaufort torpedo-bomber of No 22 Squadron Coastal Command had succeeded in penetrating the defences and in scoring a hit on the *Gneisenau*. Post-attack reconnaissance showed that the battlecruiser had moved into dry dock. Further attacks had followed, and during the night of 10/11 April Bomber Command had succeeded in registering four additional hits. The extent of this success remained unknown in London and the Admiralty had been unable to relax its precautions. But the implications for the German naval authorities were clear enough.[11]

Raeder was embarrassed by this setback but saw no case for a fundamental revision of his plans. At his next meeting with the *Führer* he presented the matter as a simple accident of war. When pressed further on the adequacy of air defences in western France, he pointed out that the risk to ships under repair in Wilhelmshaven or Kiel was just as great. The *Bismarck* and the *Prinz Eugen*, he told Hitler, would sail for the Atlantic at the end of April as planned. He conceded, however, that until defences were strengthened or until safer bases were made available, large ships would 'put into Brest only in exceptional circumstances'.[12]

* * *

Of the written orders rushed forward to meet the deadlines set for the start of 'Rheinübung', only those of the Fleet Commander betrayed an inkling of new difficulties now that the *Bismarck* and the *Prinz Eugen* would be operating alone. Whatever his private opinions, Lütjens could say little about the broader strategic issues. 'Rheinübung' could be no more than the pale shadow of that ambitious war of manoeuvre that the Naval Staff had envisaged at the time of his recall from the Atlantic. But it was for others to point out the growing gulf between conception and reality. Lütjens could only scale back his operations to match the capabilities of the force at his disposal, and this he proceeded to do.

The *Bismarck* and the *Prinz Eugen* were, he recognised, ill-matched; it was far from clear how they should be handled in the presence of the enemy. He would have to assume that convoys were protected by a heavy ship and, as in the case of SL.67, by one or two cruisers as well. Since the strength of the escort would seldom be known beforehand, he could never allow a lightly armoured ship like the *Prinz Eugen* to test the strength of the enemy defences. This had to be a job for the *Bismarck* alone. Lütjens' orders were explicit. If the *Prinz Eugen* sighted a convoy, she was to hold off at the extreme limit of visibility, taking care not to reveal her identity, until the *Bismarck* had probed the defences and given permission to close.[13]

On the idea that the *Bismarck* might somehow succeed in drawing off the heavy escort, Lütjens was openly sceptical. Success seemed to depend on the enemy making a tactical blunder – an uncertain basis for planning. It was far more probable that the escort would hold its position close to the convoy and make it impossible for either of his ships to close without risking an engagement. Under these conditions, Lütjens would have no option but to break off the attack. If, against the odds, the *Bismarck* did succeed in drawing the heavy escort away, experience suggested that the *Prinz Eugen* might still encounter a cruiser. The Fleet Commander's orders were again explicit. If this happened, the cruiser was to break off her attack immediately and report the matter.

Lütjens went on to discuss the case of the weakly defended convoy. This, he assumed, would almost certainly scatter. If it did, the aim would be to disable as many ships as possible. They could then be sunk at leisure, though not until everything capable of moving had been brought to a stop. He then gave precise instructions on weapon calibres, fuse settings, and aiming points that would best conserve ammunition and warned his captains not to be diverted from their task by rescue operations. The safety of their own ships came first.

Because he could see no sure way of dealing with the protected convoy, Lütjens gave equal emphasis in his orders to attacks on independent shipping. Single ships were no longer to be regarded as secondary targets suitable for attack only when all else had failed. They were to be sunk or taken from the beginning. And, influenced no doubt by Staff concern at the strain on Axis sea transport, the Fleet Commander laid considerable stress on the capture of fast motor ships, tankers and refrigerator ships. Past mistakes in the handling of prizes were to be avoided. Movements would now be staggered and some prizes might have to lie low in remote areas of the Atlantic for several weeks before starting their passage eastwards.

The emphasis on prizes (and on prize crews) caught the ships of the task force unprepared. Time was short. Captain Ernst Lindemann of the *Bismarck* noted in his War Diary that the extra equipment needed 'could not be procured by normal means . . .'[14]

* * *

It remained for the staffs of the Fleet Commander and of Group North to settle the details of the departure and break-out plan and to choose a scheme that would minimise the risk of early detection by the enemy. The problem was a familiar one. The staffs could draw on a series of lessons beginning with Vice-Admiral Marschall's raid on the lines of the Northern Patrol in November 1939 and ending with the recovery of the *Hipper* and the *Scheer* in March 1941. The record had contained moments of high tension. Lütjens knew this as well as anyone; but, so far, no major warship had been lost in the attempt.

Few commanders by this stage of the war could bank on reaching the Atlantic without giving the enemy at least some clue to their movements. British intelligence and reconnaissance had become too active to allow such illusions to persist. The main weakness in the British system lay in its ability to sift the truth from the fragments of evidence presented to it and then to react in time. For German commanders, the best hopes of success lay in moving fast, in maintaining momentum and, if they could not conceal their movements completely, in delaying the moment of disclosure for as long as was humanly possible.

The British drew their information on German shipping movements from air reconnaissance, including photo-reconnaissance of the main fleet bases, and from agents in occupied Denmark and Norway. Of the two sources, air reconnaissance was seen as the greater threat since reports would reach command authorities more or less immediately. Agents, on the other hand, had to report through a clandestine and unreliable network. Their information would reach British decision-makers only after considerable delay, the generally accepted estimate being twenty-four hours.

In the light of these factors, the staffs quickly rejected the option of departing from the Elbe. Passage of the Kiel Canal would mean lightening the *Bismarck* and reloading her at the far end. The inevitable delay would mean disclosure – perhaps even attack.[15] The only alternative was to leave the Baltic by way of the Great Belt and the Kattegat, the route that had been used during Operation 'Berlin'.

Thereafter, the issues were less clear cut. The advance of spring made some aspects of the departure easier and some more difficult. With the narrows clear of ice, a night passage of the Great Belt had become feasible. It would be easy to minimise the risk of observation from the shore. On the other hand, the opening of the Belt and the Sound and the longer hours of daylight increased the risk of meeting neutral shipping. It was decided that traffic in the Kattegat would be suspended during the critical period of the task group's passage.

Everything now pointed to an arrival off the Skaw in late afternoon, a dusk transit of the mine barrier which guarded the Baltic entrance and a night passage of the Skagerrak. Here, at least, the task group would be free from observation from the air. But the early dawn and the lengthening hours of daylight meant danger in the Shetland–Norway narrows, where enemy air surveillance would be intense. There was little doubt as to the best course to follow if the weather were foul; but what if it were clear? Was it better to press on and loiter in the Arctic until the right moment for a break-out came or to put into a Norwegian fjord in the hope of avoiding detection altogether? Lütjens leaned towards the latter course. His ships would be well hidden on the broken coastline south of Bergen and the *Luftwaffe* could be relied on to keep would-be intruders at arm's length. He had insisted on the Korsfjord option at the start of *'Berlin'*, though in the event he had not needed to use it. And the *Scheer* had been glad of it during her return to Germany at the end of March. But there was now an additional point in its favour. It would provide an opportunity to top up the *Prinz Eugen* and thus increase freedom of action during the critical break-out phase that was still to come.

Admiral Carls, CinC Group North, doubted the value of this Norwegian bolt-hole but was content to accede to the Fleet Commander's wishes provided that he kept his visit short.[16] He issued his orders on 22 April. The task group was to pass through the Great Belt with *Sperrbrecher* and mine-sweeper support and was to be clear of the swept channel off Kristiansand by 2030 on the third day of the operation. It was then to proceed at high speed (and with destroyer escort), keeping to the deep-water channel off the Norwegian coast so that it could enter Korsfjord on the morning of day four. It would remain at anchor during daylight hours and the *Prinz Eugen* would refuel. It would weigh at dusk and leave the fjord by the northern exit. From there it would steam north at high speed and release its destroyers on passing Sognefjord. Movements thereafter would be at the discretion of the Fleet Commander.[17]

Although the handling of the task group from this point on was a matter for Lütjens rather than for the shore command, Admiral Carls felt it proper to advise on the matter. He believed that if weather conditions were right for a break-out the task group should make direct for the Iceland–Faeroes passage, keeping well clear of the land to allow scope for evasive manoeuvre. If conditions were unfavourable – if the Home Fleet were at sea, or if the weather were clear – the ships would make for the Arctic Ocean and lie low until the right opportunity presented itself. He had warned Lütjens about the use of the Denmark Strait at the time of 'Berlin' and he now did so again. The Strait, he suggested, was narrow, detection a near certainty. The Home Fleet occupied a central position and would be operating on interior lines. It would move quickly to support scouts that had established contact in the far north. The route south of Iceland was shorter; fuel was less likely to become a critical factor. If the enemy did find out that something was afoot, an early attempt on the southern route would test his speed of reaction to the utmost and give the task group the best chance of getting a head start over the heavy forces waiting in Scapa Flow.[18]

Lütjens took a very different view. His orders were brief; he referred simply to an 'unobserved break through to the North Atlantic via the Denmark Strait. Probable refuelling from the tanker *Weissenburg* [off Jan Mayen] beforehand.'[19] It was characteristic of the man that he would keep his options open until he could see more clearly how enemy dispositions and the weather might affect his plans. But that dawn encounter with British cruisers three months before seems certainly to have coloured his thinking. The passage south of Iceland had many advantages; but it was closely watched by surface and air patrols and it was the natural point of concentration for the heavy units of the Home Fleet. With the lengthening hours of daylight and the coming of spring weather, he would be more vulnerable to detection than ever. Surprise encounters with equal or superior forces could never be ruled out. In the Denmark Strait he would certainly have to contend with cruiser patrols; but there would be no light forces and air reconnaissance would be sparse. There would be no immediate risk of meeting heavy ships and the chances of finding low visibility off the ice-edge would remain very good indeed.

* * *

The orders of Group North and those of the Fleet Commander were delivered to the *Bismarck* on the morning of 25 April. Admiral Lütjens and his staff were expected next day and the task force would sail from Gotenhafen on the evening of the 28th. All would now be put to the test. But, within hours, new orders arrived from Fleet Headquarters postponing 'Rheinübung' for 'seven to twelve days at least'. The *Prinz Eugen* had set off a ground mine in the approaches to Kiel. The extent of damage was unknown, but the cruiser had been shaken from end to end and a thorough survey would be needed to ensure that hull and machinery were still sound.

Instead of embarking on 26 April, Lütjens called on Admiral Raeder in Berlin to discuss the implications of this latest setback. How far the Fleet Commander felt able to express his reservations about the effectiveness of the *Bismarck*/*Prinz Eugen* combination is not clear. His position was a delicate one.[20] It is certain, however, that he spelt out the advantages of waiting until the *Scharnhorst* had completed her overhaul or even until the *Tirpitz* had reached operational readiness.

Raeder was not to be moved; the operation was to go ahead as soon as the *Prinz Eugen* was ready. Raeder conceded later that Lütjens had not been wholly convinced that this was the right course to follow. But the meeting had ended in 'complete mutual understanding'. Was there a rational case for pressing ahead? The original concept set out in the Naval Staff directive had been bold, even visionary. Sober reflection must now have suggested that the chances of any major success against the British convoy system were slim. At worst, the *Kriegsmarine* would be risking the piecemeal destruction of its surface fleet.

In his later attempts to justify the decision, Raeder chose to stress the adverse trends in Germany's relations with the United States. American neutrality, he claimed, had become a fiction; war with the United States was 'staring us in the face'. Before long, the whole weight of American sea power would be thrown on to the side of the enemy.[21] There is something to be said for these arguments. Raeder had every reason to believe that the balance of naval power was shifting irrevocably against him and that things would get worse rather than better. The fate of the *Gneisenau* was sufficient in itself to demonstrate the dangers of delay. But he can have had few illusions that the coming operation – the 'fag-end' of a much more ambitious plan – could have any decisive impact on the flow of British supplies. His motives must be sought elsewhere. The Navy was losing the strategic debate. Its warnings were being ignored and its claims to a proper share of the nation's resources were going unheeded. Impervious to argument, the national leadership seemed bent on courses of action that would confine the Navy, perhaps permanently, to a secondary and subordinate role. It had to assert its claim to strategic significance in the only way it could.

That said, Raeder could hardly have risked a force with so much institutional and national prestige invested in it if he had not believed that the risks could be kept within reasonable bounds. This may have been one of the less helpful lessons of Operation 'Berlin'. He may have felt that, in Lütjens, he had found a worthy successor to the masters of evasion and disengagement that he had served himself and who had brought their ships home safely after a dozen heart-stopping but ultimately inconclusive actions. 'Deliberate and careful operations are indicated,' he told his Fleet Commander at this final meeting. 'It would be a mistake to risk a heavy engagement for limited and perhaps uncertain results. Our objective with the *Bismarck* and later with the *Tirpitz* must be continuous, sustained operations.'[22] Here was a man uniquely qualified by aptitude and experience to pull the plan off. He was decisive yet coldly analytical, a man who weighed the odds carefully, a cautious and vigilant commander, never rash, who could be relied on to impose his own qualities on impetuous or casual subordinates. He knew exactly what the Naval High Command had in mind and would carry out his orders to the letter.

* * *

Lütjens embarked in the *Bismarck* on 13 May 1941, bringing with him a staff of more than sixty officers and men. The day was devoted to command team training and to exercises with the *Prinz Eugen*. On 15 May Group North sent the code word 'Marburg' which was to signal the start of 'Rheinübung'. There followed another eleventh-hour postponement. The *Bismarck*'s port crane, a source of anxiety since the beginning of the ship's trials programme, broke down and Lütjens decided that a thorough overhaul was essential. The ship entered Gotenhafen and operations were postponed for three days.

On the morning of 18 May Lütjens held a final briefing for his commanding officers, Captain Lindemann of the *Bismarck* and Captain Helmuth Brinkmann of the *Prinz Eugen*. He made it clear that, if weather conditions were right, he would bypass the Korsfjord and make direct for the Arctic

Ocean. Captains should also be prepared, if conditions for the break-out were adverse, for a longish wait in Trondheim. His preference thereafter was for a fast break-out through the Denmark Strait, taking full advantage of low visibility along the ice-edge; ships would maintain full speed even in fog, keeping station by radar. If he met enemy cruisers in the Strait, he would probably fight them off; but he would have to conserve ammunition for the cruise as a whole and the decision would rest with him.

He touched on the vexed question of aircraft. Embarked aircraft were to be kept on a tight rein. Orders for a sortie were to be given clearly and in writing. Aircraft on search missions were never to attack; they were to do their best to keep out of sight. They would be launched only on his orders. He stressed that security was of prime importance. Ships' companies could be told that the squadron was going on a 'cruise to the Arctic Ocean'. The break-out could be announced when he gave permission. Ships were to meet at 1100 the next morning in the southern approaches to the Great Belt.[23]

At midday on 18 May 1941 the *Bismarck* slipped from her berth in Gotenhafen. The fleet band, formed on her quarterdeck, struck up *Muss i Denn*, the traditional anthem marking the start of a long cruise; the head of the Naval Intelligence Service would wonder much later whether this had not been a most dangerous lapse in security.[24] That afternoon the *Bismarck* dropped anchor off Gotenhafen to top up with fuel and provisions. At 0200 the next morning she weighed anchor and sailed west to rendezvous with her escort in the approaches to the Great Belt.

Notes to Chapter 4

1   Report of CinC Navy to the *Führer*, 27 December 1940. *Führer Conferences*, p. 160.
2   A crack *Luftwaffe* unit specialising in anti-shipping operations.
3   Report on Conferences with the *Führer* and Supreme Commander of the Armed Forces at the Berghof (Obersalzberg) 8 and 9 January 1941. *Führer Conferences*, pp. 169–72.
4   Report of the CinC Navy to the *Führer*, 4 February 1941. *Führer Conferences*, pp. 174–9.
5   Report by the CinC Navy to the *Führer*, 18 March 1941. *Führer Conferences*, pp. 182–9.

6   Raeder appears to have given a similarly cautious assessment in his report to Hitler on 18 March, indicating that 'more vigorous action' would be taken against British convoys when four battleships were available. *Führer Conferences*, p. 182.

7   Tonnage sunk by the battlecruisers and by the *Hipper* amounted to 148,428 tons; the U-boat total for February and March came to 439,803 tons. Roskill, Vol. I, pp. 372, 379, 616.

8   PG20418, Operations and Tactics; Evaluation of Important Experiences in the War at Sea, Book 3, *The Atlantic Operation of the Combat Group Bismarck and Prinz Eugen* (Berlin: October 1942), p. 5 (German text).

9   The Naval War Staff was still hopeful that Hitler would allow operations in the Pan-American Neutrality Zone.

10   PG20418, p. 7. In the end, two reconnaissance ships, the *Gonzenheim* and the *Kota Penang*, were assigned to 'Rheinübung'. They were stationed, initially, 300 miles south of Cape Farewell, Greenland.

11   Flying Officer K. Campbell RAF, pilot of the Beaufort torpedo-bomber which damaged the *Gneisenau* on 6 April 1941, was later awarded a posthumous Victoria Cross.

12   Conference of 20 April 1941. *Führer Conferences*, p. 191. The safer alternatives discussed at this time were Ferrol and Trondheim. Hitler seems to have contemplated renewed pressure on Spain after 'Barbarossa'. Franco would, surely, become more compliant. He also wanted the Todt Organisation to build a large dry dock in Trondheim. Raeder may well have regarded both ideas as visionary; neither solved the problem of basing and repair in the short term.

13   This summary of Lütjens' operation order is based on PG20418, pp. 10–11, and on PG47895, a draft report compiled by the OKM in the immediate aftermath of the *Bismarck* sortie.

14   PG47897, *Bismarck* War Diary, 16 April 1941. Knowledge that the *Bismarck* had embarked prize crews gave London an important clue as to her intentions. Bletchley Park had been able to break naval Enigma traffic for certain days in April 1941, but only after a prolonged delay. See Hinsley, Vol. 1, p. 341.

15   Comments by Group North on planning and execution of 'Rheinübung', PG4789, p. 58.

16   Comments by Group North on the planning and execution of 'Rheinübung'. PG47895, p. 58.

17   PG20418, p. 9.

18   *Ibid.*, p.12.

19   *Ibid.*, p. 9.

20   Roskill observes that Lütjens was in the 'unenviable position of opposing a daring plan which he himself would have to carry out. This weakened his case . . .' Roskill, *The War at Sea*, Vol. 1, p. 394.

21 Raeder, pp. 346, 351–3.
22 Cited in Müllenheim-Rechberg, p. 86.
23 PG47895, pp. 5–6.
24 PG20418, p. 33.

5

Break-Out

British naval strategists reflecting on events in the Atlantic during the spring of 1941 had little reason for self-congratulation. A disaster of major proportions had been avoided, but costs, measured in terms of fleet effort and in the dislocation to convoy schedules, had been high and the enemy had gone unpunished.

Some comfort could be taken from the deterrent effect of attaching heavy escorts to convoys. This tactic had proved itself on at least two occasions. Following the *Hipper*'s actions against SLS.64 in mid-February and Lütjens' operations off the American eastern seaboard later in the month, the Admiralty had directed area commanders to provide battleship cover, or, failing that, cruiser cover, to all eastbound convoys on the transatlantic routes. But this was easier said than done. Overseas commands attempting to balance operational requirements with essential maintenance and refit schedules had been unable to make ends meet. The brunt of the escort task had thus fallen on the ships of the Home Fleet, and for much of March Admiral Tovey had found himself reduced to a single capital ship.[1] German cruiser warfare theorists were being proved right in their predictions.

What was the answer? As the German operations of spring 1941 came to a close, there was a growing consensus in British circles that any durable solution to the problems of ocean warfare had to be found in the northern passages. The problem was one of cruiser numbers. To keep even a single cruiser on station in the Denmark Strait or in the Iceland–Faeroes passage with fuel enough to respond to the challenge if it came implied a healthy surplus of ships and, after escort commitments and minimum fleet requirements had been met, the necessary surplus had seldom been available. The watch on this vital strategic area had relied too heavily on early warning (demonstrably unreliable) and on the dubious tactical capabilities of the armed merchant cruisers and trawlers of the Northern Patrol. Tovey and his predecessor had long since identified the problem; so far, their representations had met with little success.

The events of winter 1940/41 threw the weaknesses of existing arrangements for controlling the northern passages into sharp relief. A succession of German ships, disguised raiders and auxiliaries as well as warships, had passed through British lines undetected. Intelligence on their movements had been unreliable or missing altogether, and the first evidence of their passage had come, as often as not, with a surprise sighting (or unexplained sinking) in the Atlantic. The return of the *Hipper* and the *Scheer* at the end of March, however, had demonstrated the weakness of existing arrangements with unusual clarity. A break-back by one or other of these ships had been widely expected, but both had reached home waters as secretly and as easily as they had left. In the case of the *Scheer*, radio intelligence had even provided indications of route and timing (she would be passing Iceland on 29 March) and a cruiser force had been deployed to the east of the Iceland–Faeroes mine barrier in an attempt to catch her. It had seen nothing.[2] There could be little doubt, after these incidents, that standing cruiser patrols had to be seen from now on as an essential component of British strategy.

But the necessary changes could hardly have come about if German actions during the spring of 1941 had not encouraged a sense of expectation in British minds. The main lines of German strategy were becoming abundantly clear. Evidence from French sources was beginning to suggest that the two battlecruisers, *Scharnhorst* and *Gneisenau*, would remain immobile for some time to come, but there was little doubt in London that other ships were getting ready to take their place. The new battleship *Bismarck* had completed her trials and training programme. It was puzzling that she had not put in an appearance already; the Admiralty had half expected her to assist in the recovery of the battlecruisers in the final stages of Operation 'Berlin'. The pocket-battleship *Lützow* had finished repairing damage received during the Norwegian campaign, and the *Prince Eugen*, and several light cruisers, were also believed to be ready.[3]

By mid-April this sense of expectation was reaching fever pitch. On the 19th reports reached London that the *Bismarck* had been seen passing the Skaw. Tovey strengthened his cruiser patrols in the northern passages and sent the battlecruiser *Hood* to support them; but the report proved false.

Three days later air reconnaissance over Narvik found a force which appeared to include one heavy and two light cruisers. The evidence seemed conclusive. The Admiralty assessed the ships concerned as the *Lützow*, the *Emden* and the *Köln*. This report proved to be false as well, but from now on Tovey scheduled his cruisers to provide a constant watch on the Denmark Strait and the Iceland–Faeroes passage; and at times of particular sensitivity he sent a battlecruiser forward to Hvalfjord to support them.

During the second week of May (while Lütjens and his staff were joining the *Bismarck* and beginning command team training) British radio intelligence noted an increase in *Luftwaffe* reconnaissance activity between Greenland and Jan Mayen. German aircraft were also showing renewed interest in Scapa Flow. It had seemed possible, at first, that the Germans were preparing for some kind of joint operation in the north. There had been rumours of troop movements in northern Norway, linked, perhaps, to an expedition against Iceland.[4] Jan Mayen had seemed another possibility; on 14 May Tovey had ordered FOIC Iceland to report on the ice conditions in that remote outpost. But opinion had hardened in favour of a purely naval operation, although whether this was to be a break-out or a break-back could not be known for certain.

On 18 May (while the *Bismarck* was making her final preparations for departure) Tovey warned the heavy cruiser *Suffolk* then on station in the Denmark Strait to keep a careful watch for ships approaching from the east and from the west, particularly near the ice-edge. But the *Suffolk*'s fuel state was already close to operational margins. On 19 May (the date of the *Bismarck*'s departure) Tovey sailed the *Norfolk* to relieve her, so that, if need be, he could call on two heavy cruisers capable of sustained operations.

There was nothing, as yet, to justify further precautionary moves. Normal business continued. The westbound convoys OB.325 and OB.326 sailed as planned. The incoming convoys HX.126, and SC.31, now passing Cape Farewell, held course for the North Channel. The heavy escort earmarked to cover WS.8B, the monthly Middle East troop convoy, was mustering in the Clyde. The battleship *Rodney*, long overdue for refit, was preparing to sail for Boston, Massachusetts, with the liner *Britannic* and an escort of four destroyers. The newly commissioned carrier *Victorious* was off Scapa Flow completing her trials. Her hangar was full of crated Hurricane fighters for shipment to Gibraltar and she, too, was due to sail with WS.8B. A scratch air group assembled for the occasion – it consisted of nine Swordfish torpedo-bombers and six Fulmar fighters, all that the carrier could accommodate in present circumstances – waited at RNAS Hatston, the wind-swept naval air station in the Orkneys, to begin deck-landing training.

But the sense of expectation among units of the Home Fleet was strong. It was on 19 May that Captain J. C. Leach, commanding officer of the new battleship *Prince of Wales*, called on the Commander-in-Chief to report his ship ready for operations.

* * *

The German task group and its escort passed Kristiansand towards sunset on 20 May. Their passage of the Great Belt and the Kattegat had been free from the muddle and delay that had marked the start of Operation 'Berlin' and they were running almost exactly to time. The intelligence picture as presented by Group North seemed favourable. The Home Fleet was in Scapa Flow. The *Luftwaffe* had sighted an aircraft carrier, three battleships and a number of cruisers in the anchorage shortly after mid-day. Photographic analysis had confirmed this report; one of the battleships appeared to be the *Hood* and the number of light cruisers present was now established as six.

Yet there was plenty of reason for anxiety. Lütjens had cleared the Sjaellands Rev, the narrow neck of land marking the northern limit of the Great Belt, at sunrise, and, leaving the island of Anholt on his port hand, had shaped course for the Skaw and the defensive minefields guarding the Baltic approaches. Early overcast had given way to a bright clear day; one eye witness later described it as 'radiant'. War seemed remote. In early afternoon, as the *Bismarck* and *Prinz Eugen* with their escort of destroyers and mine-sweepers were approaching the latitude of Gothenburg, look-outs made out a warship standing clear of the Swedish coast. It was soon identified as the Swedish cruiser *Gotland*; the ship had increased speed and turned north-westward to match the movements of the German task group and had remained in sight for an hour or more before disappearing to the south-east.

An encounter of this kind, unforeseen by German planners yet now seemingly so predicable, raised difficult questions about the security of the operation. Lütjens felt it necessary to report the incident. 'At 1300 ... cruiser

Gotland passed in clear view,' he told Group Headquarters, 'anticipate formation will be reported.' Admiral Carls attempted to restore a sense of perspective. 'Given Sweden's strictly neutral stance,' he replied, 'I do not consider the risk of compromise any greater than that posed by well-established and systematic enemy surveillance of the Baltic approaches.[5]

The effect of this unwelcome development on the Fleet Commander's decisions must remain a matter for speculation. If the news did reach unfriendly ears – and Lütjens seems to have had few illusions about this – the British would reinforce their patrols in the northern exits and strengthen their watch on the Norwegian coast. But how long would it take for the news to filter through to London? If the intelligence network was slow and inefficient and British commanders were slow to react, there was much to be said for making direct for remote Arctic waters. Lütjens had spelt out the advantages of this course at his pre-sailing conference. But if the network was efficient and the enemy reacted quickly, daylight would see the narrows alive with British aircraft. It would then be better to lie up in the fjords during daylight and move on after darkness returned. The Admiral had foreseen just such a possibility; all preparations were in place. The balance was a fine one. Weather and visibility along the Norwegian coast on the morning of 21 May would decide the issue. Until then, the proper course was to adjust alert states to reflect the latest assessment of risk. As Lütjens rounded the southern coast of Norway in the dark hours, leaving the comparative safety of the Skagerrak for the uncertain waters of the North Sea, he brought his ships to the full action state so that his main and secondary batteries would be at instant readiness for a night encounter.

As dawn approached, Lütjens reduced his state of alert to the normal war cruising condition. And it was probably in the half-light of that May morning, when he could judge the cloud base and visibility for himself, that he made his final decision in favour of the fjords. Shortly after 0700 he turned his squadron towards the entrance to the Korsfjord. The ships reached the shelter of the land at 0900, and two hours later the *Bismarck* was secure in Grimstadfjord, a T-shaped cleft in the rugged coastline four or five miles south-west of Bergen. There she remained until evening, her crew painting over her camouflage stripes with ships-side grey, pausing occasionally to admire the virtuosity of the *Luftwaffe* pilots as they wheeled their Me 109 fighters between the bluffs.

The *Prinz Eugen* continued up the narrows for a further ten miles before coming to anchor in Kalvanes Bay, where she refuelled from the tanker *Wollin*. Lütjens' parting instructions to her were to meet him south of Kalvanes at 2000 that evening and to be at immediate readiness for action on leaving the land.[6]

* * *

Lütjens regained the open sea as the sun was setting and steamed rapidly northwards overnight. He had spent a bare twelve hours in Norwegian waters and had left as soon as it was safe to do so. On passing the latitude of Trondheim he released his destroyers and continued with the *Prinz Eugen* alone, leaving no clue to his further intentions.[7] He still faced a fundamental choice. He could make for the Arctic and loiter there as he had done in January or he could make an immediate attempt on the northern exits. What he needed most of all was reliable information on the enemy's state of alert and on his fleet dispositions. For the moment, there was little solid information to go on.

Luftwaffe reconnaissance over Scapa Flow that afternoon had failed; the latest unambiguous evidence on the position of the Home Fleet (obtained at noon on the 20th) was nearly 36 hours old. Radio intelligence, on the other hand, had seen nothing in the patterns of enemy signal traffic to suggest that the British might be on a heightened state of alert or that the Fleet might be on the move. There was just a single snippet of evidence suggest otherwise.

In the early morning of 21 May, as Lütjens was making his decision in favour of Korsfjord, German intelligence had intercepted a message from a British signal station warning aircraft to be on the look-out for two battleships and three destroyers moving north. Group North had relayed this information to the task force, although his signal does not seem to have reached Lütjens until the late afternoon. Admiral Carls had pointed to the efficiency of British agents in the Great Belt and had added that the report provided clear evidence that the departure of the task force 'had not gone unobserved'. He had wanted to make sure that Lütjens would not linger in Norwegian waters too long.[8]

Twenty-four hours after the event, the report had lost a good deal of its former significance, and by the morning of 22 May Admiral Carls was beginning to play the matter down. The *Luftwaffe*, he told the Fleet Commander, had linked the message to air operations west of the Faeroes. If this were true, the enemy were badly off the scent. His next intelligence assessment reached Lütjens at 0935. It read:

> Nothing of special interest in aircraft W/T; no operational wireless traffic; no observable results from departure of task force or from British order to search for battleships; only reinforced air reconnaissance in north-east sector.[9]

Within the hour Group North had been forced to modify his line. Enemy aircraft, he told Lütjens, had dropped flares and bombs over Kalvanes Bay not long after the task force had left, and, since dawn, reconnaissance of the Norwegian coast had become intense. But enemy air activity was centred too far south to have any prospect of finding the *Bismarck* and there was no sign that her departure from the Bergen area had become known.[10]

By noon on 22 May Lütjens was approaching latitude 66°N. He was more than 400 miles from British bases in the Shetlands and safe from observation from the air. The wind was a little east of south, the weather increasingly overcast. Forecasts suggested that, over the next thirty-six hours, a weather front would move northwards to cover Iceland and the waters to the north of it. At 1203 Lütjens altered course to the north-west and passed the *Prinz Eugen* his intended route to the Denmark Strait. He was careful to add, however, that if the weather changed he would break off and rendezvous with the *Weissenburg* in the Arctic Ocean.

At 2015 that evening Lütjens received the latest intelligence on Scapa Flow. Weather had prevented photography, but visual reconnaissance had identified four large ships, one apparently an aircraft carrier, six light cruisers and several destroyers. There had been no change, Group North commented, since the photo-reconnaissance of 20 May. The passage of the Norwegian narrows, he suggested, had gone unnoticed.[11]

For the rest of the day the task force held its course to the north-west. The wind had veered south-westerly and the visibility had started to close in; watch-keepers in the *Prinz Eugen* put it at 300–400m. They could see nothing of the battleship ahead of them and kept station on her wake. Captain Brinkmann recorded that the weather seemed 'made for a break-out'. His forecasters saw every possibility that it might last until the ships reached the southern point of Greenland. There could be no better opportunity.

Towards midnight – the term had little meaning at this latitude for it remained as bright as day – the ships turned to the west. Soon afterwards they got a message from Group North to speed them on their way.

(1) No operational moves by enemy naval forces so far.
(2) Major U-boat successes south of Greenland during past few days.
(3) Landing in Crete proceeding according to plan.
(4) After today's sinking of four British cruisers off Crete and damage to others, Group expects grave threat to British sea power from immediate appearance of Task Force on Atlantic routes.[12]

By noon on 23 May the *Bismarck* and *Prinz Eugen* were approaching the longitude of 20°W. Six hours steaming would bring them to the North Cape of Iceland, the narrowest and shallowest part of the passage. Lütjens brought his ships to the highest state of readiness and ordered degaussing equipment to be switched on. There had been no change to the intelligence assessments issued the evening before. So far, the air waves had offered no hint that enemy surface forces might be on the move, and it was now more than thirty-six hours since the task force had left Bergen. Meanwhile, as the ships pressed on towards the narrows, they remained shrouded in a blanket of fog. The forecast continued to show the northward movement of warm air over the Denmark Strait; visibilities, according to Group North, would be poor to very poor. The planned reconnaissance sortie along the ice-edge had been cancelled because of the weather and there was no prospect of its being revived until the weather cleared. The coming hours would inevitably be anxious ones, but there was no reason for pessimism.

* * *

The first direct evidence that a new German operation might be under way reached the Admiralty in the late hours of 20 May. The warning message from the British Naval Attaché in Stockholm, Captain H. W. Denham, read:

Kattegat today 20 May. (a) This afternoon eleven German merchant ships passed Lenker North; (b) at 1500 two large warships, escorted by three destroyers, five escort vessels, [and] ten or twelve aircraft, passed Marstrand course north-west.

When Home Fleet staff officers were summoned to Tovey's cabin they found the Commander-in-Chief on the telephone, discussing the news with the Director of Naval Intelligence and with Admiral Sir Tom Phillips, Vice-

Chief of Naval Staff. The intelligence seemed to be reliable. One of the ships was probably the *Bismarck*; the other might be a pocket-battleship or a *Hipper* class cruiser. The presence of the *Tirpitz* seemed unlikely. Was it right to assume some connection between the heavy units and the merchant ships mentioned in Denham's signal? If so, what kind of operation was this, and what could its objectives be? There was a good deal of speculation that night both in London and in Scapa Flow, but it seemed premature to draw any firm conclusions.

Meanwhile what was Tovey's proper course of action? By morning the enemy might be passing Bergen, but he could hardly be further on than that, and, if he were intending to break out, it would be a further twenty-four hours before he came within range of British patrol lines in the Iceland–Faeroes passage. There were serious dangers in deploying forces too early: as at the end of January, Tovey could find his ships running low on fuel just as the critical moment came. For the time being he could afford to wait. Reconnaissance sorties at first light on 21 May, already the subject of joint discussions between the Admiralty and Headquarters Coastal Command, would help him to time his next moves.

In the early afternoon of 21 May the second of two photo-reconnaissance Spitfires assigned to cover Norwegian coastal waters from Oslo westwards flew over Bergen at a height of 25,000ft and took photographs which have since become famous.[13] When he landed at Wick on the Pentland Firth, Pilot Officer Michael Suckling reported seeing two cruisers and a number of merchant ships; but an analysis of his photographs quickly established the presence of the *Bismarck* and a heavy cruiser of the *Hipper* class. The news reached London and Scapa Flow within the hour. Plans were set in hand for an immediate attack by bombers of Coastal Command; there would be more attacks during the morning of the 22nd. Furthermore, unknown to the Admiralty and to the Commander-in-Chief, the commanding officer of the naval air station at Hatston, Captain H. St J. Fancourt, moved the Albacore torpedo bombers of 848 Naval Air Squadron to the forward base at Sunburgh in the Shetlands to be nearer the objective.[14]

Meanwhile speculation about German intentions had reached fever pitch. Cryptographic evidence suggested a raid on the sea lanes and, during the evening of 21 May, the Admiralty warned commanders-in-chief accordingly.[15] But the stop in Bergen, a place in easy reach of British reconnaissance, had seemed inconsistent with this interpretation and the presence of merchant ships close to the *Bismarck* and the cruiser had continued to hint at other possibilities. Reports of a U-boat north of Iceland and of an air attack on the wireless station at Thorshaven in the Faeroes provided additional, if rather dubious, clues.[16] Tovey was not yet ready to bank all on a single assumption, but by evening he had decided on two preliminary moves. In a nicely calculated risk, he ordered the cruisers *Manchester* and *Birmingham*, on watch in the Iceland–Faeroes passage, to fuel immediately and then return to their stations. As he later noted, 'it was obvious that fuel would become a vital factor before the operation was completed'. At the same time, he felt that the moment had come put some additional weight off south-western Iceland to stand behind his patrol lines. At 2000, Vice-Admiral L. E. Holland sailed for Hvalfjord with the heavy ships of the newly formed Battle Cruiser Squadron, the *Hood* and the *Prince of Wales*, and an escort of six destroyers.

* * *

Admiralty planners, meanwhile, had been in constant touch with their opposite numbers in Coastal Command Headquarters defining the search areas to be investigated from dawn 22 May. They would cover the Norwegian coast from Kristiansand to Trondheim. At the same time, urgent steps were being taken to reinforce the Commander-in-Chief. As the ships of the Battle Cruiser Squadron left the anchorage, Tovey learned that the *Repulse* (then in the Clyde awaiting the departure of WS.8B) and the *Victorious* (then embarking her new air group and giving some of its younger pilots their first attempt at a deck landing) were to be placed at his disposal. These additions were welcome; but a brand new carrier with a scratch air group was something of an unknown quantity. Tovey needed to form an opinion about its fighting capabilities as a matter of urgency. A hastily convened meeting provided a modicum of reassurance. The ship's Swordfish squadron (825 Naval Air Squadron) seemed well led and fired with enthusiasm for all its inexperience: Tovey was impressed by what he saw of Lieutenant-Commander Eugene Esmonde, its commanding officer.[17] But the Fulmar fighters of 800Z Squadron were barely trained; as far as could be foreseen, they had no clear part to play in the coming operation. The urgent need was to bolster the Fleet's reconnaissance and torpedo strike capability and the

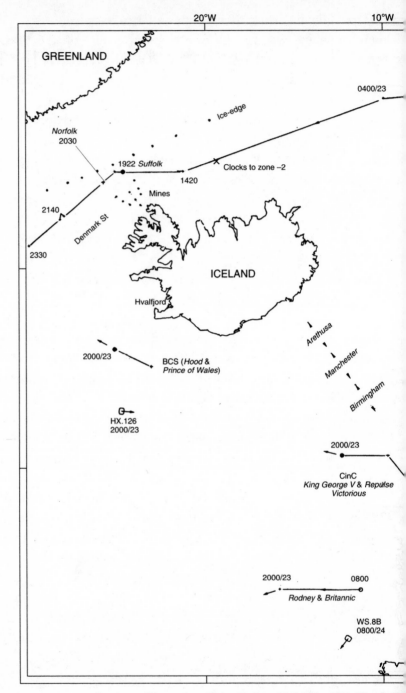

Break-out of Bismarck *and* Prinz Eugen *, 21–23 May 1941. Time B (zor*

100

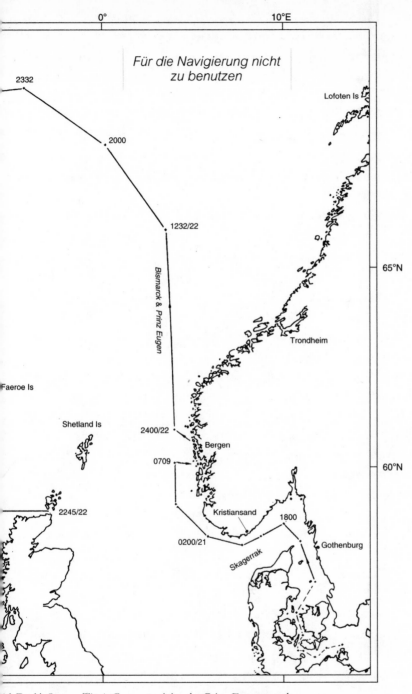

obvious answer lay with the Albacores of 848 Squadron. Urgent enquiries were made, and it was found that the Albacores had been ordered to the Shetlands in preparation for an attack on the fjords. In a late-night telephone conversation with the First Sea Lord, Tovey was given *carte blanche* to change the composition of the *Victorious*'s air group as he saw fit, keeping Coastal Command informed. But the balance of advantage was difficult to determine. Should he stop the squadron's move and spoil an attack opportunity? Would he find that his carrier was tied up exchanging squadrons just when he needed it most? He decided, by default, to let existing orders stand. Later on, people would come to sense an opportunity missed.[18]

Forecasts now began to show ominous signs of a deterioration in the weather. They were confirmed by events. Few of the Coastal Command bombers launched against Bergen during the final hours of 21 May reached their objective and none succeeded in identifying a target. They bombed blind. The first aircraft to reach the Norwegian coast in early hours of 22 May found the cloud base at 200ft and conditions 'extremely adverse'. As the morning progressed conditions became worse still, and at midday Coastal Command suspended further operations.

Tovey waited on tenterhooks in Scapa Flow, knowing that he faced critical decisions. Twenty-four hours had elapsed since the last sighting of the *Bismarck*. If he could be sure that she had sailed and certain that she was bound for the northern passages his proper course of action would be clear enough: he would reinforce his cruiser lines and get his fleet to sea. But what if she was still in Bergen? What if she had sailed on some different mission? If Tovey's deployments were premature or wrong, he would find himself poorly placed to deal with alternative contingencies. In the event, matters were settled for him by one of the more bizarre episodes in the history of naval warfare.

At Hatston, Captain Fancourt had been reflecting on what he might do to assist the situation and his thoughts had turned to Commander G. A. Rotherham, an Observer specialist of legendary experience (and now Hatston's Executive Officer) and to a pair of obsolete Maryland bombers used by the fleet for target-towing and height-finding. Rotherham had fallen in with his captain's ideas at once, and by 1400 Fancourt had got the agreement of the operational authorities, obtained guidance on German air defences in the Bergen area and assembled an all-volunteer crew.

Rotherham took off at 1630, crossed the North Sea with barely a glimpse of the surface and, using the methods of the aviation pioneers, descended to make a near-perfect landfall at the entrance to Korsfjord. Inside the island chain, cloud and visibility lifted. The aircraft looked into Grimstadfjord and went on to Kalvanes. Finding both empty, it flew the circuit again. It then passed low over the town and harbour of Bergen, attracting a hail of anti-aircraft fire, and turned for home. After several failed attempts to raise Coastal Command, the aircraft telegraphist succeeded in getting through to Hatston on the target-towing frequency, and at 1939 Fancourt passed the news on. His signal read: 'Following received from Hatston reconnaissance aircraft over Bergen. Battleship and cruiser have left.'

At 1942 Tovey ordered his fleet to prepare for sea and made his final dispositions. Of the various courses of action open to the enemy, an Atlantic break-out appeared the most likely and the most dangerous. Precedent suggested that the enemy would choose the Denmark Strait, but a break-out south of Iceland could not be excluded and it was this that would put him under the greatest pressure. He ordered the cruisers *Manchester* and *Birmingham* to resume their patrols in the Iceland–Faeroes passage and sent the *Arethusa* to join them. He sailed the *Suffolk* from Hvalfjord to join Rear-Admiral W. F. Wake-Walker (Rear-Admiral First Cruiser Squadron) in the Denmark Strait and ordered Vice-Admiral Holland with the Battle Cruiser Squadron to cover both patrol lines. Tovey himself, with the *King George V*, the *Victorious* and the cruisers *Galatea* (Rear-Admiral Second Cruiser Squadron), *Hermione*, *Kenya* and *Aurora* sailed to pass the Hoxa boom at 2300 on 22 May and set out to the north-west at economical speed. He intended to cover the passages south of the Faeroes while keeping open a 'reasonable possibility of interfering' if a threat to Iceland developed.[19] He ordered the *Repulse* to join him at noon the next day and called for a comprehensive programme of air reconnaissance to cover the northern passages, the approaches to Iceland and Norwegian coastal waters.

The stage was now set. At 1000 in the morning of 23 May the heavy cruiser *Suffolk*, newly refuelled, joined Rear-Admiral Wake-Walker in the approaches to Isafjord, a deep cleft in the glacial coastline of north-western Iceland, close to the minefields than guarded the narrows. To exploit the potential of her new Type 284 radar, a system designed primarily for fire control but which had already demonstrated its capabilities in the surface warning role, the Rear-Admiral gave her a patrol line running north-east/ south-west within radar range of the ice-edge. Wake-Walker's flagship, the *Norfolk*, less well equipped, took up a parallel patrol line a few miles to the southward.[20]

* * *

As the *Bismarck* task group approached the narrows, the fog that had shrouded it since the evening before lifted a little, giving visibilities of 400– 500m. From time to time, dim shapes materialised before the eyes of edgy look-outs, only to resolve themselves into ice-floes. Alarms were frequent, and as they skirted the ice-edge the ships took violent avoiding action to reduce the risk of hull or propeller damage. As evening approached, the weather became clearer. To starboard, over the icefields, the sky brightened and visibility extended to the horizon. To port and towards the land it remained murky with patches of fog. Ahead lay a broad corridor of clear water extending to the south-west.

The German record of the evening's developments is not wholly reliable. Captain Brinkmann's war diary, much used in historical reconstructions, shows every sign of having been written up after the event when one incident had merged into another and when it had become impossible to recall the exact sequence in which things had happened. This much seems clear. At 1922 the *Bismarck* signalled the alarm. Peering ahead, look-outs in the *Prinz Eugen* glimpsed a dim shape disappearing into the mist about twenty degrees on the port bow. It was taken to be an auxiliary cruiser; but the encounter had been so sudden that neither ship had been able to make a definite identification and neither had been able to bring its guns to bear. Radar showed a contact at 13,000m; it was opening rapidly to the southward. Within minutes radio intelligence teams intercepted an enemy report: 'Emergency, repeat back; one battleship, one cruiser in sight bearing 020°, range 7 miles, course 240.'

Thereafter radar and hydrophone contact showed the bearing of the enemy moving slowly astern. He was soon following in the wake of the German ships; he was matching their speed and he could be glimpsed from time to time at the extreme limit of visibility. This was something more than an auxiliary. At 2015 Lütjens signalled Group North, 'Quadrant AD 29, one heavy cruiser.'

Within minutes radar detected a new contact closing from the port bow. At 2030 it broke clear of the mist at a range of about six miles, the heavy superstructure and three funnels revealing it as an 8in cruiser of the 'County' class. The *Bismarck*'s main battery came into action at once. The enemy turned away abruptly under cover of smoke and disappeared into the murk, the splashes of the *Bismarck*'s 15in shells cascading around him.

As they fled south-westward at flank speed, the German commanders tried to gauge from radar, hydrophone effects and radio intelligence, and from occasional glimpses of the enemy, the strength of the forces that were following them. There was at least one heavy cruiser in pursuit. The *Prince Eugen* had caught a brief glimpse of her at 2044 and thought that she had seen the flash of gunfire. Lütjens had at once ordered her to the head of the formation. But radio intelligence had quickly established the presence of two British units exchanging plain-language information on the task group's position, course and speed – information that seemed amazingly prompt and accurate – and sending urgent coded messages to Scapa Flow. It was about now that the radio intelligence section in the *Prinz Eugen* formed the view – or contributed to the rumour – that the radio call-sign of one of the units in pursuit was that of the battleship *King George V*.[21]

* * *

The fact that the enemy had established contact in the Denmark Strait caused no immediate alarm in German command circles. There was, however, mounting criticism of the *Luftwaffe*: its failure to get a look into Scapa on 23 May was later described as 'highly deplorable'. But there was still no sign in the patterns of enemy signal traffic that a major fleet movement had started. Watching from the sidelines, Admiral Saalwächter, Commander-in-Chief Group West, drew the rather obvious conclusion that German intentions had been recognised. But he was not pessimistic:

> Based on an evaluation of the situation as a whole [he recorded in his War Diary], I consider it appropriate for the task force commander to continue the break-out since I see no particular danger . . . An approach by heavy forces from Scapa, which, according to the latest photo-reconnaissance, are in Scapa, is hardly to be expected for the time being.[22]

They felt much the same in the *Prinz Eugen*. 'It is assumed on board,' wrote Captain Brinkmann after reading the latest intelligence summaries, 'that the break-out through the Denmark Strait has been successful.'[23]

It seems unlikely that Lütjens would have shared this complacency. All his experience in ship and fleet command must have told him that his first priority was to break contact with his shadowers as soon as a reasonable opportunity came his way. Initially at least, the odds would be against him. The ice-edge was close on his starboard hand and the coast of Iceland not far to port. His freedom of manoeuvre was severely restricted. But his course was taking him towards open waters and within hours he would be able to take advantage of a snow squall or perhaps the brief period of Arctic twilight to make his decisive move.

He had touched on the question of engaging enemy scouting forces during his pre-sailing conference with Brinkmann and Lindemann and must surely have considered the option now. But, again, circumstances were far from ideal. The enemy was holding contact at extreme range and he was visible only at intervals. Turning back in the hope of engaging a distant and elusive target would only delay progress towards open water. If the opportunity came he was ready to seize it. He had reversed the order of his line for a number of reasons – to protect the *Prinz Eugen* and to restore radar warning in the ahead sector (the *Bismarck*'s forward system had not survived the shock from her main batteries), but primarily to give himself a clear field of fire astern. Towards 2200, it seems, he made the attempt. Müllenheim-Rechberg, the *Bismarck*'s Third Gunnery Officer, recalls that, under cover of a rain squall, Lütjens turned the ship, hoping catch his pursuers unawares, but when he drew clear of the rain there was nothing to be seen. He quickly resumed his course to the south-west.[24]

Towards midnight, at the change of the watch, the task force commander decided that his decisive moment had come. He had gained the sea-room that he needed. The sky was heavily overcast and the north-west wind was bringing periodic flurries of snow which reduced visibility to a few hundred metres. In the gloomy half-light, the ships laid smoke and altered abruptly to the southward.

For more than two hours Lütjens had every reason to believe that his manoeuvre had been successful. The enemy's shadowing reports, so prompt and accurate up to now, changed. A few minutes after midnight, unit 'K3G', the more active of the shadowers, had reported 'Enemy hidden by snow; my course 180°; my speed 29 knots; my position 65°47′ North, 27°57′ West.'[25] Her reports had continued in the same vein. At 0028 she had reported the visibility as one mile, at 0131 as two miles and at 0231, after an hour's silence, as one mile once more. The key ingredients in her reports – enemy position, course, and speed – had been missing; shadowing in the prevailing conditions was clearly impossible.

But at 0228 came a new alarm. Look-outs reported a cruiser closing from astern. The *Bismarck*'s after radar had given no warning; the *Prinz Eugen* was now charged with watching the stern sector as well. Any lingering hope that the enemy might have lost the scent dissolved. The next enemy report, timed at 0247, read, 'Emergency; repeat back; have detected enemy surface craft by RDF bearing 180°, 10 miles; my position 64°47′ North, 29°02′ West.'

Reports reaching Lütjens from his *B-Dienst* section in the hours that followed showed that the shadowers were tracking his squadron with an efficiency that was unprecedented. How were they doing it? They could hardly be relying on visual means alone; they were out of sight for hours on end. Everything pointed to some new technical development, and, worryingly, to one which seemed to outperform equivalent German devices. The Fleet Staff reached the conclusion (possibly on the basis of radio intelligence) that, contrary to all earlier assumptions, British ships were now equipped with a highly effective radar system. Not everyone agreed. Captain Brinkmann was sure that the enemy was using a passive directional sensor and fixing position by triangulation. The presence of two shadowers, widely spaced, seemed to point firmly to that conclusion. He thought that hydrophones were the probable answer – the Admiralty had long been interested in acoustics – although he could not rule out radar, or (short-wave) radio-intercept.[26] There were some in high places who found it convenient to support his views.

* * *

But, whatever these developments might mean for future break-out attempts, the immediate implications for the *Bismarck* task group did not appear unduly serious. The Home Fleet must certainly have sailed by now, but there was no reason to suppose that the German squadron had not gained a healthy head start. The open Atlantic lay before it; the coming day would provide ample opportunity to test the mettle of the shadowing cruisers. Lütjens resumed his south-westerly course, and at 0358 in the morning of 24 May he stood down from the action state.

Notes to Chapter 5

1   ADM 234/327, p. 291.
2   The timing had been wrong; the *Scheer* had come though the Denmark Strait in low visibility and passed north of Iceland twenty-four hours earlier. Roskill, *The War at Sea*, Vol. 1, p. 371.
3   PRO ADM 234/327, p. 291. The Admiralty's Naval Intelligence Division seems to have kept its information on the *Scharnhorst* and *Gneisenau* under close wraps, presumably to protect highly sensitive sources. Senior commanders, including Admiral Somerville of Force H, were not kept informed of their operational status.
4   German plans for the occupation of Iceland ('*Ikarus*') had been in existence since June 1940 but were now dormant. Admiral Raeder had opposed them for lack of sufficient surface forces and because he could not guarantee resupply. *Führer Conferences*, p. 112.
5   Müllenheim-Rechberg, p. 104. See also reconstruction of Fleet War Diary for 20 May 1941, PG47895, p. 7.
6   PG47897, diary entry for 21 May 1941. (This reconstruction of the *Bismarck*'s War Diary was undertaken by Group West after '*Rheinübung*'. It was based on the signal logs and war diaries of the major shore commands and of the *Prinz Eugen*.)
7   PG47895, chronology of events, 22 May 1941. Admiral Carls was annoyed by his silence; he suggested in his War Diary that Lütjens was relying on the weather or other factors to help him make up his mind.
8   *Ibid.* Group North's comments are included, misleadingly, in the chronology of events for 20 May 1941. There is some evidence that the intelligence report may have reached Lütjens earlier; the *Prinz Eugen* appears to have received it from the Naval High Command at 0645 on 21 May. If it did, it may have been a factor in the Fleet Commander's decision to enter Korsfjord. Eye-witness accounts suggest the later time. Müllenheim-Rechberg, pp. 113–14.
9   PG20418, p. 14.
10 PG47897, diary entry for 22 May 1941.
11 PG47895, chronology of events, entry for 22 May 1941; PG47897, diary entry for same date.
12 *Ibid.*, chronology of events, 22 May 1941. The Group North War Diary shows

that this message was a deliberate hint. Admiral Carls had long favoured the idea of breaking out rather than sneaking out and still hoped that Lütjens would take his advice.

13 The version given opposite p. 400 in the British Official History has been printed back to front.

14 This move was not cleared with the naval authorities because, as a disembarked squadron, 848 NAS came under the operational control of Coastal Command. The need to keep other commands informed seems to have been overlooked in the heat of the moment.

15 Admiralty Message 1828 (B) of 21 May. Admiralty opinion was based on a partial reading of German Naval Enigma during April. This showed that the *Bismarck* had been exercising with the *Prinz Eugen* and that she had embarked prize crews and appropriate charts. Hinsley, Vol. 1, p. 341. The decryption of naval Enigma was running up to a week late during May 1941; it thus played a peripheral part in the events now about to unfold.

16 PRO ADM 199/1188, p. 122.

17 Grenfell, p. 27. Lt-Cdr Esmonde was killed ten months later while attacking the *Scharnhorst*, *Gneisenau* and *Prinz Eugen* during their escape up-Channel (Operation *'Cerberus'*). He was awarded a posthumous VC.

18 Tovey blamed the Admiralty for the muddle over 848 NAS and the controversy simmered on for some months. See minutes DNAD to VCNS in PRO ADM 199/1188, pp. 27 and 33. The charitable conclusion would seem to be that the complex command arrangements governing disembarked Fleet Air Arm squadrons were too inflexible to meet the demands of a fast-moving situation.

19 PRO ADM 199/1188, p. 9.

20 *Ibid.*, p. 125. The text of RA 1CS signal 1009 (B), 23 May 1941, is given in Broom, *Make a Signal* (London: Putnam, 1955.) For technical and tactical developments in radar, see Howse, Derek, Radar at Sea: The Royal Navy in World War 2 (Annapolis: Naval Institute Press, 1993).

21 PG47897, *Bismarck* War Diary (as reconstructed by Group West), entry for 23 May 1941; PG47895, chronology of events, same date. The origins of this mistake are obscure. German sources suggest, implausibly, that the idea came from the ship's *B-Dienst* section, but it seems more probable that it arose from a misunderstanding between the *B-Dienst* and the Command. The *Suffolk*'s radio call-sign was 'K3G'.

22 PG47895, chronology of events, entry for 23 May 1941. The latest photo-reconnaissance was in fact three days old, although a partial visual reconnaissance had been made 30 hours earlier.

23 *Ibid.*, chronology of events, 23 May 1941. The Naval Staff found Brinkmann's remark 'surprising'; this was later amended to 'totally incredible'.

24 Müllenheim-Rechberg, p. 134. Captain Ellis's ROP is consistent with this

evidence. At 2154 the *Suffolk* caught sight of the *Bismarck* as she emerged from rain. She seemed to be at a fine inclination. Ellis at once reversed course, believing that she might be returning to the Denmark Strait. PRO ADM 199/1188, p. 270.

25   HMS *Suffolk*'s shadowing reports are listed in PRO ADM 119/1187, p. 345.
26   PG47895, Section E, *Prinz Eugen: Lessons Learned.*

6

'An Unlucky Hit'

The heavy ships of the Battle Cruiser Squadron which sailed for Iceland on the evening of 21 May made an ill-matched pair, though hardly more so than earlier *ad hoc* groupings. Pressure of commitments and wear and tear after twenty months of war meant that commanders-in-chief had to cobble together battle groups as best they could.

Admiral Holland's flagship, the *Hood*, was a ship with a reputation to uphold. She had been completed in 1920, too late for service in the Great War, and had been seen as the most powerful ship afloat for the best part of two decades. She was classed as a battlecruiser; her main machinery developed 144,000 shaft horsepower and gave her a speed of 31kts. But speed had not been bought at the expense of firepower and protection; she had been armed and armoured as a battleship and her design had reflected the best of contemporary ideas. The result had been a leviathan. The ship had emerged with a displacement of nearly 42,000 tons and a price tag to match, an escalation in scale and cost that post-war governments had been unwilling to emulate. The later ships of her class had been cancelled. In an era of naval limitation, the *Hood* had remained unique, a symbol of British maritime pre-eminence and a 'problem' for the wargamers of rival navies.

For all that, the *Hood* had been the product of her time. Her designers had emphasised vertical protection (a sensible priority in the 1914–18 context) but had seen little reason to enhance the ship's horizontal protection beyond the accepted standards of the day. Specialists had been uneasy from the start, and additional armour had been placed above magazine spaces during the course of the build, though not enough to stifle criticism. Within a decade of the *Hood*'s completion, experts, aware of developments in fire control and in long-range gunnery, had warned that the ship would be vulnerable to plunging shellfire. Later, they had pointed to the growing risk from the armour-piercing bomb. But nothing had been done. Although the crises of the late 1930s had again focused attention on the *Hood*'s shortcomings and a programme of improvements had been agreed, the work had never been put in hand.

Her consort, the *Prince of Wales*, was the second in a new class of battleships (the *King George V* class) ordered under the 1936 naval rearmament programme. In terms of protection she incorporated the very latest ideas. Her vertical and horizontal armour was exceptionally strong and took the form of a single, heavily armoured box on the principle of 'all or nothing'. The Admiralty had few worries on this score. The shortcomings of the class – which would be brought into sharp focus by the events of the next few days – had their origins in the Washington Treaty of 1922 and in subsequent attempts to get a quart into a into pint pot. Balancing the competing claims of speed, protection and firepower on a displacement of 35,000 tons had never been easy. And there was now the air threat to be considered as well. The Admiralty had seen little alternative but to reverse past trends towards ever-larger calibres and accept a main armament of ten 14in guns; they had hoped to find compensation in increased rates of fire. And in a further attempt to save weight, to preserve stability and to concentrate protection where it really mattered, the Admiralty had decided to mount the main armament in two turrets of four guns and one of two guns.

The result had been a developmental nightmare, and serious delays had resulted. Ammunition supply and the provision of electrical and hydraulic power to the turrets had been particular areas of difficulty. Infuriated by signs that Germans were winning the race to get the new battleships to sea (the *Bismarck* had shipped her guns while those of the *King George V* were still in the shed), Churchill had accused the Admiralty of 'improvidence' and had threatened to leave off 'the lagging two-gun turret' and put a dummy in its place.[1] Later, many would come to believe that reliability had been the main casualty in this difficult design and development process.[2]

The full truth about the main armament in ships of the *King George V* class would be revealed only under the test of action, but the Vice-Admiral Battle Cruiser Squadron can have had few illusions about the battleworthiness of his consort. Captain Leach had reported his ship ready for operations only two days beforehand. His work-up, widely acknowledged to have been cut to the bone, had been dogged by breakdowns, and contractors' workmen were still on board setting things to rights. Opportunities for exercising the main battery as a whole had been few, and the need to concentrate on elementary problems had delayed progress towards more complex evolutions. The battleship was an uncertain quantity, and the Admiral had every excuse for treating her as such.

During his passage westward Holland conducted simple tactical exercises and set out his action policies. These were unremarkable. He referred simply to standing instructions on concentration of fire and on marking the fall of shot. He said nothing that could be interpreted as allowing Captain Leach any discretion in his conduct of an action; he intended, evidently, to adjust his plans to suit the circumstances and to control matters himself. His squadron was, after all, newly formed and wholly untried. The only topic that seems to have attracted a genuine exchange of views was the use to be made of the *Prince of Wales'* Walrus aircraft. It was decided that its primary function would be to locate and report the enemy; its secondary role would be spotting for the *Prince of Wales*.

News that the *Bismarck* had left Bergen reached Admiral Holland's flagship during the evening of 22 May and brought these leisurely proceedings to an end. Tovey's precautionary moves now had a clear purpose. To allow for the possibility of extended operations south-west of Iceland, Holland sent two of his destroyers to fuel and told them to re-join him south of Hvalfjord the next day. When, twenty-four hours later, the flagship intercepted the *Suffolk*'s enemy report, tension reached fever pitch. The plot showed that the *Bismarck* and her consort were 300 miles to the northward. If the German task group held its course for the Atlantic and if the cruisers maintained contact, there was every possibility of an interception. At 1939 on 23 May Holland ordered steam for full speed, imposed radar silence and turned his ships to a course of 295°. When it was clear that the enemy was holding on to the south-west, Holland worked his heavy ships up to 26, 27 and finally 28kts, warning his destroyers that, if they could not keep up, they should follow at their best speed.[3]

Attempts to recapture Admiral Holland's appreciation of the situation at this critical time are inevitably speculative, but the main features of the tactical problem confronting him are obvious enough. With 300 miles – perhaps eight hours' steaming – separating him from contact with the enemy, Holland would have realised how much depended on the men in

113

the shadowing cruisers. At any moment the *Bismarck* might turn on them or attempt to break away in low visibility. He had every incentive, therefore, to make contact with the enemy as quickly as he could. The state of the light might or might not become a factor; in these northern latitudes, a successful gun action might well be possible at any time of day. Delay risked everything.

Then there was the question of surprise. There was no knowing how the enemy might react to the approach of heavy ships. Precedent suggested that he would attempt to evade; he might even scuttle back to German waters by the way he had come. Even a simple change of course would complicate the interception problem unless it were quickly reported by the cruisers. There were reasons beyond mere tactical orthodoxy for maintaining radio silence, even if this meant that the movements and actions of the heavy ships and the shadowers were imperfectly coordinated.

While the interception problem was complex in itself and likely to demand precision, quick thinking and fine judgment, most specialists have agreed that the conduct of the coming action would already have been uppermost in the Admiral's mind. He would have been thinking in particular about how to shape an approach which would minimise exposure to plunging shellfire and bring him to effective gun range quickly. Here, he would hope to use his superior weight of fire to decisive effect.[4] He needed high closing rates and open arcs of fire, conditions best met by shaping a course that would cross a little ahead of the enemy and bring about an engagement on his (Holland's) starboard bow. If all went well, the *Bismarck*, keeping south-west with the icefields on her starboard hand, would be presented, suddenly and unexpectedly, with an enemy closing from the port bow. He would be closing quickly and with A-arcs open.

This, at any rate, seems to have been Holland's preferred solution to the problem. His initial westerly course aimed for a position well ahead of the enemy; had he continued it indefinitely, he would have passed fifty or sixty miles ahead of the *Bismarck* at about 3 o'clock in the morning. But he had no intention of waiting that long. It seems that, having gained a forward position that would ensure high closing rates during the approach to contact, he intended a starboard turn to intercept the *Bismarck* on a course of 340°, for at 2120 he gave warning that he would spread his destroyers on a line of bearing of 070° to form an advanced screen.[5]

But by 2300 Holland had concluded from the cruisers' shadowing reports that the *Bismarck* was further on than expected and that his planned approach course was becoming increasingly unfavourable. He needed to 'gain bearing'. At 2311 he adjusted his course 10° to port and asked the *Prince of Wales* whether she could go faster. The reply was 'not without risk'. With his final approach course now uncertain, he postponed the deployment of his destroyers and, for the moment, put them in a close screen ahead.

As Holland held on to the westward, observing each new plot of the *Bismarck*'s position and watching for any hint of change, tension in the flagship mounted. Patches of fog and flurries of snow were beginning to affect the shadowing task; but the *Suffolk* was holding on to the enemy – just. At 2306 she had caught a glimpse of both ships at a range of eighteen miles; she reported their course and speed as 232°, 28kts. So far so good: the *Bismarck* was keeping to her south-westerly course; the geometry was still right; and contact would be made in a little over two hours.

But towards midnight things began to change – and change for the worse. At 2341 the *Suffolk* reported the *Bismarck* as altering 20° to port. Her next report had read 'Emergency. My 2341; enemy hidden in fog near ice. Estimated course 200°'. On the stroke of midnight she reported again. She had obtained a brief glimpse of the *Bismarck* and had confirmed the alteration of course. Minutes later the enemy had been 'hidden by snow'.[6]

What did these reports mean for Holland's plans? The *Bismarck* was now a little east of north at a range of 120 miles. A D/F bearing of the *Suffolk* taken by the *Prince of Wales* had helped to tie things together. If the reported course change was correct, the Battle Cruiser Squadron was already crossing the enemy's bow. Further westerly movement served no purpose; and it would leave the south-easterly quadrant uncovered. The time for decision had come. At eight minutes past midnight Holland reduced speed to 25kts and turned to a course of north. With the two battle groups now closing at a combined speed of more that 50kts, action could not long be delayed. The Admiral told his ships that he expected to make contact at any time after 0140. He ordered them to assume the first degree of readiness and to hoist battle ensigns.[7]

Roskill has described the situation now facing Admiral Holland as 'fraught with dangerous possibilities'. He had made his decision on the slenderest of evidence. Observation of the *Bismarck* had become intermittent, and there was no knowing whether her alteration of course had been temporary or something more. If he held to his northerly course too long and missed the enemy, Holland risked more than his favourable position on the enemy's bow: he risked a stern chase that he could never hope to win. He seems certainly to have sensed the danger. Towards 0030 it became clear that the *Suffolk* had entered snow and that visibility had dropped to less than a mile. Holland warned his ships that if the enemy was not in sight by 0210 he would alter course to the south until the cruisers had regained touch. But action remained uppermost in his mind. At 0032 he gave orders that the *Hood* and the *Prince of Wales* should concentrate their fire on the *Bismarck* and leave her consort to the two cruisers.[8]

Captain Leach shared his admiral's sense of anticipation. He prepared to launch his Walrus. But visibility dropped sharply and it was held on the catapult. At 0130, with no sign of the weather lifting and with battle expected at any moment, Leach gave orders for the Walrus to be defuelled and stowed.

As the 2 o'clock deadline came and went with no further reports to guide him, Admiral Holland turned his heavy ships to a course of 200° – the enemy's last reported course – and ordered the *Prince of Wales* to sweep the north-eastern horizon with her gunnery radar as he did so. The radar would not cover the arc ordered and a request to use the search radar instead was refused. In the circumstances prevailing, further northerly movement was beyond legitimate risk. But Holland remained sure beyond reasonable doubt that the enemy was still to the north of him for he ordered his destroyers to continue their search in that direction. Having settled on his new course, he increased speed to 26 and then to 27kts to keep ahead of the enemy, and, with the chances of an immediate encounter now slight, he allowed his guns' crews to rest.[9]

This period of uncertainty and of mounting anxiety came to an end at 0247 when the *Suffolk* regained contact. Her radar had detected a ship to the southward at a range of 19,200yds. Ten minutes later she had detected a second ship close to the first. Captain Ellis had reported the enemy's course and speed as 240°, 28kts. (The change of course had been short-lived.) From 0300 onwards the visibility had opened up, and at 0319 Ellis had gained a clear view of the *Bismarck* and the *Prinz Eugen* at a range of twelve miles. He had confirmed their course and speed. All doubts now resolved, the *Suffolk* had manoeuvred to open the range and had continued to watch the enemy from a position fifteen miles on his starboard quarter, alert for any sign of aggressive intent.

With up-to-date information on the enemy's position, course and speed, and helped by frequent D/F bearings on the two shadowing cruisers, Holland could begin to develop a clearer picture of relative position. The situation revealed by the flagship's plot was far from ideal. The enemy was close; his range at 0300 was calculated as fifteen miles. But he was not to the north, as had been hoped, but to the north-west. And he was steering a slightly diverging course. Holland was not on the enemy's bow but on his beam, and, with the *Bismarck* forging on at 28kts, he had no prospect of regaining a forward position.

At 0321 Holland turned 20° towards the enemy to close the range. Minutes later he turned a further 20° and increased speed to 28kts. At 0400 the enemy was judged to be twenty miles to the north-west. Visibility was improving. The *Prince of Wales* again prepared her Walrus for launch; but the fuel was contaminated and the aircraft sat uselessly on the catapult. Towards 0500 Holland put his ships into quarter line and ordered the first degree of readiness. At 0530 look-outs made out a suspicious object on the north-western horizon. The range was estimated as seventeen miles ; the bearing was exactly as predicted.[10]

With the enemy in sight broad on his starboard bow, Holland turned 40° towards him and adjusted his consort's position in the quarter line. At 0549 he gave the order to concentrate fire on the left hand, or leading, ship and executed a further 20° turn in the direction of the enemy.[11]

The view from the compass platform of the *Prince of Wales* was now something like this. Forty degrees on the port bow at the standard distance of four cables loomed the grey bulk of the *Hood*, white water boiling under her stern, her battle ensigns stretched taught and her funnel gases, sooty black, streaming away to port and obscuring the southern horizon. The ships were head to sea; as bows punched into the Atlantic swell, sheets of spray came whipping over upperworks to sting the faces of men in exposed positions and drench the optics of directors and rangefinders. Forward main batteries in the two ships were trained 40° to starboard, the elevation of each gun adjusted to provide the required spread in range. Observers following the line of the guns could make out the enemy – two ships, well spaced and moving from right to left, their broadside silhouettes looking, at this extreme

117

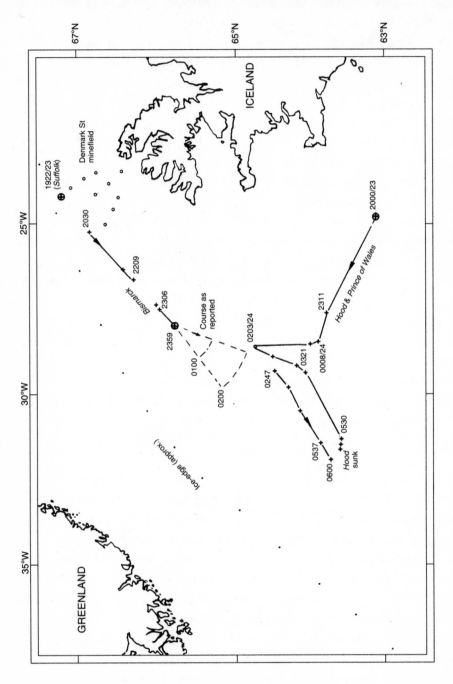

The battle off Iceland: approach to contact, 1922(B) (zone –2), 23–24 May 1941 (based on records of HM ships Suffolk *and* Prince of Wales*)*

range, deceptively similar. The after turrets in the *Hood* and the *Prince of Wales*, trained to the forward limit of their firing arcs, pointed well astern of the enemy. A port turn would be needed to bring them to bear.

As the range approached 26,000yds the *Hood* opened fire. Although, moments before, Holland had corrected his fire-distribution orders and ordered a concentration on the second ship in the enemy line, it appears that his initial salvos were aimed at the *Prince Eugen*. Gun directors in the *Prince of Wales* who had been watching the *Bismarck* from the first saw no sign of the *Hood*'s salvos; they were later adamant that only their own shots had fallen around the prime target. Most of these had been long.

The *Bismarck*, for her part, had opened fire on an almost exact range. She had straddled the *Hood* with her second or third salvo and the splashes of her 15in shells had seemed to tower above the battlecruiser. Three minutes into the action, with the range approaching 20,000yds, Holland executed a two-point turn to port to bring his after turrets to bear. (He would soon need to make another as his ships reached the chosen fighting range and turned to parallel the enemy. The flag hoist '2 Blue' was already flying at his yardarm, awaiting his executive order.) It was now that observers on board the *Prince of Wales* saw the flash of fire on the flagship's boat deck. It had started port side, close to the after 4in mounting, and expanded to cover the whole midships area. It had flickered for a few moments and then died down. It had been followed by a gush of flame from the base of the *Hood*'s mainmast. The *Suffolk* had seen it from a range of nearly 30 miles; it had looked like a pillar of orange flame. The *Norfolk*, much closer, had seen it as 'a high sheet of flame like a fan or inverted cone'. To Captain Leach, it had seemed like a 'vast blow lamp'. There had been no ear-shattering detonation; the most that any witness had heard was a muffled rumble; the *Hood* had seemed to burn through like a damp firework, leaving only a massive pall of smoke.[12]

Leach had little time to reflect on the fate of his leader. As he drew clear of the smoke cloud, he found himself under the combined fire of the *Bismarck* and the *Prinz Eugen*. They found his range quickly. The *Prince of Wales* was soon drenched with spray and shuddering under the impact of heavy hits. At 0602 a 15in shell came hurtling across the compass platform, severing communications with wheelhouse and gun direction positions and leaving the place a charnel house. Splinters from the same salvo put out both forward HA directors, damaged the radar office and left the Walrus, still on its catapult, a riddled hulk; it was ditched over the side. Stunned but unhurt, Captain Leach re-established command on the lower bridge. All semblance of central direction had gone; controllers were blinded by spray or blanked by smoke, and the main armament was firing in local control, its salvos increasingly ragged. Unable to counter the German onslaught, Leach turned away under cover of smoke. As the ship leaned under emergency wheel, a heavy shell broke loose in 'Y' turret, leaving the shell-ring jammed and the four guns with a bare two rounds apiece. He needed a respite.[13]

* * *

Bad luck or bad judgement? Before continuing the narrative, it seems right to attempt an assessment of Admiral Holland's handling of the Battle Cruiser Squadron in the hours leading up to the fatal action off the Denmark Strait, an action which culminated in the loss of more than 1,400 men, which reopened questions about the adequacy of magazine protection in Britain's older capital ships and which exposed the deficiencies of the Admiralty's more recent weapon policies.

Contemporary criticism, some of it reaching the Admiralty through informal channels, focused on two main issues. Critics wondered, first, why Holland had adopted an angle of approach that denied his ships the use of half their main armament. It was as if the British squadron had gone into action with one hand tied behind its back – a matter which, as Admiral Pound himself acknowledged, 'certainly wanted some very good reason'.[14] The second line of criticism echoed post-Jutland controversies on the relative merits of central control and individual initiative. The close formation adopted by Holland had denied the *Prince of Wales* the freedom of manoeuvre to open firing arcs or to avoid incoming salvos, and, just as seriously, had allowed the enemy to shift target to the battleship with the minimum adjustment to range and deflection.[15]

Both arguments had some basis in fact. It is far from certain, on the other hand, that Holland had any genuine choice in the matter. Given the adverse relative position that he found himself in on the morning of 24 May, he had to choose between evils. He chose the course best calculated to get him to effective gun range quickly; it was a choice that entailed risk. His alternative was to adopt a course which gave slower closing rates but which brought all guns to bear. This, too, carried risk; and it is by no means clear, given the material deficiencies of the British ships, that a long-range gun duel would have led to a different or a better outcome.

The issue of formation is, perhaps, a more substantial one; within days, critics had been able to point to another action in which open order and freedom of manoeuvre had made a vital contribution to success. But the circumstances had been different. Holland was constrained by the laws of relative velocity. Deviation from the ordered course whether to bring guns to bear or to avoid the enemy's salvos could only have lessened the chances of getting both ships to effective gun range simultaneously. The issues were finely balanced. With all the facts before them, the naval staff historians could reach no verdict. They left it to the reader to decide.[16]

Faced with this same difficulty, later historians have looked for the origins of the disaster in earlier tactical decisions. They have wondered how it was that Holland came to throw away his position of advantage on the enemy bow. And they have been drawn to that critical turn to the northward at 0008 on morning of 24 May. Some have seen it as a response to the *Suffolk*'s loss of contact; others as an attempt to advance the timing of the encounter and to make better use of the light. Neither explanation matches the facts. Holland turned because he judged, from the *Suffolk*'s reports, that the *Bismarck* had altered from south-west to south. His new course was the course to close.

It was an unfortunate accident of timing that Holland's turn coincided with an interruption in what, up to then, had been a reasonably steady flow of information from the shadowers. He recognised the dangers. He knew that he had to set a time limit to his northerly sweep and then turn to match the enemy's last reported course. The key judgement that he had to make was where to set the limit. There were many uncertainties. How exact was his knowledge of the *Suffolk*'s position? How accurate were the cruiser's latest measurements of the *Bismarck*'s position, course and speed? How might enemy course and speed have changed since the last report? The potential for error was large.[17] Holding on to the northward after contact had been lost took confidence and nerve. Holland cut the safety margin very fine indeed.

Others have wondered whether Holland made the best use of the forces available to him. Wake-Walker knew nothing of his approach until he intercepted a report from the *Icarus*, one of Holland's destroyers, at 0445. If he had known sooner he might have been able to position himself better to take part in the action or to report the fall of shot. Yet the case for radio and radar silence was undoubtedly a strong one. An attempt to alert the shadowers to the approach of heavy forces or to make contact with the search aircraft that were now coming forward from their bases in Iceland risked warning the Germans that the net was closing around them. The best hopes for an interception lay in keeping them in the dark until it was too late for them to evade. It is true, on the other hand, that Holland found no effective use for assets which were under his immediate control and which he could contact by signal lamp – his four destroyers and his consort's aircraft. Uncharacteristically, he left decisions on the use of the aircraft to the captain of the *Prince of Wales*. He sent his destroyers on a futile sweep to the northward in conditions of worsening visibility, leaving it to them to decide how far to go and what to do if their search failed. His orders deprived them of any part in the coming drama; had things gone differently, their presence at the scene of action might have been useful.

But these are peripheral matters. It is difficult to fault Holland's decisions on matters of substance. He made a successful interception over a considerable range and in conditions that were far from easy. He achieved total surprise. Despite his unfavourable relative position, he brought his squadron to effective gun range undamaged. (Plunging shellfire was not the issue.) The outcome turned on the lethal accuracy of German gunnery, on weaknesses in British weaponry and training standards and on deficiencies in the *Hood*'s protection. The origins of the disaster are to be found in institutional weakness rather than in command error.

* * *

The small knots of German officers who met to share impressions of the action pieced together a remarkable and, in some respects, disturbing story. There had been the occasional scare during the night hours; most had started with the *Prinz Eugen*'s over-zealous hydrophone operators. But the first genuine warning, it was now clear, had come only fifteen minutes before the action opened. It had come from the *B-Dienst*; it had detected transmissions to the south-east at 0537 and had reported two new radio call-signs on the British net. Moments later, look-outs had seen the tell-tale sign of smoke on the south-eastern horizon. The British, it was assumed, were bringing up extra shadowers.

By 0545 it had been possible to make out the ships themselves. They were in quarter line and in close formation. Identification had been difficult: the angle of approach had been too fine to give a clear view of funnels or superstructure. Indeed, it had been difficult to pick out anything useful against the smoky eastern horizon. Adalbert Schneider, the *Bismarck*'s well-liked and imperturbable Gunnery Officer, had called them out as cruisers. But they had not behaved like cruisers. At 0552 Lütjens had signalled the shore authorities 'Am engaging two heavy ships.'

The *Prinz Eugen* had taken even longer to determine the enemy's identity. Commander Jasper, directing the *Prinz Eugen*'s main armament, had been so certain that he was dealing with cruisers that he had loaded high-explosive contact ammunition rather than armour-piercing shell. He had thought that his targets were ships of the *Exeter*, *Birmingham* or *Fiji* classes and had not realised that he had been firing at battleships until the engagement was over.[18]

Yet, despite the lack of warning and problems with identification, the battle had ended in triumphant success. Some of the more vivid eye-witness accounts were provided by Lieutenant-Commander Paul Schmalenbach, who had observed the action from the *Prinz Eugen*'s main AA director. He had seen the splashes of the *Bismarck*'s second or third salvo erupt around the leading enemy ship, closely followed by the smaller detonations of his own ship's 8in ammunition. A fierce blaze had flared up at the base of the enemy's mainmast; it had looked like a petrol fire. The next salvo had produced even more dramatic effects:

> The smoke from the explosion [he wrote in his after-action report] rose in a yellow-white incandescent cloud over the after turrets. Debris was flying about. One particularly noticeable glowing piece was thrown aft where it lay burning and emitting black smoke for a long time. This probably caused the ignition of fuel oil on the surface of the water. Within the cloud of the explosion, one could see detonating ammunition exploding like stars upwards and in all directions. I think that after the explosion, the forward turrets fired one more salvo.[19]

Schmalenbach had then seen the whole fore part of the ship rear up, mast, funnels and superstructure intact, before turning over and sinking stern first. He had suspected the presence of heavy ships from the beginning, but it was

123

only now that he recognised the target as the *Hood*, from the characteristic shape of the stem.

Following this cataclysmic event, the Fleet Commander had ordered a shift of target. (It had been his only order.) The *Prinz Eugen* had just found the range when the surviving ship, straddled repeatedly and almost certainly hit, had turned away to the south-east and disappeared behind an impenetrable black fog. As it turned, Schmalenbach had recognised the jutting bridge structure, the tripod mast and the twin funnels with the deep cleft between them. It was a battleship of the *King George V* class. The *Prinz Eugen*'s Torpedo Officer had been watching this ship too. Unwilling to chance a shot at extreme range, he had been waiting for the target to reach the 'positive 500 metres' mark on his torpedo calculator. It had never quite got there.[20]

It had been a remarkable outcome – eloquent testimony to the lethality of German gunfire and to the effectiveness of German training methods. People were reminded of Jutland. But why had the Fleet Commander not pressed home his advantage? A chance like this might never occur again. There was an uneasy sense of opportunity missed and there were rumours –nothing more – of sharp exchanges on the *Bismarck*'s bridge.

As the excitement of the moment died away, new and rather different questions began to assert themselves. Why had German intelligence given no warning? What was the future of *Rheinübung*? The task force had faced a dangerous encounter with enemy capital ships at the very beginning of its operations. Air reconnaissance and radio intelligence, both key ingredients in operational decision-making, had clearly failed. There had been cruisers in the Denmark Strait. That had been predictable; but why had no one warned the task force that British ships could now keep contact at extreme range and in conditions of low visibility? Failures in operational and in technical intelligence had come together to produce crisis.

Nor did the Fleet Commander's personal handling of events escape scrutiny. There had been little sign of a guiding hand during that sudden and unexpected encounter. The *Prinz Eugen* had emerged from the ordeal unscathed but it had been a close-run thing; she had avoided one tightly spaced salvo only because her sound room had suddenly reported torpedoes. Brinkmann had ordered an emergency turn away; he claimed later that he had seen the torpedo tracks for himself.[21] Had Lütjens appreciated the extreme risks that the cruiser had run? Had he considered ordering her to the

Bismarck's disengaged side, the station prescribed for lightly armoured ships when heavy units were engaged? Had it been a deliberate decision on his part to keep her in the line, where her guns could play a part and her presence help divide the enemy's fire? In the absence of orders, should Brinkmann have acted on his own initiative? Views differed. But it was hard to escape the conclusion that Lütjens had been unprepared. He had thought hard about how best to employ the *Prinz Eugen* when in contact with the enemy – he had wanted her well clear of the action – but he had been thinking about convoys and their heavy escorts, about probing the enemy's defences, about engagements in which he held the initiative and had the freedom to pick and choose. This had been different. Action had been forced on him in circumstances he had not foreseen. It had never been envisaged that the *Bismarck* and the *Prinz Eugen* would fight together in this way. There were no policies; there had been no discussion. There was nothing in the orders.[22]

* * *

In the lull following the storm, Lütjens sent the signal 'Battleship, probably *Hood*, sunk. Another battleship, *King George* or *Renown*, turned away damaged. Two heavy cruisers still in contact.' After a brief interval he sent the short coded message 'Have sunk a battleship in quadrant AD73.' He got no receipt or acknowledgement from shore.

If Lütjens was tempted to settle matters with the injured battleship, the temptation was short-lived. His mission was cruiser warfare. If he was to pose a sustained threat to British shipping he had to keep out of trouble and minimise the risk of damage to his ships. Success depended on caution and self-restraint, on following the plans and policies that he had developed during Operation 'Berlin'. A change now would have meant more than flexibility of mind; it would have implied a revolution in his ideas. The priority now was to see what could be salvaged from 'Rheinübung'.

The *Bismarck* emerged from the battle down by the bow and with a nine-degree list to port. One heavy shell had passed between funnel and mainmast, causing trivial damage on the upper deck, but two hits (both, it seemed, from the '*King George*') were more serious. The first had struck the forward part of the ship just above the waterline, passing through from port to starboard without exploding but leaving an exit hole more than a metre across. Two forward compartments were flooded. Damage control parties were already busy shoring bulkheads and assessing how best to stem the inrush of water. Engineers were planning to counter-flood void spaces aft in an attempt to bring the ship on to an even keel and correct the trim.

The second heavy shell had struck port side below the bridge. It had passed under the belt armour and burst against the torpedo bulkhead, splitting welds in the bulkhead between No 4 turbo-generator compartment and the forward port boiler room and allowing both spaces to flood. Damage control teams were at work here too, plugging leaks, pumping out and trying to maintain steam and electrical supplies. Fuel oil was seeping from shattered service tanks close to the point of impact.

What did all this mean? With her forward compartments open to the sea, the *Bismarck* was restricted in speed – a matter of grave concern to anyone who understood the art of cruiser warfare. Reports from below suggested that the flooding in the area of the port boiler room was containable. Perhaps it was; but the loss of that compartment would place further limits on mobility. Contamination of boiler feedwater was another possibility – remote, perhaps, but nonetheless worrying. The ship's armament and main machinery were intact; that was a source of encouragement. With dockyard assistance, hull repairs would be quick and easy; but the *Bismarck* was in no condition to set out on the sustained period of operations that Lütjens and Raeder had discussed the month before. Before long, she would have to make for port.

'Rheinübung' might be in the balance, but all was not yet lost. The *Prinz Eugen*'s lucky escape meant that something, at least, could be saved from the original plan. The shadowing cruisers were the main obstacle to progress. The *Prinz Eugen* would need fuel within forty-eight hours and it was vital that the cruisers did not follow her to the tanker rendezvous. How would they behave if the force divided? Would both concentrate on the *Bismarck*? Would one follow the *Prinz Eugen*? Could one or other, or both, be brought to action? There was no telling.[23] Lütjens knew that, somehow or other, he had guarantee a clean break and that the *Bismarck* still had an indispensable part to play in bringing it about. Until the right moment came, it would be best to make ground towards the tankers and open the distance from British naval and air bases in Iceland.

Once the *Prinz Eugen* had been released, the *Bismarck* could make for a German or a German-controlled port. The nature of the her injuries meant that the choice could be made on operational rather than technical grounds; all that was needed was a suitable drydock. Lütjens could only guess at what the British might be doing. (He was getting nothing from Group North that he did not already know.) But Force H would surely have sailed for the Atlantic: that was a near-certainty, whatever the situation in the eastern Mediterranean. And it was a safe bet that the Admiralty was already trying to cobble together a new fast task force to replace the old one. Some elements would be coming from home waters, others from convoy duty; but, as long as the shadowers remained in contact, everything would be converging on his position. The conclusion was obvious. He would choose the destination and route that gave him the best prospect of breaking away from his shadowers and thus of minimising the risk of another encounter with heavy ships.

The distance to Bergen from his 8 o'clock position was 1,150 miles. The passage south of Iceland was the quickest route to German air cover. If he moved quickly he might even profit from the dislocation caused by the recent disaster. This was hard to judge. What was inescapable was that the direct route was flanked by British naval and air bases. This was the enemy's main area of concentration. Patrol strength would be at its most intense, and behind the patrols the Home Fleet would deploy whatever strength it could still muster, flotillas and strike aircraft as well as capital ships. The chances of an undisputed passage were low.

Trondheim via the Denmark Strait was 1,400 miles. (This was the option favoured later on by desk-bound strategists in Berlin.) It avoided the main area of enemy concentration and offered the chance of evasion in the wide expanses of the Arctic Ocean once the narrows had been negotiated. But a turn towards the Strait and towards British naval and air outposts in western Iceland could only help the enemy's scouting and shadowing operations. If the enemy held contact through the narrows and continued the pursuit to the eastward – low visibility gave little protection against pickets fitted with radar – Home Fleet units, acting on interior lines, would concentrate east of Iceland and again threaten the passage to Norwegian waters. This option was hardly better than the first.

The best prospects for evasion lay in the open Atlantic. Here Lütjens could escape the attention of shore-based aircraft and test the endurance of the shadowing cruisers or of any other ships that were sent in pursuit. The darker nights of more southerly latitudes would help him. Once he had released the *Prinz Eugen* and broken away himself, there was little chance that, in the immensity of the Atlantic, the enemy could assemble enough scouting effort to find him again. (Did not the whole concept of cruiser warfare rest on this proposition?) Once clear, he could make for the Biscay coast and effect his repairs. The distance to the French coast was 1,700 miles, perhaps 2,000 allowing for detours. He was losing oil from his port service tanks at a rate that was difficult to assess. Lütjens may have known by now that the flooding forward was preventing access to pump rooms that controlled the distribution of fuel oil from the forward tanks. But, at this early stage, endurance did not present itself as a critical problem, and, with several promising ideas for restoring supplies yet to be tried, it was much too soon to rule out all hope of repair.

It would be the French west coast. It can hardly have escaped Lütjens's notice that this destination offered the best prospects for an early resumption of Atlantic operations: the hazards of another break-out through the northern passages during the summer months would be avoided.

At 0801, roughly two hours from the end of the action, Lütjens signalled his assessment of damage received and an outline of his future plans. His signal read:

1. Number 4 generator out of action.
2. Port 2 boiler room taking water. Can be contained. Water in foreship.
3. Maximum speed 28 knots.
4. Denmark Strait 50 nautical miles [wide]. Drifting mines. Enemy has radar.
5. Intentions: Enter St Nazaire. Sea God [*Prinz Eugen*] cruiser war. No casualties.[24]

* * *

As yet the German shore authorities knew nothing of what had happened, and they would remain in ignorance for several hours to come. Group North had read the *Bismarck*'s first contact report during the evening of 23 May, but since then he had been relying on intercepts of British signal traffic to keep abreast of the situation. He knew, therefore, that the two shadowing cruisers were still in contact, and soon after 0530 on 24 May he had become aware that another British unit had gained touch. But it had not been heard from again.[25]

Above left: : Navalist ambition: Erich Raeder, in the uniform of Grand Admiral.
(Bundesarchiv)
Above right: Günther Lütjens on appointment as Fleet Commander. The
formal portrait captures the intensity of the man. (IWM)
Below: Raeder inspecting ships of the surface fleet. (Bundesarchiv)

Above: The battlecruisers *Scharnhorst* (foreground) and *Gneisenau*. Their availability in the early months of the war was lamentable. (Bundesarchiv)
Below: A historic moment: Lütjens arrives in Brest after Operation *'Berlin'*, 22 March 1941. (Bundesarchiv)

Above: The *Gneisenau*, Lütjens' flagship during Operation *'Berlin'*, shows the wear and tear of sixty days at sea. (Bundesarchiv)
Below: A veteran of the Atlantic convoy routes: HMS *Ramillies* in the Mediterranean, 1940. (IWM)

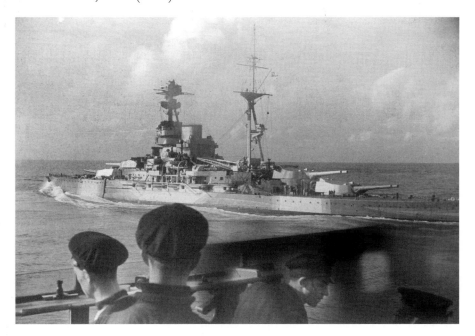

Above: : 'Needed to be pretty artful': Admiral Somerville with his Chief of Staff
on board the *Renown*. (IWM)

Below: Tough-minded and stubborn: Admiral Tovey on board his flagship,
December 1940. He is seen here with 'Daddy' Brind, his Chief of Staff. (IWM)

Above left: More technocrat than tactician: Admiral Wake-Walker, Flag Officer First Cruiser Squadron, during the chase of the *Bismarck*. He is seen here as a Vice-Admiral after his appointment to the Admiralty as Third Sea Lord. (IWM)

Above right: Helmut Brinkmann of the *Prinz Eugen*, in happier times. (Bundesarchiv)

Right: Helpless bystander: General-Admiral Alfred Saalwächter, CinC Group West. (Bundesarchiv)

Above: The *Bismarck* in the North Sea, 21 May 1941. Her camouflage stripes were painted out during her brief stop in Norwegian waters. (IWM)
Below: The Norwegian bolt-hole: the *Bismarck* approaching Grimstadtfjord, 21 May 1941. (IWM)

Right, upper: Crucial
evidence: Flying Officer
Suckling's photograph
of the *Bismarck* in
Grimstadtfjord, 21 May
1941. The merchant
ships are well placed to
obstruct torpedo attack.
(IWM)
Right, lower: Important
early initiative: Captain
H. St J. Fancourt, seen
here talking to a
Swordfish crew at
Hatston. With him is
Rear-Admiral Moody,
Flag Officer Naval Air
Stations. (IWM)

Above: HMS *Norfolk* leaving Isafjord for her station in the Denmark Strait. The photograph was taken from her consort, HMS *Suffolk*. (IWM)
Below: Able Seaman Alfred Newall of the *Suffolk*, a Londoner and the first man to sight the *Bismarck*. (IWM)

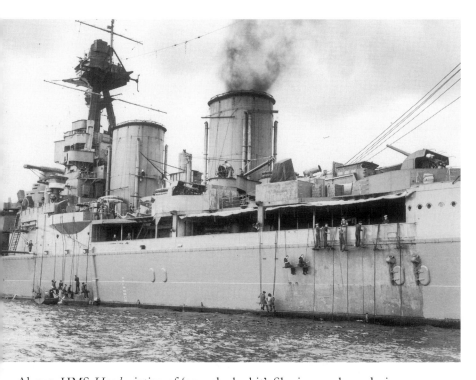

Above: HMS *Hood*, victim of 'an unlucky hit'. She is seen here during a maintenance period in Scapa Flow. (IWM)
Below: HMS *Prince of Wales* at anchor in Scapa Flow. The second ship of the *King George V* class ordered under the 1936 rearmament programme, she was plagued by 'teething troubles' during operations against the *Bismarck*. (IWM)

Above: A salvo from
'Caesar' and 'Dora' turrets:
the *Bismarck* in action with
the *Hood* and the *Prince of
Wales*, 24 May 1941. (IWM)
Left: He knew that his
actions would'invite the
most critical examination':
Captain J. C. Leach of the
Prince of Wales. (IWM)
Right, upper: Master of
naval warfare as applied
science: Captain R. M.
Ellis on the bridge of the
Suffolk during the chase of
the *Bismarck*. (IWM)
Right, lower: 825 Squadron
Swordfish on the deck of
the *Victorious* before their
gallant but unsuccessful
attack on the *Bismarck*, 24
May 1941. (IWM)

Above: The famous 'Stringbag'. Aircraft like these played a key role in operations against the *Bismarck*. (IWM) Left: Teamwork: Admiral Somerville (right) with Captain L. E. H. Maund on the flight deck of the *Ark Royal*. (IWM)

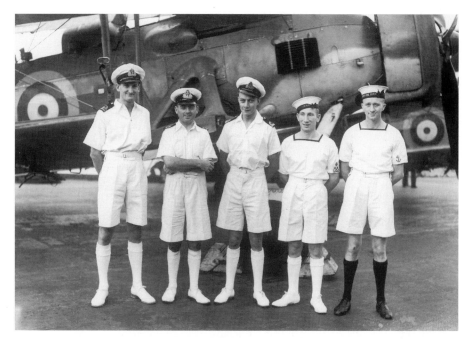

Above: 825 Squadron, key players in the *Bismarck* drama, at the later awards ceremony. From the left: Lt P. D. Gick DSC, Lt-Cdr Eugene Esmonde DSO, Sub-Lt V. K. Norfolk DSC, APO(A) L. D. Sayer DSM, and ALS(A) A. L. Johnson DSM. (IWM)

Below: HMS *Rodney* in Atlantic weather. She was en route to Boston for refit when diverted against the *Bismarck*. (IWM)

Above: HMS *Nelson* exercising her secondary armament. (IWM)
Below: Phillip Vian, Captain (D) 4th Destroyer Flotilla, on the bridge of the *Cossack*. He was one of the coolest tacticians of his generation. (IWM)

Above: The *Prinz Eugen*, Brest, summer 1941. (IWM)
Right: The *Prinz Eugen* during the Channel breakthrough, February 1942. (Bundesarchiv)

Left: Brinkmann addressing his ship's company on leaving the *Prinz Eugen*, May 1942. (Bundesarchiv)
Below: The pattern of things to come. (Bundesarchiv)

For Group North, the situation remained worrying but in no sense critical. The *Bismarck*'s silence, Admiral Carls presumed, was another example of the Fleet Commander's extraordinary (and unnecessary) reticence. Lütjens, he thought, would be searching for a way to refuel the *Prinz Eugen* without compromising the position of the tankers. He might try to drive the shadowers off or he might attempt to draw them over a U-boat trap. If so, there were good reasons for an early transfer of operational command; Group West's Paris Headquarters was far better placed than his to coordinate plans with U-boat Command. Admiral Carls signalled in mid-morning:

> Take advantage of enemy contact to report [your] position and intentions. Assume intentions are:
> (a) to drive off shadowers and refuel *Prinz Eugen*.
> (b) to draw enemy over U-boats.
> CinC U-Boats knows your position from enemy shadowers.
> From 1200, command passes to Group West.
> Three destroyers remain Trondheim for the moment.
> *Weissenburg* is in position.[26]

The truth began to filter through to Group Commands from 1330 onwards. News of the action that morning came as a complete surprise. Details remained sketchy but Admiral Saalwächter captured the mood of the moment. 'It can already be stated,' he wrote in his War Diary, 'that this is the first time since the Battle of the Skagerrak [Jutland] that a German battleship has measured itself against a superior enemy and emerged the victor.' But he was puzzled by the Fleet Commander's references to the '*King George*' and the *Renown*. Neither could be in the north. The *King George V* had been seen off Gibraltar; as for the *Renown*, radio intelligence showed that she had left Gibraltar only the evening before with the *Ark Royal* and *Sheffield* in company, bound, presumably, for the Atlantic. The ship concerned could only have been the *Prince of Wales*; the latest information showed that she had been working with the *Hood*.

Admiral Saalwächter gave his full endorsement to the Fleet Commander's plans. It was right, he thought, to release the *Prinz Eugen* – the cruiser was clearly undamaged – and he grasped immediately that the Fleet Commander's choice of destination had been driven by the need to break contact with the shadowers. The presence of radar in British ships, he remarked, was going to have a serious impact on the future conduct of the war. In the circumstances, a 'retreat' via the northern passages might well be unwise. The enemy could still put powerful forces on the routes to Norway. Meanwhile he would have to take immediate steps to prepare for the *Bismarck*'s arrival on the French west coast. The ship could be expected at any time from the morning of 27 May onward.[27]

Notes to Chapter 6

1   Churchill to First Sea Lord, 28 January 1940; PRO ADM1/10617.

2   Russell Grenfell was one of the Admiralty's sternest critics. He was scathing on the subject of 'teething troubles', the excuse much used at the time. See *The Bismarck Episode* (London: Faber & Faber, 1948), p. 199.

3   A number of sources give the time of receipt of the *Suffolk*'s enemy report as 2004(B) on 23 May. The account given here is based on Captain Leach's narrative in ADM 199/1188, pp. 223–4.

4   See Roskill's analysis in *The War at Sea*, Vol. 1, pp. 398–400. There was no ideal fighting range. The so-called 'immune zone' – the zone within which a ship was safe from both flat-trajectory and plunging shellfire – was a theoretical concept. The muzzle velocities of German heavy guns were known to an accuracy of plus or minus 10 per cent only. Holland probably felt himself reasonably safe from the effects of 15in fire between the ranges of 20,000 and 27,000yds. (The *Prince of Wales*'s figures were better – 15,000yds to maximum gun-range.) But Holland would have been just as interested in the penetrative power of his own shells – another unknown factor – and the accuracy of his fire. He would have chosen a range of about 15,000yds.

5   *Prince of Wales* narrative, PRO ADM 199/1188, p. 223.

6   Transcript of HMS *Suffolk* enemy reports, PRO ADM 199/1187, p. 345.

7   Official dispatches, *Prince of Wales* narrative, PRO ADM 199/1188, p. 223.

8   *Ibid.*, p. 224.

9   *Ibid.* The radar search arc ordered by Admiral Holland (020° to 140°) was probably intended to cover the possibility that the *Bismarck* had been steering south or even a little east of south since the *Suffolk*'s last report.

10   *Ibid.*

11   *Ibid.* See also ADM 234/321 pp. 4–5.

12   Report of (Second) Board of Inquiry, PRO ADM1/11726.

13   Official dispatches, *Prince of Wales* narrative, PRO ADM 199/1188, p. 223. See also Grenfell, pp. 52–5, and Kennedy, pp. 106–8.

14   Roskill, *The War at Sea*, Vol. 1, p. 402.

15   See, for example, letter to First Sea Lord from Rear-Admiral Roger M. Bellairs

in ADM 199/1188, p. 48. Although Bellairs declined to name his sources, it seems clear that his information came from the Navigating Officer of the *Prince of Wales*, who had been wounded in the action.

16 PRO ADM 234/327, BR 1736 (48) (2), p. 311

17 Taking the mean of the position reports made by the *Norfolk*, *Prince of Wales* and *Hood* on sighting the *Bismarck*, Captain Ellis calculated his navigational error as 110° 14 miles. His next sight confirmed it. *Suffolk* ROP, PRO ADM 199/1188, p. 270.

18 PG47895, Section E II, Report by Chief Gunnery Officer.

19 *Ibid.*, Section E II, p. 47.

20 *Ibid.*, Part C 1, chronology for 24 May 1941. Captain Brinkmann was later admonished by CinC Cruisers (Rear-Admiral Schmundt) for delays in getting his tubes ready and for missing this opportunity.

21 *Ibid.*, Part F. The *Prinz Eugen*'s sound room was prone to false alarms and this may have been one of them. There is no evidence that the *Hood* fired torpedoes although the possibility cannot, perhaps, be totally discounted: in the coming days other British ships would fire torpedoes at equally extreme ranges.

22 The German operational staffs found it difficult to reach a united view on these matters. Admiral Schmundt (CinC Cruisers) took the view that the *Prinz Eugen* should have been treated as a lightly armoured unit. Admiral Carls (Group North) disagreed. He acknowledged the cruiser's part in the outcome of the battle and warned against tactical dogma. PG47895, Parts F and G.

23 Admiral Wake-Walker had covered the possibility of the enemy separating in his orders to the *Suffolk* nearly twenty-four hours earlier. The *Norfolk* was to follow the *Prinz Eugen* and attempt to bring her to action; the *Suffolk*'s job was to shadow the *Bismarck*. RA 1CS signal 1017(B), 23 May.

24 PG47897, *Bismarck* War Diary, 24 May 1941.

25 German staff officers later advanced a number of theories to explain why the Fleet Commander's signals failed to get through. Some suspected action damage, although evidence from the *Prinz Eugen* did not support this. Others blamed radio propagation conditions; but German shore stations heard the British cruisers clearly. It seems likely that the *Bismarck*'s radio transmitters were below par.

26 PG47897, *Bismarck* War Diary (reconstruction), 1036, 24 May 1941. For Group North's appreciation of the situation, see his War Diary extracts in PG47895, chronology of events, p 14. The tanker *Weissenburg* was stationed off Jan Mayen.

27 Extracts from Group West War Diary, PG47895, chronology of events, 24 May 1941.

7

The Admiralty Intervenes

It fell to Rear-Admiral Wake-Walker (RA 1CS), an experienced seaman though more technocrat than tactician, to save what could be saved from the wreckage of Tovey's plans. The smoke had barely cleared before the *Norfolk* passed through the scene of action, continuing her pursuit to the south-west. Captain Leach was attempting to restore some semblance of control; he gave the Admiral a preliminary assessment of the damage to the *Prince of Wales* and followed him. An hour later he was able to report all but two of his heavy guns ready for action. He was still dealing with floodwater in the after part of the ship, but he thought he could make 27kts. Wake-Walker told him to open out to the eastward so that the *Norfolk* could fall back on him if the enemy became aggressive. It was a cautious plan, certainly, but one which seemed to make due allowance for the battleship's doubtful fighting qualities.

But had the *Bismarck* been damaged in the recent action? This was the burning question for Wake-Walker and for a growing circle of onlookers in the hours following the battle. The *Norfolk*'s gun directors were sure that one or two salvos had straddled the target; some thought that they had seen a burst of black smoke from the *Bismarck*'s midship section. It had appeared as if all the soot collected in funnel uptakes had been shaken loose and carried away in the funnel gases. Something unusual had certainly happened, but, seen from a distance of fifteen miles, no one had been sure what it was. Hopes had risen briefly when, towards 0800, the *Suffolk* had reported that the *Bismarck* had slowed down and that she seemed to be on fire. A Sunderland flying boat had been sent to investigate but had quickly dispelled the illusion. There was no sign of fire and the *Bismarck* was holding her course to the south-west at 30kts. The *Norfolk*'s plot told much the same story. A brief report 'losing oil', made as the Sunderland left for Iceland, was interpreted by the *Norfolk* as 'an unfortunate personal ailment affecting the aircraft'.[1]

British commanders knew nothing of the film of oil spreading out from the *Bismarck*'s wake until well after midday when FOIC Iceland (Rear-Admiral R. J. R. Scott) broadcast the results of the aircrew debriefing.

Wake-Walker's terse signal reporting the outcome of the battle reached Admiral Tovey towards 0800. The Commander-in-Chief, with the main strength of the Home Fleet, was 300 miles to the eastward. He had been steaming hard since receiving the *Norfolk*'s enemy report the evening before but he had been in no position to give early support his Battle Cruiser Squadron. (This was the penalty for having tried to cover all conceivable possibilities.) Tovey had been preoccupied with the idea that the enemy would avoid an encounter and turn for home. He had been determined to make no move that would leave the enemy's escape routes uncovered.

But the Battle Cruiser Squadron had neither stopped nor diverted the enemy. The *Bismarck* was holding her course to the southwest; she was following the line of the ice-edge and her speed remained high. Tovey found that his closing rate was no more than a knot or two at best and, in the absence of some radical change in the enemy's course and speed, it was hard to see how he could avoid a long and possibly futile stern chase.

Staff officers called to the flag bridge to deal with this sudden and unexpected crisis found the Commander-in-Chief analysing the situation in his usual calm and methodical way. The enemy had a number of options. It was still conceivable that, with an important tactical success under his belt, he would turn back for the Norwegian coast, passing either south of Iceland or retreating north-eastwards through the Denmark Strait. If these possibilities were to be covered, Tovey would need to keep north of the line best calculated to close the enemy even if, for an interim period, the *Bismarck* might gain a little ground.

Although there was little evidence to support the idea, it remained conceivable that damage inflicted during the course of the battle would force the *Bismarck* to seek the assistance of a dockyard. A return to German waters was already covered. But she might choose the French west coast; this was an obvious destination – perhaps too obvious. There were other possibilities as well – Ferrol, Dakar, even a Mediterranean yard, perhaps French, perhaps Italian. Speculation ranged over all of them.[2] Her choice would depend on how urgent her problems were: she might turn in a matter of hours or she might make a longer excursion into the Atlantic. If the basic premise was correct, one thing was certain: at some point Lütjens would have to turn east, and the longer he left it the greater the turn would have to be. Provided that the shadowers succeeded in holding on to their quarry, this was the enemy course of action that Tovey felt he was best placed to counter. He would be operating on interior lines.

A far more dangerous possibility, and one that came to dominate Tovey's thinking as fears of a break-back to German waters receded, was that Lütjens would keep down the coast of Greenland and, when clear of Cape Farewell, strike out to the westwards.[3] The *Bismarck* would need fuel before long and there were strong reasons to suspect that her oilers would be concealed along the Greenland coast or waiting in the Davis Strait; the Azores were another possibility; they were already under investigation.[4] A successful fuelling had to be prevented at all costs. With the Home Fleet itself getting close to safe margins as it carried the pursuit into the western Atlantic (the endurance of the *Repulse* was already giving rise to concern), a German task group, restored to full mobility, would be very difficult to catch. The consequences were unthinkable: if the Home Fleet were forced to make for Newfoundland, the nearest source of fuel, it would leave the convoy routes uncovered and surrender the advantages of central position to the Germans.

Through the forenoon of 24 May Tovey resisted the advice of staff officers who urged him to turn to an intercept course. Closing the range quickly was not the key issue. Tovey had to preserve his ability to respond to the 'worst case' situation. He kept half an eye on Cape Farewell and refused to be drawn too far to the southward.

* * *

For the naval authorities in London, the weekend of 24/25 May was one of exceptional tension and anxiety. The Admiralty faced not one crisis but two. The battle for Crete was reaching its climax, and, with the *Luftwaffe* dominant over the Aegean, the cost of continued support to the island garrison was becoming clearer by the hour. Hard decisions were pending.[5]

Most of the Royal Navy's senior hierarchy were at their posts during these anxious days, monitoring developments in the Admiralty's Operational Intelligence Centre (OIC) or 'on call' within that warren of a building that divides Horse Guards from Whitehall and the Mall. They included the First

Sea Lord, Admiral Sir Dudley Pound, a reserved and now rather careworn figure, and his able though abrasive deputy, Vice-Admiral Sir Tom Phillips. Both had been closely concerned with decisions to reinforce the Home Fleet and both had remained in regular touch with Tovey until the fleet had sailed. The Prime Minister had left for Chequers on the Friday afternoon, but there could be no doubt of his continuing personal interest. When told that the *Bismarck* and *Prinz Eugen* had left Bergen, Churchill had telegraphed a warning to President Roosevelt and had asked in characteristically histrionic style for the help of the (still neutral) US Navy in marking the enemy down.[6]

It had seemed, on that Friday evening when the cruisers made contact in the Denmark Strait, that all essential steps to counter a German break-out had been taken. There were eleven convoys at sea in the North Atlantic, five outbound and six homebound, but the Battle Cruiser Squadron would be somewhere south of Reykjavik and the rest of the Home Fleet not far behind it. If there was a worry, it was for the troop convoy WS.8B, which had been stripped of its heavy cover to reinforce the CinC and which was now moving south-westwards down the Irish coast with an escort of cruisers and destroyers only. If events in the north were part of the now familiar pattern and signalled the start of a two-pronged attack on the Atlantic convoy routes, WS.8B, with its crowded troop transports and vital war material for the Middle East theatre, would be standing into danger. At 0050 in the morning of 24 May the Admiralty sailed Force H to join WS.8B but warned Somerville that if one or both of the battlecruisers in Brest were found to have left, his orders were liable to change.

Somerville left Gibraltar at 0200 on 24 May with the *Renown*, the *Ark Royal*, the *Sheffield* and an escort of five destroyers. At dawn, as momentous events were taking place in the north, he was rounding Cape St Vincent.

Through the night of 23/24 May, as Admiralty teleprinters chattered out each new report on the movements of the *Bismarck* and the *Prinz Eugen*, Pound and his colleagues found it impossible to dismiss the idea that if Lütjens got wind of what lay in wait for him he would turn back into the Denmark Strait. They therefore warned the three cruisers that were on watch in the Iceland–Faeroes passage – and two more which they wrongly assumed were deployed south of the Faeroes – to be ready to rendezvous off the north-east coast of Iceland 'in the event of the enemy breaking back'.[7] And this proved to be the first of many precautionary moves ordered by the

Admiralty when, towards 0800 in the morning of 24 May, first reports of what had happened to the Battle Cruiser Squadron reached London.

The Admiralty's other moves were more overtly offensive. They dismissed the loss of the *Hood* as an 'unlucky hit'. It was much more than that. It was an uncomfortable reminder of Jutland and of the defects in design and drill that had brought disaster to the battlecruisers *Invincible*, *Indefatigable* and *Queen Mary*. The loss of the *Hood* was a blow to the prestige of a proud institution and to the reputations of those who led it.[8] As the hours passed and individual orders and instructions began to shape themselves into a pattern, it became clear to all concerned that London had steeled itself to accept quite abnormal levels of risk in its attempts to bring the *Bismarck* to action.

Wake-Walker was among the first to get evidence of London's new single-mindedness. (He would get more later.) As he continued his pursuit of the *Bismarck*, he was told plainly that he would have to risk running out of fuel in order to bring the CinC into contact. An hour later the cruiser *Edinburgh*, searching north of the Azores for enemy tankers and blockade-runners, was given orders to similar effect. She was told to steer to intercept the *Bismarck* and to be ready to take over shadowing duties:

> Fuel should be conserved reasonably while closing, [the message read] and a speed of 25 knots is suggested, but after contact NO consideration of fuel must allow you to lose contact.[9]

These were early signs of the large-scale strategic redeployment that was now being organised in London, a design that could only be put into effect at the expense of the convoy escort task. If this too involved risk – the *Bismarck* or *Prinz Eugen*, or perhaps both, might break away at any time – Pound accepted it without hesitation. Ships on convoy duty in mid-Atlantic or fuelling in Halifax were relieved of existing commitments and ordered to close the enemy. The movement involved ships from both sides of the Atlantic and from all points of the compass. Some were within 500 miles of the centre of interest and would be in position after twenty-four hours' hard steaming. Others were more than a thousand miles away and would take two days or more to bring their influence to bear. But by midday the Admiralty had orchestrated a general movement towards the central North Atlantic designed to support the CinC. Its first situation report, issued at 1238 on 24

May, named fifteen ships of cruiser size and above that were in contact with, or converging on, the enemy. It included estimates of their various positions and a brief summary of the orders that had been given to them.[10] It was now for individual captains to adjust their plans in the light of the broader picture.

The battleship *Rodney* was among the first to be diverted by the Admiralty. At 0800 she had been 500 miles west of the North Channel with the transport *Britannic* and an escort of four destroyers; she had been making for Boston Navy Yard, her decks cluttered with the spares and stores needed for a refit that was long overdue. She had been some 700 miles south-east of the *Bismarck*. The Admiralty had first told her to close the enemy at her best speed, keeping her screen and the transport with her; it had then changed its mind. In mid-morning Captain Dalrymple-Hamilton had detached the *Britannic* with a single destroyer and steered to close the *Bismarck* from the eastward using as much power as his time-worn machinery allowed.[11]

The *Ramillies*, a veteran battleship of the 'R' class and, as has been seen, a regular convoy escort, was eastbound in mid-Atlantic with HX.127. At 0800 on 24 May she was 800 miles south-south-east of Cape Farewell and a thousand miles south of the German task group. The Admiralty instructed her to leave her convoy and steer for a position west of the *Bismarck* in order to 'place the enemy between the *Ramillies* and the CinC'. Captain Read saw his situation as a delicate one. The *Bismarck* seemed to be coming straight towards him, bound, he thought, for the South Atlantic. There seemed every likelihood of a meeting within twenty-four hours. Common sense dictated that he should avoid becoming heavily engaged until other heavy units were in position to support him. But he might have little choice in the matter; the *Ramillies* was hardly agile enough to keep out of trouble if it came her way.[12]

In late morning the Admiralty earmarked the *Revenge*, a second convoy veteran then resting in Halifax, for possible use if the *Bismarck* moved to the west. She was ordered to raise steam with all dispatch and proceed to sea. In the afternoon urgent messages went to the US and Canadian Navies asking for long-range aircraft to be held ready in Newfoundland in case of need, while on the other side of the Atlantic the cruiser *London*, homebound off the coast of Spain with a Gibraltar convoy, was ordered to close the enemy at economical speed with a view to taking over the shadowing task in the longer term.

Towards evening the Admiralty began to promulgate the logistic arrangements that it had put together. (They were hardly sufficient to meet the needs of this unprecedented situation.) An oiler was on its way to St John's, Newfoundland, and capital ships could refuel in emergency from a tanker in Conception Bay. There were commercial tankers with fuel oil in convoys HX.127 and 128, the second just clearing Halifax. Two further oilers, one fitted for refuelling at sea, were being assigned to patrol areas north and west of the Azores, although neither could reach its station for five or six days. Meanwhile the Admiralty was investigating the possibility of American help.[13]

Force H, now approaching the latitude of Lisbon and steering to meet convoy WS.8B, was being seen increasingly as a potential asset for use against the *Bismarck* in the longer term. At 2138 the Admiralty warned Somerville to be prepared for extended operations and told him to send his destroyers back to Gibraltar before it became necessary to give them fuel. Minds in London were turning more and more to the *Bismarck*'s fuelling options and her progress during the day had pointed to the Azores. As 24 May drew to a close, the Admiralty ordered Somerville to steer to intercept the *Bismarck* from the southward and warned him that her movements might guide him to the oiler in question.[14] But by the time these messages reached Somerville in the early hours of 25 May, the situation had changed radically.

* * *

Wake-Walker, meanwhile, the hub (and linchpin) of the entire concentric movement, was beginning to face new difficulties. In the hours following the battle, visibility had remained good and the shadowing cruisers, one on each quarter, had been able to watch the enemy from positions of relative comfort, well beyond effective gun range. The *Bismarck*'s speed seemed to have dropped a little, and her course seemed nearer south than south-west. But from mid-morning onwards a sullen drizzle had set in and the enemy had disappeared from view. The *Prince of Wales* closed in to follow in the Admiral's wake. (She was still trying to sort out the wreckage of her bridge, but nine of her ten guns were now ready for action.) On the *Bismarck*'s starboard quarter the *Suffolk* moved forward to re-establish contact by radar.

By midday visibility was two or three miles at most and Wake-Walker was beginning to feel distinctly uncomfortable; he was shadowing blindfold. He judged that he was only some 20° abaft the enemy's beam. If the *Bismarck* made a further alteration to port, she might come looming out of the murk quite suddenly and at dangerously close range. The *Norfolk*'s primitive Type 286M radar would give no warning and the *Prince of Wales*'s sets were reported as unreliable. He needed to drop back four or five miles. At 1228 Wake-Walker began a 360° turn and ordered the *Prince of Wales* to conform to his movements. His premonition was soundly based. Within the hour, a brief opening in the visibility revealed the *Bismarck* at a range of only 16,000yds. If he had not turned, the range would have been point blank; even now, good sense called for a turn away under cover of smoke.[15] While out of sight, the *Bismarck* had edged round to a course of south.

For the rest of the afternoon Wake-Walker had to be content with occasional glimpses of the enemy as the visibility rose and fell. The *Suffolk*'s unaccustomed silence showed that she, too, was out of touch, her calculations thrown out apparently by the *Bismarck*'s change of course. But at 1609 she had reported a radar contact, and minutes later a second, close to the first; and shortly after 1700, she had followed this up with a sighting of the *Bismarck* and the *Prinz Eugen*.

While Wake-Walker was treading the fine line between enterprise and discretion, he became aware that his operations were attracting intense interest in higher quarters. Signals about fuel could be dismissed for the moment, however peremptory their tone. His fuel margins were comfortable and his plot suggested – wrongly, as he later admitted – that the CinC would make contact soon after midnight.[16] But a second signal needed careful analysis. Embedded among innocent questions about the *Bismarck*'s fighting capability and ammunition expenditure, and among cheery reminders to be on the look-out for U-boats, was the ominous sentence, 'Request your intentions as regards the *Prince of Wales* re-engaging?'[17] Coming as it did from an institution which a generation earlier had court-martialled an admiral for neglect of duty in circumstances not far removed from his own, and which, much more recently, had summarily relieved one senior admiral and instituted formal enquiries into the conduct of another, the signal gave warning of trouble ahead.[18]

Writing after the event, Wake-Walker presented the issues in terms of a simple choice. He could give priority to shadowing, a choice which, with the support of the *Prince of Wales*, offered reasonable prospects of bringing the Commander-in-Chief into contact; or he could provoke an action himself. If he chose the latter, the outcome would be unpredictable. He had been able to judge the *Bismarck*'s fighting capability at first hand and had seen the British battleship's very ragged reply. He might be lucky and succeed in slowing the *Bismarck* down. It seemed more likely, on the other hand, that a progressive weakening in the firepower of the *Prince of Wales* – the result of damage and material failure – would leave the cruisers dangerously exposed. If either of these were damaged, the chances of continuing the pursuit were slim.[19]

Wake-Walker's reply was carefully phrased; as he remarked later, he gave his 'opinions' rather than his 'intentions'. 'Consider *Prince of Wales* should not re-engage until other heavy ships are in contact unless interception fails,' he told the Admiralty at 1619. 'Doubtful if she has speed to force action.'[20] There matters were allowed to rest, at least for the moment. But what had been said could not be unsaid and the hint of criticism, real or imagined, seems to have nudged the Admiral towards courses of action that he might otherwise have rejected.

Judging that some more active policy was required of him, he conceived a plan for delaying the *Bismarck*'s southerly advance and drawing her to the eastward. This, he hoped, would help Admiral Tovey close the range. The essence of the plan was this. He would put the *Prince of Wales* in the van and adjust course to creep up astern of the enemy. As the *Bismarck* came into view through the murk, he would open fire and evade to the eastward, hoping that the *Bismarck* would follow. He envisaged a brief exchange of fire only. As he told Captain Leach (a willing accomplice in this scheme), he had no intention of becoming heavily engaged until the CinC was close by.[21]

A little before 6 o'clock Wake-Walker was ready to put his plan to the test. Using the *Suffolk*'s reports to guide him, he increased speed and adjusted course to close the invisible enemy from astern. Thirty minutes later the *Suffolk* came into view about twelve miles to the westward. It was clear at once that she would find herself in an exposed position when the action opened; Wake-Walker ordered her to close to supporting range. At this point Wake-Walker's schemes were frustrated by the actions of the *Bismarck* herself.

* * *

In the hours following the battle, the *Bismarck* had been preoccupied with her damage. Something had to be done to contain the flooding forward, correct the trim and restore mobility, but, with the enemy close astern, Lütjens had found his choices limited. The option of heeling the ship to expose and patch the damaged plating was considered but rejected.[22] It could hardly be done in the presence of the enemy, especially now that a battleship had joined the pursuit. The best that the repair teams had been able to offer was to plug the holes with collision matting. This they had done, and their efforts had brought a measure of relief. With the inrush of water checked, divers had been able to run hoses to the forward compartments and begin the transfer of fuel from forward to aft. As time passed, people had begun to notice a definite improvement in the trim.[23]

With these essential, if temporary, repairs complete, Lütjens had turned his attention to the release of the *Prinz Eugen* and had told Brinkmann soon after midday:

> Intend breaking contact as follows. During rain squall, *Bismarck* will turn off, course west. *Prinz Eugen* will maintain course and speed till forced off or three hours after *Bismarck*'s departure. [She is] then released to fuel from *Belchen* or *Lothringen*. Then independent cruiser warfare. Execute code-word on 'Hood'.[24]

Lütjens was now in a position to state his requirements for the U-boat trap that Group North had suggested earlier that morning. 'Assemble west boats in quadrant AJ 68.' he had signalled U-Boat Headquarters, at 1442. 'I am coming from the north. Intend drawing heavy forces shadowing *Bismarck* through AJ 68 dawn tomorrow.' The shore commands had anticipated his requirements fairly accurately and they now made final adjustments to their plans.

At 1540, as a belt of rain enveloped his two ships, Lütjens signalled the code-word 'Hood'. The *Prinz Eugen* watched as the *Bismarck* put her wheel over, revealing more and more of her impressive length as she turned slowly to a westerly course and disappeared from view. In minutes she was back, taking up her former position in the cruiser's wake. Her signal lamp blinked out, 'Cruiser to starboard.'

The German shore commands, at this time, were still adjusting themselves to the stunning news of the morning battle. As the news spread, senior admirals, Raeder among them, began to put their initials to a succession of congratulatory signals. War diaries and signals give a glimpse, too, of the worries created by the *Bismarck*'s impending arrival in a Biscay port. The drydock at St Nazaire had to be got ready. Difficulties might arise if the battleship's draught forward was greater than normal. Air defences would need strengthening. Coast defences had to be alerted and E-boat flotillas positioned to shepherd the casualty in. Group North, believing that Lütjens might, even now, decide that Norway was the better option, ordered the Sixth Destroyer Flotilla to Bergen and asked Dönitz to establish U-boat patrols in the northern passages.

British operations in the eastern Atlantic still lacked any discernible pattern. All that was known for certain was that Force H had left Gibraltar; the rest was speculation. Group North called on the Commander Fifth Air Force to mount additional reconnaissance sorties over Britain's northern bases. (He was told, early that evening, that there were still three battleships in Scapa Flow, a finding that seemed a little implausible and which he passed on with the caveat 'possibly dummies'.) Group West trawled through what little intelligence he had and concluded that the British might have up to three fast task forces at sea in the eastern Atlantic. And the *Victorious*, he thought, was probably working with the Home Fleet. He had nothing solid to pass on to Lütjens. He was inclined to think that the British would be aiming for a fleet concentration in the approaches to Biscay like the one that they had attempted in the closing stages of Operation *'Berlin'*. If so, an immediate return to the French west coast might well be unwise. Had the Fleet Commander's decision perhaps been premature? Calculations showed that the *Bismarck* would still have more than 5,000 cubic metres of fuel remaining at midnight, an ample reserve for the time being. At 1842 Admiral Saalwächter put his reservations to Lütjens. If the *Bismarck* could shake off her pursuers, he suggested, she might do better to lose herself in some remote part of the Atlantic, if need be for a week or two, until the hue and cry had died down.[25]

But this was something for the future: first priority had to be given to the all-important business of breaking contact. In late afternoon, Saalwächter sent Lütjens the coordinates of the six U-boats that would form a submarine trap off Cape Farewell and of three more that, a little later, would lie close to his course for the Bay of Biscay.[26]

It is not known for certain whether the *Bismarck* received these signals. The *Prinz Eugen*'s communications staff thought not, and had been preparing to relay them by light.[27] But at 1814 Lütjens gave the order 'Hood' for the second time. The *Bismarck* again hauled out to starboard and this time disappeared for good behind a curtain of rain. Minutes after her departure, watch-keepers in the *Prinz Eugen* heard the reverberation of her gunfire on the wind; and, down below, the *B-Dienst* heard a British cruiser reporting the *Bismarck*'s alteration first to the west and then, unexpectedly, back to south.

* * *

The *Bismarck*'s turn to the west to release the *Prinz Eugen* played havoc with Wake-Walker's calculations. The *Suffolk* was the first to notice that something was amiss. She had last seen the enemy broad on the port bow at fifteen miles; radar now showed that he was dead ahead at a range of only ten. It looked like an ambush. Captain Ellis rang on full speed and put his helm over to open the range.

As he steadied on a course of east, the *Bismarck* emerged from the rain belt just aft of the starboard beam. The *Suffolk* put down smoke and began a series of violent manoeuvres. The *Bismarck* opened fire and some of her shots fell close enough to start rivets in compartments aft. The *Suffolk* replied, but at a price. The blast from the guns of 'B' turret, trained abaft the beam, shattered the bridge windows and dismantled the flimsy covering that had been fitted to shelter bridge watch-keepers in arctic conditions. Wind and spray now drove straight in over the bridge coaming. The cruiser had been in contact with the enemy for twenty-four tense and exhausting hours. Discomfort would now reinforce fatigue.[28]

Wake-Walker, who had expected to sight the enemy dead ahead on a bearing of south and within gun range, now found him hull-down to the westward at a range of eighteen miles. There was no time to search for explanations; the *Suffolk* was out on her own and under threat. He turned to give her support. At 1847 the *Prince of Wales* opened fire. The *Norfolk* followed suit a few minutes later, but the range was extreme and the order to cease fire was soon given. The *Prince of Wales* had fired twelve salvos. As if to confirm Wake-Walker's predictions, two guns of 'A' turret had gone down with mechanical defects. The *Bismarck* did not seem to have replied.

As this brief skirmish came to an end, Wake-Walker could only conclude that his experiment had failed. There was no sign that the *Bismarck* had wanted to trade blows with the *Prince of Wales* or that she was willing to be drawn to the eastward. If anything, his plan had produced the opposite effect. Further attempts to shepherd the enemy towards the Commander-in-Chief were likely to prove unhelpful. Wake-Walker decided that he would put no further pressure on the enemy and that, from now on, he would confine himself to the task of shadowing at a safe range.

In weighing his options, Wake-Walker must surely have considered reverting to the shadowing disposition that had served him so well up to this point. It is alleged that some members of his staff urged him to send the *Suffolk* back to her former station on the enemy's starboard quarter.[29] Wake-Walker rejected the idea. The recent incident had demonstrated all too clearly the risks attached to shadowing in conditions of low visibility. Estimates of relative position were highly unreliable; the enemy's movements were sudden and unpredictable. The *Suffolk* had come under threat and he had been in no position to support her. It seemed better, on balance, to keep his force concentrated on the enemy's eastern flank, where the guns of the *Prince of Wales* would cover all units and the *Suffolk*'s radar would give early warning of any threatening development.

Through the evening of 24 May Wake-Walker kept his three ships in loose formation on the *Bismarck*'s port quarter, watching from a distance of thirteen to sixteen miles. The enemy was now steering a course of 160°, further eastward than before, but the chances of early support seemed, if anything, to be receding. He knew now that the CinC was planning an air attack before sunset, but the heavy ships of the Home Fleet would not, it seemed, reach his area before the following morning. He was becoming concerned about the *Prinz Eugen*. There had been no positive sighting of the cruiser for some hours. She was presumably somewhere on the far side of the *Bismarck*. For the moment the *Suffolk* was best where she was, but at dusk he would send her forward to investigate with radar. 'I am anxious to locate the cruiser,' he warned Captain Ellis, 'but do not lose the *Bismarck*.'[30] There were probably U-boats about; at 1930 the shadowers began to zig-zag, altering 30° either side of their mean course every ten minutes.

Notes to Chapter 7

1   Official dispatches, PRO ADM 199/1188 p. 199. The laboured humour is, presumably, Wake-Walker's.
2   Grenfell, p. 71.

3 Official dispatches, PRO ADM 199/1188, p. 130.

4 These suspicions were strong, but they were not yet supported by definite intelligence.

5 The German airborne operation (*'Merkur'*) had started on 20 May and the garrison was now under intense pressure. The cost of maintaining naval patrols north of the island in the three days to 24 May was two cruisers and four destroyers sunk and one battleship, two cruisers and four destroyers severely damaged. On 24 May Admiral Cunningham warned the Admiralty of 'incommensurate losses' if operations continued.

6 Churchill, *The Second World War*, Vol. 3, p. 272. The text of Churchill's message, 'Give us the news and we will finish the job', is in PRO ADM 205/10.

7 Admiralty message 0120(B), 24 May, to HM Ships *Manchester, Birmingham, Arethusa, Galatea* and *Hermione*. The Admiralty was unaware that the CinC had decided to keep the *Galatea* and *Hermione* with him. The same move had been made following news of the *Scheer*'s return at the end of March.

8 Parallels with Jutland and hints at Admiralty miscalculation appeared in *The Times* on 28 May. On the same day, Pound complained to the Controller (Bruce Fraser, then a Rear-Admiral) that the *Hood* had been destroyed 'in what appears to the onlooker to be exactly the same [way] as the *Queen Mary, Invincible* and *Indefatigable . . .'*. PRO ADM 116/4351.

9 Admiralty message 1250(B), 24 May 1941. The signal to Wake-Walker was timed 1126(B).

10 There were in fact seventeen, since Tovey had elected to keep the Second Cruiser Squadron with him. There were other inaccuracies. Some of the positions were 'best guesses' and a later source of confusion. However, this report and the ones which followed it were generally held to have served an essential purpose. See Tovey's remarks in PRO ADM 199/1188, p.18.

11 Admiralty messages 0903(B) and 1036(B) of 24 May. *Rodney* ROP, PRO ADM 199/1188, p. 230.

12 Admiralty message 1144(B), 24 May.

13 Admiralty message 2030(B), 24 May 1941.

14 Admiralty messages of 2138(B) and 2331(B), 24 May. See also *Somerville Papers*, p. 270.

15 Official dispatches, R-A 1CS ROP, PRO ADM 199/1188, p. 199.

16 The CinC's position report signalled at 0825(B) in the morning of 24 May was mis-plotted in the *Norfolk*. The error seems to have been compounded by inaccurate estimates of the CinC's position in the Admiralty's 1445(B) situation report. Wake-Walker did not get an accurate estimate of Tovey's interception time until after midnight. PRO ADM 199/1188, p. 203.

17 Admiralty message 1445(B), 24 May.

18 The Board of Inquiry into Admiral Somerville's action off Cape Spartivento in November 1940 had been the latest example. It had caused widespread

resentment. See *Somerville Papers*, pp. 203–12. Many senior officers saw the hand of Churchill in this and similar cases.

19　Official dispatches, R-A 1CS ROP, PRO ADM 199/1188, p. 127.

20　R-A 1CS to Admiralty, 1619(B), 24 May.

21　Official dispatches, R-A 1CS ROP, PRO ADM 199/1188, p. 202.

22　Müllenheim-Rechberg, p. 157.

23　PG48797, *Bismarck* War Diary, 24 May 1941, citing evidence of survivors.

24　*Ibid.* The tankers *Belchen* and *Lothringen* were stationed off Cape Farewell.

25　*Ibid.* Group West's broad appreciation of the threat is given in PG47895, chronology of events for the same date.

26　This U-boat plan was signalled before the Fleet Commander's specific requirements were known. It was adjusted later.

27　The *Bismarck* certainly asked the *Prinz Eugen* whether she had received them. Lütjens may simply have wanted to assure himself that the *Prinz Eugen* was aware of the U-boat positions before detaching her.

28　HMS *Suffolk* narrative, PRO ADM 199/1188, p. 270.

29　Kennedy, p. 129.

30　R-A 1CS signal 2106(B), 24 May; PRO ADM 199/1188, p. 203.

8

A Stale Datum

News that the *Bismarck* had altered course to the southward and that her speed had dropped to 24kts or less reached Tovey soon after midday on 24 May and brought him a modicum of relief – or so he later claimed. It would be more accurate to say that the enemy's alteration of course and speed strengthened the hand of those who had been uneasy about the Commander-in-Chief's earlier compromise and who had argued for 'some choice of probabilities'.[1] It was becoming possible, in theory at least, to contemplate an interception soon after dawn on 25 May.

But there were twenty hours still to run, and the obstacles to a successful interception remained formidable. Tovey was unimpressed by reports that the *Bismarck* was losing oil: the quantities concerned might be too small to matter. The speed reduction might be nothing more than a routine measure to conserve fuel; when darkness fell, he thought, the *Bismarck* might put in a burst of speed and evade to the westward. The spectre of an escape into the western Atlantic and of a subsequent fuelling in the Davis Strait continued to haunt him. Tovey was already having to think about releasing his destroyers, and it was becoming worryingly clear that the *Repulse* would be unable to make the interception and return to Iceland at a safe speed. If everything stayed as it was – a highly optimistic assumption – the battlecruiser might just have time to fight a short action at dawn on 25 May and then make Conception Bay, Newfoundland, with 5 per cent usable fuel remaining. Tovey was aware by now of the movements that the Admiralty had set in train. The *Rodney*, he calculated, could reach him at about 1000 and the *Ramillies* an hour or so later. But the margins for error were very narrow indeed and there was still 'a grave risk of [the *Bismarck*] getting away by sheer speed'. He had to find a way to slowing the enemy down and he had until dark to accomplish it.[2]

By early afternoon Tovey had decided on a torpedo-bomber attack. He was still a good 250 miles east of the enemy, well beyond strike range, but the geometry of the situation was now such that, if he detached the *Victorious* to the south-west at her best speed, she would pass some 100 miles off the enemy's port quarter at 2100 that evening. This would allow her to launch a strike force and recover it before sunset. So far, Tovey had seen the *Victorious* and her half-trained squadrons primarily in terms of reconnaissance, and he recognised, even now, that he might need this capability badly if contact were lost overnight. But in present circumstances he had to risk a torpedo strike, even if the chances of success were small.

At 1440 Tovey ordered Admiral A. T. B. Curteis, Rear-Admiral Second Cruiser Squadron, to take the *Victorious* under his orders and, with the cruisers *Galatea* (flag), *Aurora*, *Kenya* and *Hermione*, make for the nearest position within 100 miles of the enemy. The carrier was to launch her attack from there. His signal went on:

> *Victorious* is not to come under gunfire from enemy ships. As cruisers run short of fuel they are to be detached to Reykjavik. *Victorious* is to maintain contact as long as torpedo-bombers or reconnaissance aircraft are available.[3]

At 1519 Tovey himself, with the *King George V* and the *Repulse*, turned to an interception course of 200°.

* * *

At 2200 in the evening of 24 May the *Victorious* turned into wind and prepared to launch her Swordfish torpedo-bombers. She was late and a little beyond the range ordered. The westward excursion that had surprised Wake-Walker had upset calculations here too. It was three hours to sunset and the wind was rising.

Those watching the take-off from the carrier's flight control position found the weather 'as bad as it could be', with 'dark foaming seas, rain, and scudding clouds in a leaden sky'.[4] Lieutenant-Commander Esmonde led his squadron off the deck and formed up over the carrier in three sub-flights each of three aircraft. At 2227 he took his departure and set out on a course of 255° (magnetic) at a true airspeed of 85kts. Allowing for target movement during his time of flight, he had rather more than 140 miles to run. The

Fulmar fighters of 800Z Naval Air Squadron followed an hour later with orders to shadow the enemy and provide a distraction.

Esmonde climbed to 1,500ft and flew south-westwards through broken stratus. An hour after departure, his ASV radar detected a contact fine on the port bow at a range of sixteen miles. A break in the cloud revealed it as the *Bismarck*. Esmonde judged her course as 160° and her speed as 28–30kts. He wheeled his formation to port to position himself for an attack from ahead.

As he turned back towards the target, his radar failed to regain contact. The cloud was thicker than ever and he could see nothing of the surface. Esmonde maintained height and continued his turn to the north-east. With no sign of the enemy on this heading, he began a slow turn to the westward and, almost at once, detected two targets, one to port and the other to starboard. He chose the second, certain that it would be the *Norfolk* or one of her consorts, but ready to break away if he were proved wrong. The shadowers were expecting him. The *Suffolk*'s air defence radar had detected his IFF beacon some thirty minutes earlier. As the Swordfish came into view, the *Norfolk* signalled 'enemy fourteen miles on starboard bow'.

Esmonde took his departure from the *Norfolk* at 2350. He found a radar contact almost at once and began his descent for the attack. As he broke cloud, he found a ship with distinctly unmilitary lines and the paint scheme of a US Coast Guard cutter. She seemed to be stopped.[5] As he turned away, Esmonde caught sight of the *Bismarck* six miles further on. He clung to the cloud base, intending to work round to the target's starboard bow while the second and third sub-flights attacked from port. But the enemy was on the alert and opened a brisk and accurate anti-aircraft fire. With his starboard lower aileron shot away, Esmonde decided to attack while he could still do so; he dived for the water and came in from the *Bismarck*'s port bow. As he steadied for his attack run, the target began to manoeuvre violently. Esmonde pressed through the barrage and launched his torpedo at a range of 1,000yds. He then veered off to make his getaway at wave-top height, pursued by fire from the *Bismarck*'s medium batteries until he was out of range. Some of the splashes, he said later, looked suspiciously like those of 15in shells.[6] There was no sign that the first sub-flight's torpedoes had found their mark.

The second and third sub-flights, following Esmonde at intervals of about a minute, also tried to make their attacks from the *Bismarck*'s port side. But

Lindemann's well-timed manoeuvres made it difficult to select a good line and Lieutenant Percy Gick, the squadron weapon specialist and leader of the second sub-flight, was forced to break off his initial approach and come in again at a better angle. He, too, pressed home his attack without apparent result. One aircraft, however, the last to begin its attack run, made its approach from the *Bismarck*'s starboard side and was not noticed until too late. As it made its getaway, eager observers in several aircraft saw a column of water flung high into the air, close to the target's midship section. It was followed by dense clouds of black and white smoke. As Esmonde gathered his flock and began the return flight, there were high hopes that this single hit might have caused serious damage. The weapon had been fitted with a Duplex pistol and had been set to run under the *Bismarck*'s keel. This seemed to be a non-contact hit.

On board the *Victorious*, Captain Bovell awaited the return of 825 Squadron with mounting anxiety. It was a gloomy evening, giving promise of a dark night to come; the brisk north-westerly wind was bringing outbreaks of squally rain and shortening visibility. Three of the pilots had never made a night deck landing before. The carrier had been steaming hard to close the range, but time was running short and, to make matters worse, the ship's homing beacon had gone down. Bovell began to transmit on MF to give the returning aircraft a bearing and to sweep the horizon with his signal projectors. There was 'considerable relief' when, towards 0200 and a good hour later than expected, Bovell and his team saw the flash of Esmonde's lights. All the Swordfish landed safely, but they were uncomfortably close to the limit of their endurance.

The Swordfish squadron, with its high proportion of new and inexperienced people, had excelled itself. It had made a near-perfect interception at extreme range in weather conditions that had been far from easy. Eight of its nine aircraft had attacked the *Bismarck*; one had become separated in cloud and had failed to find the target. The new airborne radar had proved itself beyond all expectation. A squadron which had done little formation flying and which was unpractised in operations against ships had pressed home its attack and scored a hit. It had returned without loss.[7] Yet spirits were subdued. The *Bismarck* continued stubbornly on her way, and there was no apparent reduction in her speed.

Two of the Fulmars which had supported the raid had gone missing. Bovell continued his attempts to home them in until he could no longer ignore his admiral's orders to stop. The *Victorious* and the ships of the Second Cruiser Squadron continued their pursuit and planned for a second torpedo strike at dawn.[8]

* * *

If his enemies were downcast by the failure of this crucial mission, Lütjens had equal reason for pessimism. It is impossible to determine precisely when the full gravity of the *Bismarck*'s fuel situation came to his attention. Until mid-afternoon there had been solid grounds for believing that damage control teams would gain access to the flooded pump room in compartment XX and transfer the fuel isolated in the forward tanks. Lütjens had still been planning a long detour to the south-west to make use of the U-boat trap. The truth became apparent sometime after this. It was certainly apparent six hours later. By then it had become necessary to quash suggestions coming from shore that the *Bismarck* should delay her return. At 2056 Lütjens signalled Group West, 'Breaking contact not possible because of enemy detection equipment. Fuel situation requires direct course for St Nazaire.'[9]

There are signs that Lütjens began to edge round to the south-east at 1900, soon after his release of the *Prinz Eugen* and his brief exchange of shots with the shadowers. And he might have turned more directly for his destination but for the concentration of ships on his port quarter. Too sharp a turn would produce a close-quarters situation and a renewal of the action that he was determined, more than ever, to avoid. Nor is it possible to reconstruct Lütjens' assessment of the air threat as that eventful day drew to its close. Like Group West, he knew that a carrier had joined the Home Fleet in recent weeks but he had nothing beyond his own deductive powers to tell him when it had sailed and where it had gone. For a deliberate planner like Lütjens, this must have been a period of acute frustration.

Unmistakable signs that an air attack was developing came at about 2330. The *Bismarck*'s look-outs caught sight of the Swordfish formation during its early (and unsuccessful) attempts to gain an attacking position and thus a good twenty minutes before Esmonde began his attack run. This helps to account for his hot reception. From that moment on, all was confusion. Anti-aircraft gun crews, the main source of eye-witness accounts, could gain no clear overall impression of what happened.[10] They were blinded by smoke,

151

deafened by the concussion of the heavier weapons and disoriented by the movements of a ship under continuous helm. Gross overestimates of the scale of the attack began to circulate and were accepted by the command. A broadcast to the ship's company in the wake of the attack claimed that twenty-seven aircraft had been involved. Five had been shot down.

There was general agreement that the single successful attack had been the work of an aircraft which had broken away from the rest and which had closed unseen against the glare of the setting sun. The torpedo, however, had run shallow and had exploded harmlessly against the armoured belt, starboard side amidships. Lights had been put out down below, there were one or two broken bones and the collapsing water column had swept a man (Chief Boatswain Kurt Kirchberg) against the hangar wall and killed him. He had been the *Bismarck*'s first fatality. But the weapon had caused no further damage.

The effects of high speed, violent manoeuvre and defensive fire, on the other hand, had been more serious. At the end of the action the *Bismarck* was once again down by the bow. The temporary repairs forward had failed under the test and the shock of heavy weapons had opened up the seams in the damaged bulkhead between the turbo-generator compartment and No 2 port boiler room. Flooding could no longer be contained and the boiler room had been abandoned.[11]

In spite of these setbacks, morale in the *Bismarck* seems to have remained high. There would be more attacks to come and anti-aircraft crews remained at their posts. Apprehension was lessened by reports – based probably on a less-than-perfect interpretation of enemy ship-to-air signal traffic – that the British had run into problems recovering their strike and that only one aircraft had made it. As night drew on, damage control teams renewed their attempts to stem the flooding forward, correct the trim and bring the ship back to an even keel.

* * *

There was a postscript to Esmonde's gallant but unsuccessful attack on the *Bismarck* in the dying minutes of 24 May. It was a episode of near-farce, and one that was sure to divide senior officers who retained a sense of the ridiculous from their more straight-laced counterparts. The unwitting agent in all this was the US Coast Guard Cutter *Modoc*, which, patrolling peacefully in its Atlantic station, had already attracted the attention of Esmonde's Swordfish as they prepared for their attack.

The shadowers had been able to follow little of what was going on ahead of them as the attack developed. An eager audience in the *Norfolk* and the *Prince of Wales*, hoping to exploit any opportunity that the attack might throw up, could see only the glimmer of the *Bismarck*'s anti-aircraft fire against the darkening southern horizon; strain as they would, they could make out nothing of the ship itself. But, as they closed the scene, they began to pick out a ship, end-on apparently, close to the expected bearing. It had to be the *Bismarck* or perhaps the *Prinz Eugen*. The *Norfolk*, still following in the wake of the *Prince of Wales*, hoisted the signals 'Enemy in sight' and 'Open fire'.

Doubts set in almost at once. Someone suggested to Wake-Walker that the air attack might not be over and that the arrival of British salvos might put the attackers off; the *Norfolk*'s gun direction officer was beginning to question the target's identity. But equally persuasive voices were describing turrets and the outline of a battleship.

As the debate continued on the *Norfolk*'s bridge, the *Prince of Wales* turned to port, away from the target, and the cruiser followed her round. The battleship signalled, 'I am not certain that was the *Bismarck*'. By now Wake-Walker had reached the opposite conclusion; there was no other logical possibility. He ordered an immediate turn back to starboard. But the *Prince of Wales* did not acknowledge his signal and for a minute or more the two ships, unresponsive to their admiral's urgent needs, continued to open from the supposed enemy. Determined to seize the opportunity before it slipped away, Wake-Walker turned to starboard, hoping that the battleship would follow, but by the time he got back to his original course there was nothing to be seen. He steadied on 200° to close the range.

Nearly an hour later look-outs picked out the *Bismarck*'s dim shadow fine on the port bow at a range of eight or nine miles. The *Prince of Wales* and the *Norfolk* turned to port to open 'A' arcs and permission to fire was given. The *Prince of Wales* fired two salvos on a radar range, but failing light and funnel smoke made accurate observation impossible. The flash of gunfire to the southward showed that the *Bismarck* was firing back, but only one round fell anywhere near the shadowers and that was well short. After a few moments the *Bismarck* disappeared from view. It was the last glimpse that the *Prince of Wales* would have of her.[12]

* * *

The *Suffolk* had been acting independently while this incident was in progress, and, with darkness approaching, Captain Ellis had adjusted course to re-establish contact by radar and to investigate the whereabouts of the *Prinz Eugen*. He succeeded much sooner than he expected. His most recent sighting had put the enemy fifteen miles away and he was taken by surprise when, minutes after his course adjustment, his radar operators began to report a contact to the south-west at a range of only ten. There could be no doubt that this contact was hostile; Ellis saw it exchange fire with the *Prince of Wales*; but his immediate instinct was that this must be the *Prinz Eugen* and that the *Bismarck* must lie some distance beyond her. Whatever its identity, the ship was dangerously close. Ellis turned away.

After a few minutes Ellis turned inwards once more, and by 0213 he had regained radar contact just west of south at a range of 22,000yds. His plot showed enemy course and speed as 160°, 20kts. By 0229 his radar was reporting two ships on the bearing, the first at a range of 20,900yds and a second some 5,000yds beyond it. They appeared to be the cruiser and the battleship respectively. Satisfied that he had established the position of both ships and that he had measured their course and speed reasonably accurately, Ellis turned to a parallel course and continued his radar watch.[13]

It was still comparatively light at a latitude of 57° north (the latitude of Aberdeen or of northern Labrador) and the visibility extended to about six miles. Because of the U-boat warnings issued by the Admiralty and his own fairly moderate speed, Ellis decided to resume his zig-zag ,and at 0236 he turned outwards by 30°. He knew that the enemy would fade from his radar screen as the range opened, but he would reappear – surely – when the *Suffolk* started her inward leg. Twenty minutes later this expectation was fulfilled: the enemy reappeared much as expected. There was no reason to revise estimates of his course and speed, and at 0306 Ellis turned outwards once again.

After an interval of ten minutes, the *Suffolk* turned back. The radar showed nothing. By 0326 it was clear that some decisive move was needed to regain contact. Ellis increased speed and searched down the enemy's last known bearing. There was still nothing. By 0400 Ellis was sure from his study of the *Suffolk*'s track and from his knowledge of her radar coverage that the enemy must either have made a wide circle to starboard and crossed under his stern, or put on a burst of speed and opened to the south-west. Ellis decided that his first priority must be to search between the bearings of 180° and 200°, a logical extension to the area he had just covered and the first step in what he clearly saw as an expanding spiral search based on the lost contact position. In a signal timed at 0401 he gave Wake-Walker his assessment of what the enemy had done and described what he intended to do to retrieve the situation.[14]

Reflecting later on these events, Ellis felt that his mental processes had been sluggish. He had been shadowing the enemy for more that thirty hours and, before that, had been on his bridge for the best part of two days while negotiating pilotage waters off the coast of Iceland. This was his fourth night without sleep. Sluggish or not, the Captain of the *Suffolk* showed once again his mastery of naval warfare as applied science. His search plan took little account of the enemy's most probable or most dangerous courses. Others would attempt to apply these criteria later, though to no better effect. In mathematical terms it was hard to fault. By 0600 Ellis could be reasonably sure that he had covered all possible escape routes between 160° and 200° for speeds of up to 22kts and was beginning to extend his search to the next 20° sector.

The first indications that all was not well reached Wake-Walker at 0445 when he received the *Suffolk*'s initial assessment of what the enemy had done. The gravity of the situation took some time to sink in. Thanks in large part to the *Suffolk*'s radar, Wake-Walker's ships had recovered from temporary loss of contact often enough in recent hours and there was no obvious reason why they should not do so again. At 0504 he received a second report indicating that the *Suffolk* was still out of touch. It was not until 0515 and the arrival of a third signal showing that more than two hours had elapsed since the loss of contact that he began to grasp the truth. After examining the chart he reached much the same conclusions as Ellis. He signalled the CinC for an air search at dawn and told him that the enemy must either have made a 90° turn to the westward or, as he put it, 'cut away' under his stern.[15]

As it grew light, Wake-Walker turned to a course of 280° to search a sector somewhat to the north of the *Suffolk*. His lethargic response meant that he

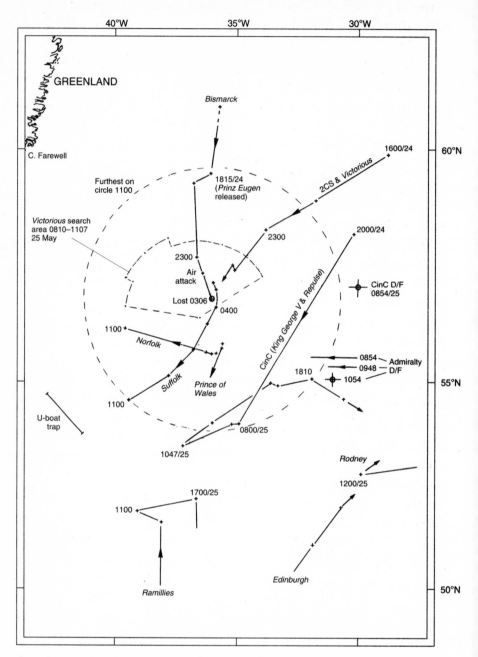

Loss of contact and search plans, period 1600(B) (zone −2) 24 May to 1800(B) 25 May 1941 (based on records of HM ships Suffolk, King George V *and* Victorious)

156

was a good way behind the enemy's 'furthest on position'. And, in a decision which indicates an uncertain grasp of priorities at this critical juncture, he detached the *Prince of Wales* to join the Commander-in-Chief.

News that the shadowers had lost contact reached Tovey shortly before 0600 and produced a situation that was distressingly familiar. Despite a shadowing operation that was already being seen as a classic of its kind, the enemy had finally succeeded in slipping through the net. The long chase was going to end in the 'blow in the air' that naval theorists had so often warned of. Instead of the dawn action that he had counted on and which the officers and men of the *King George V* and the *Repulse* had been steeling themselves for, Tovey now faced a tricky search operation around a datum position that was already three hours old. The area of uncertainty already covered nearly 20,000 square miles; it would double over the next hour and a half.

Realising that, with the assets available to him, he could search no more than a fraction of the area of interest, Tovey tried once again to look into the enemy's mind and discern his intentions. Lütjens, he thought, would either be making for a tanker or for a dockyard. If the former, he would be steering north-west for the Davis Strait or southwards for the Azores. If he had a dockyard in mind, he could be making for the North Sea, the Biscay coast, the Strait of Gibraltar or even Dakar. Tovey decided that his first duty was to cover the possibility that the enemy was looking for a tanker, since, as he put it, 'the two ships, refuelled and at large in the Atlantic, would constitute a much more serious and immediate menace to our interests than they would, damaged, in a French or German yard'.[16] The southerly quadrant was, he felt, adequately covered by the movements of the *Suffolk, Norfolk*, and *Prince of Wales*. His own force, passing still further to the southward, would cover the possibility that the enemy had put on a burst of speed. His most capable search asset , the *Victorious* and her aircraft, was best employed to the north and west of the lost contact position, covering the enemy courses that he had long recognised as the most dangerous of all. He signalled Admiral Curteis accordingly.

Tovey's instructions reached the Second Cruiser Squadron soon after 0700 and cut across plans which Curteis and Bovell had concerted between themselves and which they had been on the point of putting into effect. Despite a series of delays to recover straying Fulmars, the *Victorious* and her cruiser escorts had moved quickly south-west overnight and, on hearing that

157

contact was lost, had turned to close the datum position from the northward, calculating that an approach from this quarter would minimise the risk of meeting the enemy in the dark. Knowing that Wake-Walker's cruisers were searching to the south and west, they had planned an eight-aircraft search to the eastward that would cover the enemy's line of retreat. They had believed that, if they started early enough, their search arc would cover all likely destinations from the North Sea to Biscay. They now recast their plans. At 0735 Curteis turned his force to the north-west, spread his cruisers in line abreast at visibility distance and ordered the *Victorious* to search the north-westerly quadrant to a depth of 100 miles.[17]

As this urgent operation began, most of the ships that the Admiralty had set in motion continued to converge on the area of interest. The *Ramillies* and the *Edinburgh* were closing from the south and were, so they believed, within hours of making contact with the CinC. The *Rodney* was still some 300 miles south-east of the search centre. Her Captain, the taciturn and enigmatic Dalrymple-Hamilton, had been determined to keep his destroyers with him since leaving the *Britannic*, and progress had been slow against a rising head sea. But the *Bismarck*'s alteration to the south-south-east during the late evening of 24 May had produced a genuine chance of interception and he had decided, reluctantly, to leave his screen behind. Now, with contact lost, he had found himself well placed to counter a move towards Brest or Ferrol. He was loitering where he was to let the destroyers catch up.[18]

Force H was 1,000 miles south-east of the *Rodney*, on a course of 310° at 25kts. Somerville had just sent his destroyers back to Gibraltar and he was fretting at the lack of recent intelligence about the battlecruisers in Brest.

Later reconstructions show that the search conducted by Home Fleet units during the forenoon of 25 May was a scrappy affair, the product of haste and of inaccurate estimates of relative position. Coverage to the south of the datum was strong. By 1100 the *Suffolk* was able to report that the sector 180° to 220° was clear of the enemy. Coverage in the south was further enhanced by the movements of the *Prince of Wales* and of the Commander-in-Chief. Between west and north – the most dangerous sector in Tovey's estimation – coverage was patchy and the depth of search much less than intended. If Wake-Walker had grasped the nettle earlier, coverage in the west might have been better, but the main weakness lay elsewhere. Tovey had assumed that the *Victorious* and her escorts were well to the north of the lost contact position. In reality they were some tens of miles to the south and west. As he later admitted, the air search had not been deep enough to cover the enemy's most probable position. It was further weakened by the failure of one aircraft to start and by the disappearance of another during the course of the operation.[19] In the south-easterly sector, of course, there was no coverage at all.

There is no record of what Tovey intended to do if this search operation failed, though, as time passed, he must have given considerable thought to the matter. Given his reputation for tenacity of purpose and the strength of his conviction that the *Bismarck* would be making for a tanker rendezvous off the Greenland coast, there must be a strong possibility that he would have extended the search in that direction. But the time was surely approaching when he would have had to conclude that further searches in mid-Atlantic were unlikely to produce useful results. He would then have had little choice but to pull back and regroup in the northern passages; and London would have had to revert, as best it could, to the policy of convoy escort that it had abandoned so eagerly twenty-four hours before. That this point was not reached was due to new and unexpected developments.

* * *

During the early hours of 25 May the mood in Group West headquarters had swung from one of despondency to one of cautious optimism. At midnight the outlook had seemed bleak. Lütjens had been steering for St Nazaire direct; for some unaccountable reason, fuel had become a critical factor. He had abandoned his plan to draw his shadowers over a submarine trap and he had been pessimistic about his prospects for breaking contact. It was by no means certain that he had succeeded in releasing the *Prinz Eugen*: reports from the British cruisers had continued to suggest otherwise. Saalwächter was seeking clarification.

To make matters worse, it had become clear that the British were bringing powerful new forces to bear on the situation. News of the air attack had come as a jolt. The *Bismarck* had been lucky to escape further damage but there would be more attacks to follow. The *Luftwaffe*'s reconnaissance reports in recent days had been dangerously misleading. A close study of the photographs taken over Scapa Flow during the afternoon of 24 May now showed that the supposed battleships were no more than light cruisers and gunnery training ships. These were tense and anxious hours. There were signs that Lütjens had several important messages to pass which might throw further light on the situation; but none of them could be deciphered.[20]

Yet from 0230 onwards things had taken a turn for the better. Radio intelligence had detected a change in the pattern of British signal traffic. The plain-language enemy reports that had dominated the air waves for twenty-four hours or more had ceased – and ceased, it seemed, for good. Did this mean that, despite his earlier doubts, Lütjens had succeeded in breaking contact? Spirits rose. At 0846 Admiral Saalwächter signalled:

> Last enemy report by K3G [the *Suffolk*] was at 0213. Three digit tactical signals have continued since then but no further plain language contact reports. My impression is that contact has been lost. Operational signals being repeated to Bermuda and Halifax but not to Gibraltar. Assume Force H is in eastern Atlantic.[21]

The sudden arrival of new signals from the *Bismarck* upset this comfortable scenario. The breach of radio silence was surprising in itself; the content of Lütjens's signals was even more unexpected. In a message timed at 0727 and received by Group West some 90 minutes later, the Fleet Commander reported: '0700 [position] quadrant AK 55. One battleship and two heavy cruisers still in contact.' A second and much longer signal, transmitted in four sections between 0912 and 0948, read:

> Enemy's possession of detection equipment with minimum range of 35,000 metres affects Atlantic operations in gravest way. Ships detected in thick fog in the Denmark Strait and not let loose since. Escape attempts unsuccessful despite ideal weather conditions. Refuelling generally no longer possible unless we can outrun enemy. Running fight between 20,800 metres and 18,000 metres. *Hood* concentrated fire on *Bismarck*. *Hood* destroyed by explosion after five minutes. After that, shifted target to *King George*, which turned away making thick smoke after confirmed hits and remained out of sight for several hours. Rounds expended: 93. Thereafter, *King George* accepted action only at extreme range. *Bismarck* hit twice by *King George*: first under armour belt compartments XIII–XIV: second, compartments XX–XXI causing reduction in speed, bow-down angle of 1°, and loss of oil tanks. Release of *Prinz Eugen* achieved by engaging cruisers and battleship. Own radar prone to failure especially when firing.[22]

German staff officers who later reflected on this episode could find no satisfactory explanation. Radio intelligence had provided convincing evidence – soon supported by British accounts – that the shadowers had lost contact soon after 0230 in the morning of 25 May. Yet Lütjens had been certain that they were still in touch at 0700; he had even reported their identity and he had continued to use his radio transmitters freely for an hour or more after that time. Had there been a temporary loss of contact? Had the shadowers regained touch with the coming of daylight? Had Lütjens been able to detect their presence by the skilful use of his own sensors at a time when they could not detect him? Was it possible that the enemy did not have radar after all? The only other possibility was that the British might have changed well-established radio reporting procedures in the middle of an operation. This seemed inherently unlikely.[23]

Historians have faced similar difficulties. The riddle may be easier to understand if we dismiss the common but dubious assumption that the manoeuvre ordered by Lütjens at about 0300 in the morning of 25 May was intended – or expected – to throw the shadowers off the scent. It was not; if it had been, the Fleet Commander might have paid more attention to whether it had worked. It seems, rather, that he had excluded the possibility of breaking contact from his calculations; an effective radar in the shadowing cruisers had made it impossible. The wide circle to starboard which took him clear of the *Suffolk*'s radar coverage and which, an hour or so later, brought him across the wakes of the shadowers (the manoeuvre identified by Captain Ellis soon after the event and since accepted by most German historians) was designed to bring the *Bismarck* to the direct course for St Nazaire without risking a close encounter with the battleship that was known to be some-where on the port quarter. Lütjens fully expected the shadowers to follow him round, and, since he could neither see them nor detect them by radar, he assumed that they had done so.

The only source that might have alerted him to the true facts was his radio intelligence section. There is no reason to suppose that this was incompetent or inefficient; it was much more generously manned than the one in the *Prinz Eugen*. The key question for Lütjens was whether its reports formed an adequate basis for his tactical decisions. The record of the *B-Dienst* so far had hardly been impressive. It had given no effective warning of enemy cruisers in the Denmark Strait or of the approach of the battlecruiser squadron; the air attack had come as a bolt from the blue as well. Its advice on the progress of enemy shadowing operations had been no more reliable. According to the *B-Dienst*, the enemy had lost contact during that first evening when the task force had cleared the Denmark Strait; for two hours or more, in conditions of appalling visibility, the cruisers had done little more than exchange information on their own positions, courses and speeds. Yet, without warning, one of them had suddenly reappeared close astern. There had been another long period of silence during the afternoon of 24 May, but when Lütjens had turned to starboard to release the *Prinz Eugen* he had stumbled upon a heavy cruiser that had been tracking him through the murk with apparent ease.

Radar, Lütjens was now convinced, had given the enemy an unprecedented advantage. As long as the cruisers had the fuel to keep up with him, there was no reasonable prospect of escape. It would need more than a pause in the continuity of enemy signal traffic to persuade him otherwise.[24]

Admiral Saalwächter had little option on the morning of 25 May but to accept the Fleet Commander's reports at their face value. He quickly explained that he had signalled his impressions before receiving the latest information. Many hours would pass before the continuing silence on British wavelengths and a similar silence on the part of the *Bismarck* brought him back to his original viewpoint.

* * *

Reports that the *Bismarck* had resumed transmissions on the German ship-to-shore wavelength reached London towards 0900. They were received at first with disbelief and then with mounting excitement. There could be little doubt about the origin of the transmissions; the content of Lütjens' machine-coded messages had continued to defy the cryptologists at Bletchley Park but good progress had been made in fingerprinting the *Bismarck*'s transmitters.[25] This was almost certainly the same ship which the D/F stations had been tracking since the morning of 24 May and which had lapsed into silence an hour or so after the air attack.

But where was the *Bismarck*, and where was she going? These questions were less easily answered. Lieutenant-Commander Peter Kemp, head of the OIC's D/F plotting cell, found that many of the position lines (all from stations in the United Kingdom and none from Iceland or Gibraltar) ran parallel to one another or crossed at acute angles, producing a 'fix' that was ambiguous at best. The data needed careful interpretation, and Kemp, an acknowledged expert in the field, spent several minutes evaluating it before reaching his conclusion. The *Bismarck*'s 0854 position, he decided, had been in 55°30´N and somewhere between 32° and 30°W. Other key members of the OIC staff, including Captain Jock Clayton, the officer in overall charge, and Paymaster Lieutenant-Commander Norman Denning, head of the surface ship tracking section, agreed with him.[26] For D/F experts, at least, the implication was clear enough: the *Bismarck* was making for a Biscay port.

The Admiralty signal listing the D/F bearings taken at 0854 but, following agreed procedures, containing no estimate of the resulting position reached Tovey's flagship at 1030.[27] It came at a critical time. The search that Tovey had initiated was approaching its conclusion; nothing had been found and the CinC was facing far-reaching decisions. The pressures on the unfortunate officer who would have to make sense of the Admiralty's inconclusive data are easy to imagine.

The situation presented to Tovey after five minutes of frantic plotting was serious. The position lines drawn by the Master of the Fleet, Captain Frank Lloyd, ran north and east of the lost contact position, suggesting that, while the fleet had been searching in the south and west, the *Bismarck* had doubled back for the northern passages. She had a head start of seven hours and a lead of two or three hundred miles and there were no major units in position to block her path. At 1047 Tovey broadcast his estimate of the enemy's position (57°N, 33°W) and told his ships to 'search accordingly'.[28] He at once hauled round to a course of 055° at 27kts in a desperate attempt to overtake.

Most of the ships of the Home Fleet, spread now in a broad arc to the west of the lost contact position, followed Tovey's lead. The *Prince of Wales*, still searching for the CinC, turned towards Iceland. Admiral Curteis, less ready than others to discount the possibility that the *Bismarck* might be making for a Biscay port, found his choices constrained by lack of fuel. His smaller cruisers could never hope to overtake an enemy that was opening to the south-east, and although the *Victorious* still had 75 per cent fuel remaining he was unwilling to send her off unescorted now that the enemy was on the loose. When he had recovered his search aircraft, an operation delayed once again by attempts to home a missing Swordfish, he set course for the Shetlands, intending further air searches along the way and hoping that he could reach the Iceland–Faeroes passage in time to be of use.[29] Ellis, too, fell back towards Iceland, sure that he was out of the action for good but concerned for the safety of the carrier and its comparatively weak escort. Only Wake-Walker, eccentric as ever, turned towards Biscay. There were plenty of cruisers in the north, he thought, but few, other then the *Sheffield* with Force H, in the south and east.[30]

The ships which, under Admiralty orders, had been converging on the CinC followed the general pattern. The *Ramillies* and the *Edinburgh*, closing from the south and south-east respectively, both turned towards Iceland, although their chances of overtaking an enemy retreating in that direction appeared slim. Once her destroyers had caught up with her, the *Rodney* also turned to parallel the CinC, though Dalrymple-Hamilton, canny as ever, saw that his new track would be cutting across the cone of courses that led from the *Bismarck*'s last known position towards the Biscay coast.[31] At 0900 that morning Dalrymple-Hamilton had sent a position report; it was to be his only breach of radio silence during the entire operation.

Admiral Somerville was 1,000 miles south-east of the *Rodney*, crossing the latitude of Cape Finisterre. His destroyers had now left him; they had orders to report his position when they were 150 miles clear and to remind the CinC Plymouth that he had issued no bulletins on the state of the enemy battlecruisers in Brest for several days. Somerville was sure that Tovey's signal could not apply to him: had just received new instructions from London, and he was steering north to cover the approaches to Biscay.

* * *

The general movement towards the north-east, initiated by Tovey's signal, lasted for some five hours. If the CinC had doubts about his decision, he kept them to himself. It became clear soon enough that the Admiralty's reading of the situation differed in some ways from his own. At 1023, and again at 1100, London had ordered Force H to act on the assumption that the *Bismarck* was making for Brest and at 1158 similar orders had been sent to the *Rodney*. The Admiralty was continuing, therefore, to give at least some weight to the south-eastern sector. But these orders did not dent Tovey's confidence; the Naval Staff had probably taken the view that Somerville and Dalrymple-Hamilton were too far south to have any realistic prospect of catching an enemy who was retreating towards Iceland and were simply hedging their bets.

The early afternoon brought further D/F data. It was based on intercepts made at 0948 (a fairly long transmission) and on another at 1054.[32] London was now including estimates of position in its messages. (The enemy's longitude remained a little uncertain, but there was a definite southerly trend in his movement.) Tovey did not react; the Admiralty knew well enough what he was doing, and if they did not like it they would presumably say so. Captain Lloyd could not rest so easily, and he went back to first principles and checked the accuracy of his original fix. He did not like what he found.[33] Towards 1530 Tovey received details of yet another intercept. This one had been made on the U-boat frequency at 1320, although, according to the Admiralty, the strength of the signal indicated a surface ship.[34] The quality of the fix was said to be good. It reinforced the southerly trend established earlier.

Faced with this accumulation of evidence, Tovey wavered. At 1548 he altered course to 113°, the direct course for Brest, but almost at once a new signal was handed to him which implied that the Admiralty was having second thoughts. At 1428 London had reversed its instructions to the *Rodney*: the battleship was now to act on the assumption that the *Bismarck* was returning to Germany via the Scotland–Iceland passage. Confused, Tovey turned back to 080°, determined to steer a middle course until the conflict had resolved itself. At 1621 he asked the Admiralty whether they thought the *Bismarck* was making for the Faeroes. The wait for their reply lasted for what seemed an eternity. Eventually Tovey could wait no longer. At 1810 he turned to a course of 117°. His excursion to the north-east, unchecked by the Admiralty, had, he estimated, given the enemy a lead of at least 100 miles.[35]

* * *

To understand the ebb and flow of Admiralty opinion during these critical hours, we must retrace our steps to the early morning of 25 May when news first reached London that contact had been lost. The dangers of the situation had been recognised at once, but at this early stage the Admiralty had been content to allow Tovey's search to run its course. Their situation report, issued soon after 0900, provided an outline of the search plan and listed the positions of the principal ships involved; but it contained no clues as to the Admiralty's reading of the situation and it did not presume to advise the CinC on what should be done next. But the Naval Staff was already becoming restive; the search was half-done and Tovey's search plan, biased heavily towards the west of the datum position, had found nothing at all.

D/F specialists in the OIC thus found a Naval Staff eager for information and receptive to the idea that the German task force might have turned for home. The volume of traffic on the German wavelength had also fostered the belief that some major change of plan was in the offing. But the evidence from the 0854 and 0958 fixes did not carry sufficient weight – at least with non-specialists – to produce a settled view on the enemy's most probable destination. By 1023 the senior leadership had been prepared to agree provisionally to the diversion of Force H towards Biscay, a move which could be made without penalty Somerville's extreme southerly position, but it was not yet ready to throw its weight behind any single assumption. Reading the enemy's mind was a matter for experienced seamen and not for some 'boffin' in the OIC. Two senior staff captains, C. S. Daniel, Director of Plans, and R. A. B. Edwards, Director of Operations (Home), were sent away to make separate appreciations of the problem.

There is no contemporary record of what happened when the two officers reported back to the First Sea Lord and the Vice-Chief and other senior members of the Naval Staff. Oral evidence collected post-war suggests that both argued in favour of Brest as the *Bismarck*'s preferred destination and that both got a sympathetic hearing.[36] If Pound and his colleagues remained uneasy, it was because they recognised the weakness of the naval presence in the north and because they feared that Lütjens might seek foul weather in an attempt to elude Coastal Command's air patrols. The consensus, however, was for Brest. At 1100, and apparently in the light of these discussions, the Admiralty confirmed its orders to Somerville and, when her position became known, gave similar orders to the *Rodney*.

But the consensus did not mature, for at 1116 the Admiralty received Tovey's interpretation of the 0854 fix and the orders that had accompanied it. In the OIC, Kemp and Denning were quick to suspect human error; they urged the staff to send a signal that would set the record straight. Their pleas were rejected. The prime responsibility for the conduct of operations lay with the man on the spot; this was an established principle. Interference from the centre was unhelpful, even dangerous, as successive commanders-in-chief had been at pains to point out. Besides, the CinC might be acting on information as yet unknown in London and, quite possibly, on accurate D/F information provided by his own destroyers.[37]

Until the Admiralty's top-heavy bureaucracy had digested this new information and studied its implications, it could reach no firm conclusion. The OIC could point to a consistent trend in enemy movement; it could prevail in its attempts to include estimates of enemy position in its signals; but it could not persuade directors of operations to cross the boundary between information (which the CinC could act on or reject in the light of local factors) and guidance. It found them even less inclined to issue directions. Individuals may have arrived at firm conclusions but collective decisions still smacked of compromise. Search planning was one of the Admiralty's main preoccupations during the late forenoon of 25 May. Joint discussions with Headquarters Coastal Command on a long-range air search that would probe deep into the Atlantic towards the *Bismarck*'s last known position continued into the afternoon; plans were only finalised after the aircraft concerned – three Catalinas from bases in Northern Ireland – had taken off. Despite accumulating evidence from the D/F stations, the aircraft were tasked to sweep outwards to 30°W along the *Bismarck*'s presumed route towards Brest but back towards the Faeroes until they linked up with standing air patrols watching the northern passages. Although, as finally agreed, the plan betrayed an increasing interest in the Brest routes (they were to be covered first) it remained, in essence, a compromise. Coverage in the north could only be provided at the expense of coverage in the south.[38]

No one has ever explained how it came to pass that, at 1428 on that drowsy Sunday afternoon, the Admiralty reversed its instructions to the *Rodney* and invited her to act on the assumption that the *Bismarck* was making for Germany by way of the Iceland–Scotland gap. The burden of this signal seems so contrary to the general trend in Admiralty thinking that some have looked for a powerful constituency within the Naval Staff that was still betting on the northern passages. Others have hinted darkly at the influence of Churchillian intuition.[39] The answer is probably more prosaic. With major elements of the fleet acting on different assumptions and moving, presumably, in different directions, there were plenty of grounds for unease. How could the scattered elements, particularly the two heavy ships that held the key to the *Bismarck*'s destruction – the *Rodney* and the *King George V* – be brought together? Of more immediate importance, how could they be prevented from drawing further apart? Was some hint of these worries dropped from on high, a hint imperfectly understood or imperfectly expressed by those who had to translate it into written words? We shall never know for sure. The words, as finally chosen, made little difference to the *Rodney*. Dalrymple-Hamilton was already steering north-east across the projected routes towards Brest, hoping (somewhat against the odds) that he would stumble across the *Bismarck*. On receiving his new instructions, he simply carried on.[40] The real significance of the Admiralty's signal lay in its impact on Tovey's thinking.

As the afternoon drew on, the weight of evidence finally began to tell. At a time which can no longer be determined exactly, Bletchley Park advised the OIC that the W/T control station for the *Bismarck*'s operating frequency had shifted from Wilhelmshaven to Paris. Decrypts of *Luftwaffe* signal traffic were beginning to reveal urgent measures to reinforce air strength on the French west coast. Towards 1800, and from the same cryptographic source, came information that clinched the matter. A high-ranking *Luftwaffe* officer, visiting Athens in connection with operations against Crete, asked his headquarters about the *Bismarck*'s destination. His interest was purely personal: his son was serving as a midshipman on board. The reply was sent in Air Force Enigma, which, unlike naval variants, was being broken almost instantaneously. It showed that the *Bismarck* was expected on the west coast of France.[41]

This information reached Tovey's flagship towards 1900. The CinC had already reached his decision; he was steering south-east at 25kts but the future remained full of uncertainty. Dark was approaching and the *Bismarck* had not been found. Force H would be well-placed to make contact when daylight returned and the *Rodney*, too, would be somewhere to the south-eastward. But his own situation was beginning to look critical. He was without escort and he was closing the enemy's coast. He had 40 per cent fuel remaining and was beginning to watch his expenditures with care. If the *Bismarck* had a lead of 100 miles – a conservative estimate – he would be hard pressed to overtake her during daylight on 26 May. Yet by dawn on the 27th she could be within 200 miles of the French coast and Tovey would find himself, short of fuel and forced to economise, under increasing threat from submarines and aircraft.

It was clear, now, how much was going to depend on Force H and on the *Ark Royal's* Swordfish squadrons. They had to succeed where 825 Squadron had failed.

Notes to Chapter 8

1   Grenfell, p. 82. Grenfell attributes this view to Tovey's Chief of Staff, Commodore Brind.
2   Official dispatches, PRO ADM 199/1188, p.130.
3   CinC signal 1440(B), 24 May. For Tovey's appreciation of the situation p.m. 24 May, see PRO ADM 199/1188 pp. 11, 130.
4   PRO ADM 234/321 p. 11.
5   The ship was the USCG cutter *Modoc*. The *Bismarck* had been warned of her presence; the British ships had not.
6   825 NAS narrative, PRO ADM 199/1188, pp. 238–43.
7   PRO ADM 199/1188, pp. 131, 242. Captain Bovell was less complementary about the Fulmars of 800Z. Few had located the enemy and none had succeeded in maintaining contact. Their state of training was judged inadequate. Tovey was more charitable. He pointed out that night shadowing tested the skills of the most experienced crews and that 800Z's lack of success was hardly surprising.
8   Admiral Curteis later recalled that he cut short Bovell's attempts to recover the Fulmars with great regret. But it was now pitch dark and the shining of signal projectors was, he thought, an invitation to U-boats. PRO ADM 199/1188, p. 132. One of the Fulmar crews was later picked up.
9   PG47897, *Bismarck* War Diary, 24 May 1941.
10 Eye-witness accounts rest heavily on the evidence of *Matrosengefreiter* (Ordinary Seaman) Herbert Manthey, whose action station was No 5 starboard 20mm gun battery. His account is given in *Führer Conferences*, p. 214. The *Bismarck* War Diary, as reconstructed by Group West, follows Manthey's evidence. See also Müllenheim-Rechberg, pp. 166–9.
11 PG47897, *Bismarck* War Diary, entry for 2300, 24 May 1941. Based on evidence from survivors.
12 PRO ADM 199/1188, R-A 1CS and *Prince of Wales* narratives, pp. 204, 223. See also Grenfell, p. 94.
13 The double echo appears to have been a case of 'range ambiguity', an effect that can occur if the interval between successive radar pulses is not correctly matched to the range scale in use. I owe this explanation to Dr D. F. Dolman of the Defence Research Agency.
14 Official dispatches, HMS *Suffolk* ROP, PRO ADM 199/1188, pp. 271–3.

15 PRO ADM 199/1188, pp. 204 (R-A 1CS ROP), 271–3 (HMS *Suffolk* ROP).

16 Official dispatches, PRO ADM 199/1188 p. 133.

17 R-A 2CS ROP, PRO ADM 199/1188, p. 217.

18 PRO ADM 199/1188, p. 231. Dalrymple-Hamilton's ROP is exceptionally brief. His determination to keep his destroyers with him was based on the Admiralty's directive and on the belief that the CinC 'might be glad of them'. The *Bismarck*'s alteration to the SSE was critical for him; until that happened he had little chance of making an interception at a time that would be useful to the CinC whether he had his destroyers with him or not.

19 *Ibid.*, p. 133. In his dispatches Tovey suggested that the search to the east (as originally planned by Curteis and Bovell) would have failed too. Positional uncertainties make it hard to judge. It may be best to look upon it as a borderline case.

20 PG47897, *Bismarck* War Diary, 25 May 1941. The *Bismarck* had sent four garbled messages between 0125 and 0156 on 25 May. In an attempt to get them through she had eventually signalled the code settings that she was using.

21 *Ibid.*, entry for 1042, 25 May 1941.

22 *Ibid.*, 25 May 1941.

23 PG47895, chronology of events, 24 May 1941, note for Chief of Naval Intelligence by Operations Division of Naval War Staff. See also Müllenheim-Rechberg, pp. 177–9. Some accounts suggest that the *Bismarck* was fitted with a radar intercept set; Kennedy (pp. 277–8) says not. He is certainly right. The war diaries and staff papers covering '*Rheinübung*' make frequent reference to technical developments; other than occasional speculation that German ships might be vulnerable to detection by radar intercept, there is no mention of such a system.

24 It may be worth remembering that it took Wake-Walker more than two hours to appreciate that contact had been lost.

25 At this time German Naval Enigma was being broken by GC&CS, Bletchley Park, with a delay of 3 to 7 days, too late to have a direct bearing on current operations. *Luftwaffe* Enigma was being broken almost instantaneously. The battleship cypher used by Lütjens was never broken. The technique used to identify the *Bismarck*'s transmitters was known as RFP (radio fingerprinting). Hinsley, Vol. 1, pp. 337–42.

26 Lt-Cdr (later Vice-Admiral Sir Norman) Denning is usually credited with founding the OIC. He was a post-war DNI and the first DCDS (Int).

27 The procedure was agreed between Home Fleet staff and the Admiralty when D/F-fitted destroyers joined the fleet, but there seems to have been no previous opportunity to put it into effect. Beesly, p. 81; Hinsley, Vol. 1, p. 343.

28 PRO ADM 234/321, p. 15.

29 R-A CS2 ROP, PRO ADM 199/1188, p. 217.

30 R-A CS1 ROP, PRO ADM 199/1188, p. 205.

31 PRO ADM 199/1188, p. 231.

32 The origin of the 1054 transmission is obscure: there is no evidence for it in German sources.

33 A hot technical dispute on the origins of this error continued for some years. The principal arguments are examined in Appendix 1.

34 Later investigation showed that this transmission was made by a U-boat. Professor Hinsley makes the point that, had the GC&CS naval section been consulted, they would have advised against the Admiralty's interpretation. Hinsley, Vol. 1, p. 344.

35 PRO ADM 199/1188 p. 134. Tovey's account of this phase is skimpy; the account given here is reconstructed from Admiralty signals and from course and speed data for the *King George V*.

36 Grenfell, p. 113.

37 There may have been some rational basis for this belief. Critics have been quick to point out that none of Tovey's destroyers was, in fact, D/F-fitted and that they had all left for home anyway. This is true. But ships of the *King George V* class were also fitted with D/F and might have contributed to Tovey's fix.

38 For the coordinates of this search plan, see Grenfell, p. 114. See also reconstruction by Professor Rohwer, Müllenheim-Rechberg, p. 197.

39 Kennedy, p. 157, citing the opinion of Captain R. A. B. Edwards, Director of Operations (Home). Grenfell, pp. 122–3.

40 The *Rodney*'s behaviour during 25 May attracted very different reactions from senior officers. Tovey thought her positioning 'extremely well chosen' (PRO ADM 199/1188, p. 133); Pound saw her movements as 'very ill-judged' (minute to Tovey dated 1 August 1941, PRO ADM 199/1188, p. 25). Given the uncertainty surrounding the *Bismarck*'s position, Dalrymple-Hamilton's attempt to intercept her on the route to Brest was probably unwise. The better course – and the one probably anticipated in London – would have been to steer east as fast as possible (to remain between the enemy and his base) until things became clearer.

41 Hinsley, Vol. 1, pp. 344–5; Beesly, pp. 83–5.

9

The Riddle is Solved

The rain and drizzle that had shrouded operations in the North Atlantic during the afternoon and evening of 24 May cleared overnight and gave way to a near gale from the north-west. The new day brought a glimpse of the sun and brightening skies which lit the heavy seas that seemed to be driving the *Bismarck* towards her destination. Nothing disturbed her in her small and very private world. She saw nothing of the *Rodney*, which, in mid-afternoon, crossed 50 miles ahead of her, or of the *Edinburgh*, which, towards 1800, passed 30 or 40 miles under her stern, searching north-eastwards across the courses leading towards the Bay of Biscay. She knew nothing of the three Catalinas which, on their sweep to the north-west, exchanged identities with the *Edinburgh* and sighted some of the other ships that were still involved in the chase. (The Catalina on the more southerly track seems to have passed about 50 miles up the *Bismarck*'s port side during the late evening.) And she knew nothing of troop convoy WS.8B, which, later still and with the destroyers of the Fourth Division flung out as a picket to the westward, crossed her path from left to right at a range of less than 100 miles.[1]

Sunday 25 May was Admiral Lütjens's birthday. Raeder was fulsome in his good wishes. He complemented the Fleet Commander on his recent 'feat of arms' and looked forward to similar successes during the year ahead. Hitler's telegram was more guarded; he said simply, 'Best wishes for your birthday'.[2]

During this surreal interlude, the Fleet Commander's thoughts were full of dark foreboding. The airwaves were quiet – ominously so – but there was little doubt in his mind that the eagles were gathering. Something of his mood betrayed itself in the broadcast that he made to the *Bismarck*'s ship's company at midday. There was a lot that he could have said to steady the nerves of young and bewildered men. He could have made something of his escape from the shadowers; this was now clear beyond doubt. He could have pointed to the caution displayed by the enemy since the encounter with the *Hood* and stressed how difficult it was going to be for the British to bring up capital ships with the speed and gun power needed to defeat him; Admiral Saalwächter was already taking comfort from the thought that the enemy would 'only seek a decisive action if they were successful in bringing up the *Rodney* or a second *King George*'.[3] He might have congratulated his gun crews on their response to the air attack of the evening before and told them that, if they kept their wits about them, there was no reason why they should not break through to St Nazaire without further mishap. Instead, he spoke as if battle against overwhelming odds had somehow become inevitable. The phrase 'victory or death' set the tone of his address; and these were the words which stuck most firmly in people's memories. It was a message that few were prepared for. His men, it seems, went back to their stations not with a new sense of purpose but with the uneasy feeling that things were now desperate.[4]

Captain Lindemann did his best to counter the darkening mood. In his rounds of the ship and in a later broadcast of his own, he stressed the positive aspects of the *Bismarck*'s situation and he seems to have been least partially successful in lifting the spirits of his men. But one eye-witness, Müllenheim-Rechberg, saw the mood of depression as 'contagious'; from this point on, he began to sense a growing indifference to the military formalities, a carelessness in matters of detail, a tendency, among some, to retreat into sullen introspection, and the first signs of fatalism among the men of the *Bismarck*.[5]

It was to keep men from brooding on their predicament – rather than with any definite military purpose in mind – that, during the afternoon of 25 May, the command authorised the construction of a dummy funnel. Spare hands from the anti-aircraft batteries spent hours assembling this contraption from canvas and sheet-metal and painting it grey. It was going to be hoisted above the flight deck, but it was never finished. Below decks, engineering and damage control parties had more serious matters to attend to. Divers in the ship's flooded forepart renewed their attempts to transfer fuel from forward to aft, while, in a further attempt to lighten the bow and correct the trim, shipwrights let go the two bower anchors and their associated chain cables.[6] The threat of contamination to boiler feedwater supplies (essential for propulsion and the generation of electrical power) had become serious since the forced evacuation of No 2 port boiler room. The ship's four evaporators were kept at full stretch throughout the day to avert the threatened crisis. By midnight, it seems, they had won the battle.

* * *

The German naval commands ashore remained in a state of some uncertainty as to whether Lütjens had broken contact with his shadowers or not. Group West was trying to glean what he could from the analysis of British signal traffic. (It was his only source of information; air reconnaissance over the Bay of Biscay by the long-range FW 200 Condors of *I./KG 40* had found no sign of the enemy.) Channel radio had sent a series of high-priority messages to Force H and a dozen other addressees. Saalwächter guessed that the British were concentrating their forces between the latitudes of 52° and 53°N and beyond the range of German aircraft. He sent Lütjens a warning to this effect and told him (with Raeder's approval) that he could consider using a northern Spanish port if the situation required. Was *'Rheinübung'* going to end in a new humiliation for the naval leadership? Parallels with the *Graf Spee* incident of December 1939 cannot have been far from people's minds.[7]

But, with the passage of time, the conviction that the enemy had lost contact began slowly to reassert itself. Towards 1800 Group West told Lütjens that nothing had been heard from units K3G and 1UY (the former shadowers) for nearly twelve hours. Indeed, from midday onwards there had been nothing at all on British tactical wavelengths. 'If enemy still in contact,' Group West's signal ended, 'report your position and best speed.' There was no reply; the outlook was beginning to seem brighter. Contrary to earlier indications, signal traffic for Force H was still being routed through Gibraltar. And a convoy had been reported as leaving the Straits that afternoon. One of the enemy's priority signals had included both Force H and a convoy commodore in its address. Was there some connection? Was it possible that the release of the *Prinz Eugen* had forced the enemy on to the defensive? Had it been wrong to assume that Somerville's mission was an offensive one? Had he been deployed to cover the movement of the northbound convoy?

As they closed their journals for 25 May, Group Commanders were taking an increasingly sanguine view of developments. Admiral Saalwächter thought that the shadowers might have run short of fuel or that their detection equipment had failed. The enemy's usual 'defensive mentality' seemed to be reasserting itself; the British were reverting to convoy protection. To encourage this helpful trend, Saalwächter called on the *Prinz Eugen* to show herself on the western part of Halifax route as soon as she had finished fuelling.

Admiral Carls noted 'a marked improvement in the *Bismarck*'s situation' provided, of course, that she could maintain her speed. He shared Saalwächter's view that Force H might be acting in support of a northbound convoy. And he recorded other hopeful signs. There was a storm brewing in the eastern Atlantic: with any luck, it would make carrier operations difficult and hamper the deployment of light forces.[8]

It was assumed, meanwhile, that Lütjens was maintaining his course for St Nazaire. Preparations for his reception were now in full swing. Signals reaching the *Bismarck* through the night of 25/26 May gave details of the support that would be available on arrival. The *Luftwaffe* would provide strike groups out to 14°W (about 300 miles west from the Brittany peninsula); there would be comprehensive reconnaissance to 15°W and some as far as 25°W. Five U-boats would be spread out along the *Bismarck*'s estimated approach route at intervals of twenty miles. There would be three destroyers to escort her in. Harbour approaches would be under full control and anti-aircraft defences in St Nazaire would match those available at Brest. The drydock would be ready by 27 May and all necessary torpedo protection measures would be in place if the *Bismarck* had to unload before entering dock.[9]

* * *

British attention that evening was beginning to focus on a broad arc of ocean 500 to 700 miles north-west of Cape Finisterre, where, during the daylight hours of 26 May, the Royal Navy would have to find the *Bismarck* and strike a decisive blow. The consequences of failure were becoming obvious to all: if the *Bismarck*'s movement towards the French coast continued unchecked, dawn on 27 May would find the heavy ships of the Home Fleet close to safe margins of fuel and facing the full fury of the *Luftwaffe*. The cost of extending the pursuit would become heavy, possibly unacceptable. The likelihood of

U-boat concentrations in the Bay of Biscay added to the general sense of anxiety.

Two groups of ships were converging on this critical area. Approaching from the north-west and scattered loosely along the line joining Cape Farewell and Brest were the battleships *King George V* and *Rodney* (the latter still with her three destroyers) and the two cruisers, the *Norfolk* and the *Edinburgh*. None knew where the others were. With fuel supplies dwindling, commanding officers were beginning to find themselves torn between the urge to participate in great events and the instincts of self-preservation. They were setting deadlines for themselves and speculating on the deadlines of others.

Admiral Somerville, with the *Renown*, the *Ark Royal* and the *Sheffield*, was approaching from just east of south. Somerville needed to concentrate all his resources on finding and striking the *Bismarck*, but the possibility of a surprise appearance by the *Scharnhorst* and *Gneisenau* was continuing to nag at his mind. He had planned to keep security patrols airborne throughout the 25th as a precautionary measure, but heavy seas and worsening visibility had forced him to cancel his flying programme.[10] At midnight, the two groups were still nearly 600 miles apart.

Staffs at sea and ashore worked far into the night on search plans for the coming dawn. Somerville intended three consecutive search operations across a 300-mile front that would allow for a 'substantial detour' to the south of the direct route and which would cover enemy speeds from 25 down to 15kts. His dawn search would allow for the higher speeds; the second, starting at noon, and a third, finishing by dusk, would cover the intermediate and slower speeds respectively.[11] Each search would need ten Swordfish from the *Ark Royal*'s complement of twenty. Three additional aircraft, fitted with long-range tanks, would be held in reserve throughout the day to take over shadowing duties when the enemy was found. Captain L. E. H. Maund of the *Ark Royal* was worried, nonetheless, that his search effort would be spread too thinly; he planned to thicken it with Fulmar fighters.

Free now to concentrate its search effort on one enemy escape route rather than two, Coastal Command drew up plans that were very similar to Somerville's. Air Marshal Sir Frederick Bowhill, CinC Coastal Command, had served at sea himself and understood well enough how a large ship, uncertain of her position after several days without sight of sun or stars, might make her landfall on a dangerous coast. He rejected the uncritical assumption shared by the Admiralty and a number of commanders at sea that the *Bismarck* would approach her destination directly. Bowhill argued that she would make her approach from a direction well south of west, having first, possibly, made a landfall off Cape Finisterre. The more southerly route would, he was convinced, have the added attraction of keeping the *Bismarck* further from British airfields and of reducing the risk of early detection and attack. He persuaded the Admiralty that the patrol areas to be occupied by his Catalina flying boats from dawn on 26 May should extend well to the south of the direct route and cover an initial approach towards the north-western coasts of Spain. He established two cross-over patrol areas in longitude 20°W to cover the necessary arc.[12]

The Admiralty, meanwhile, had been turning its attention to broader questions. Saalwächter's calculation that, with the *Prinz Eugen* on the loose, the British would revert to defensive policies was not wholly unfounded. Shortly after 1400 on 25 May the two eastbound convoys HX.128 and SC.32 were ordered to reverse course for twelve hours and then resume their passage on the route ordered. The *Revenge*, twenty-four hours out of Halifax, was sent to support them. The veteran *Ramillies* was sent to find the *Rodney*'s former charge, the *Britannic*, and cover her passage westward.[13]

Anxieties about the *Prinz Eugen* and memories of German actions during the final stages of Operation 'Berlin' lay behind the Admiralty's continuing preoccupation with the northern passages and with other potential bolt-holes. Shortly after midnight the cruisers *Arethusa*, *Manchester* and *Birmingham* (then refuelling in Hvalfjord) were ordered to resume their patrols in the Denmark Strait and the Iceland–Faeroes passage and the battleship *Nelson*, then in Freetown, was ordered to Gibraltar at her best speed.[14]

Despite the accumulation of evidence in favour of a French destination, the Admiralty's worries about an escape into the Mediterranean persisted well into the following afternoon. At 1220 on 26 May the submarine *Severn*, westbound with the *Cairndale* to set up a tanker rendezvous northwest of the Azores, was ordered back to Gibraltar at maximum speed 'in case the *Bismarck* or *Prinz Eugen* endeavour to pass into the Med'. The area Flag Officer was given a similar warning and he was told that, on this occasion, 'Spanish territorial waters need NOT be respected . . .'[15]

Meanwhile the need to provide anti-submarine support for the two Home Fleet battleships had become a matter of primary concern. By evening on 25 May Admiralty planners could be certain that any original destroyers had either left for home already or would do so within hours. With the two heavy ships moving rapidly towards an area of submarine danger, urgent decisions were becoming necessary. Discussions between Captain Edwards in the Admiralty and the Chief of Staff to Admiral Sir Percy Noble, Commander-in-Chief Western Approaches, showed that the only feasible option, given the estimated positions of the ships concerned and the urgency of the situation, was to detach the Fourth Destroyer Division (HM Ships *Cossack*, *Maori*, *Sikh*, *Zulu* and the Polish destroyer *Piorun*) from convoy WS.8B and direct it to join the battleships. The risks attached to this course of action were self-evident. A military convoy bound for the Middle East with 40,000 troops and the *matériel* to support them was not to be trifled with. It was judged, however, that WS.8B was already clearing the area of greatest danger, that encounters with U-boats were becoming increasingly improbable and that the convoy's cruiser escort was sufficient to deter any remaining surface threat. At 0159 in the morning of 26 May Admiral Noble issued the necessary orders, and at 0330 Captain P. L. Vian – whose role in the *Altmark* affair had already attracted public attention and who would show himself, in due course, to be one of the coolest tacticians of his generation – turned his destroyer division to the north-eastwards and set off in pursuit of the Commander-in-Chief.[16]

* * *

It blew strongly through the night of 25/26 May and, with his ships punching into a steepening head sea, Somerville found himself obliged to reduce speed first to 23, then to 21 and finally to 17kts. He had hoped for a quiet night so that he would be fresh for the coming day, but this was not to be: the progressive reduction in speed meant continuous adjustment to his search plans.[17] By 0300 in the morning of 26 May he was already two hours behind schedule and it was becoming clear that the first search operation, planned for 0700, would have to be postponed. Somerville altered course from north-west to north to allow for the additional forward movement of his target and moved his search area 35 miles to the south-eastward.

Dawn broke to reveal a turbulent scene. The wind was north-west force 7, the sky overcast and the visibility ten miles or less. Gusts over the deck of the *Ark Royal* registered 50kts and the rise and fall of the ship's stern was measured by sextant as 50ft and more. Conditions were marginal for Swordfish; the use of Fulmars was out of the question. There was still no news about the German battlecruisers; 'Can't make out why the people at home so lack imagination,' Somerville noted at the time.[18] Shortly after 0700 a single Swordfish was sent to patrol north and west to guard against a surprise encounter. The *Ark Royal* then turned out of wind to range aircraft for the morning reconnaissance.

The evolution was a slow one. Decks were running with water and flight-deck crews, manhandling cumbersome aircraft between lift and take-off spot, had to strain every muscle to prevent them from sliding bodily across the deck.[19] By 0830 all was ready. Crews manned their aircraft. The *Ark Royal* then turned slowly into wind to begin the launch sequence, her command alert for those elusive moments when the pitching of the ship would ease a little. From the bridge of the *Renown*, Somerville watched with his heart in his mouth as, one by one, the ten Swordfish gathered momentum along the carrier's deck and rose over her bow, some of them hidden for seconds at a time behind curtains of spray.

The credit for finding the enemy, however, went to Coastal Command. Towards 1030 Catalina 'Z' of No 209 Squadron, searching low over a stormy sea in the more southerly of Air Marshall Bowhill's patrol areas, spotted a dim shape at the extreme limit of visibility. Flying Officer Dennis Briggs and his American co-pilot, Ensign Leonard B. Smith, turned to close their contact, seeking the safety of cloud cover to mask their approach.[20] Moments later the cloud parted to reveal the *Bismarck* at dangerously close range. Smith swung the lumbering flying boat away and opened full throttle in an urgent attempt to gain height while Briggs left his seat to put together a sighting report. The enemy was on full alert. As, engines throbbing, the Catalina clawed its way back into the cover of cloud, its crew felt the concussion of anti-aircraft shells bursting around them and heard the rattle of shrapnel against the hull. When they had recovered themselves, the enemy was nowhere to be found.

The Catalina's report reached Force H at 1038. Somerville was steaming northwards, close to the eastern boundary of his search area, waiting for his

Swordfish squadrons to return. His plot showed the *Bismarck* a little abaft his port beam at a range of 112 miles. Enemy course and speed was given as 150°, 20kts. With the range closing, geometries were beginning to favour an early strike and time was of the essence. But half his available striking force was away on its search mission and there would be danger in calling it back. A general recall might alert the enemy and prompt him to evade; it might even put the carrier herself at risk. And a sudden change of plan could result in muddle and delay. Somerville let the reconnaissance mission continue according to plan and, meanwhile, held on to the north. This was what his returning aircrews would expect. He gave the *Ark Royal* emphatic orders not to break radio silence; her aircraft could be left to find out about developments all in good time.

But it soon seemed possible that the enemy might slip from his grasp. At 1114 Somerville got word that the Catalina had been holed by shrapnel and that its crew was asking Coastal Command for instructions. His immediate inclination was to launch two of the Swordfish that he had been holding in reserve to relieve Catalina 'Z' in the contact area, but before he could do so a new report reached the *Renown* showing that contact had been lost. Relocation was now urgent. Maund advised that, to allow for errors in relative position, up to six Swordfish might be needed.[21] Somerville ordered 'at least four'. But within minutes he heard that two of his own aircraft had made contact with the enemy as they were returning from their mission. Swordfish '2H' was shadowing what appeared to be a cruiser; '2F', flying an adjacent track, was in touch with a battleship. The two positions compared well; they showed that the enemy, whatever his identity, was closer than expected, only 70 to 80 miles west of the *Renown*.[22]

By noon aircraft from the morning search were gathering around the *Ark Royal* awaiting the signal for recovery. Captain Maund launched two shadowers with long-range tanks to relieve '2H' and '2F', recovered the rest and began immediate preparations for a full-scale strike. To secure his hold on the enemy, Somerville detached the *Sheffield* (Captain C. A. A. Larcom) to 'close and shadow the enemy battleship and supplement aircraft reports'. (Few could have predicted that this decision would produce near-fatal consequences.) As the *Bismarck* passed clear to the south of his formation, Somerville manoeuvred to keep position 50 miles to windward of his target. Here the *Ark Royal* would be free to launch and recover aircraft without fear of interruption. It would also be the most favourable (and safest) direction from which to attack if, as a last resort, the *Renown* had to engage the *Bismarck* unsupported.[23]

* * *

The Commander-in-Chief, meanwhile, was well to the northward, steering for the French coast at 25kts. Renewed contact with the *Bismarck* did little to ease his anxieties. The position given by the Catalina was so far south of the expected line that Tovey suspected a case of mistaken identity. The contact, he thought, might well be the *Rodney*, and he asked the Admiralty to take the matter up with Coastal Command. Reports from Somerville's aircraft soon eliminated this possibility, but the picture that they revealed was far from encouraging. The flagship's plot showed the enemy a good 130 miles to the southward. If he maintained course and speed, an interception before nightfall was out of the question. Tovey held on to the south-east at his best speed, aware, more than ever, that the outcome would turn on whether or not Somerville succeeded in slowing the enemy down. For the moment, he kept his worries to himself, but he was beginning to face the unwelcome prospect that, if the *Bismarck*'s speed had not been reduced by midnight, he would be forced to break off the pursuit and return home for fuel. The captains of the *Norfolk* and the *Edinburgh*, who had also found themselves well to the north of the enemy's line of advance, were coming to very similar conclusions.

Vian had no such worries. He had been steering north-east, expecting to sight the Commander-in-Chief in early afternoon. The Catalina's report showed him that the enemy was broad on his starboard bow at a range of 40 or 50 miles. With barely a moment's hesitation he spread his destroyers in scouting line and turned to the south-east. As he later told Tovey, 'I knew you would wish me to intercept the enemy and altered course accordingly'.[24] As the destroyers of the Fourth Division turned down-sea and increased to maximum speed, white water came surging forward along their weather decks, penetrating hatches and ventilators, drenching compartments below and threatening to sweep away men in exposed positions. Commander Plawski of the Polish destroyer *Piorun* found his ship 'sheering wildly' and heeling over at times to 60°. Vian reduced the speed of his formation to 27kts.

The mystery surrounding the *Rodney*'s position was resolved towards midday. As the *King George V* continued her pursuit, an unmistakable silhouette became visible just forward of the port beam. The *Rodney*, too, was steering to the south-east and two of her destroyers were still in company. Through the afternoon hours, the two battleships slowly converged until, by 1700, the *Rodney* had slipped quietly into station astern of the Commander-in-Chief. Tovey then reduced speed to 22kts to conserve fuel and to allow his elderly consort to keep up. He was now waiting on tenterhooks for news of Somerville's attack.

* * *

The fifteen Swordfish of the *Ark Royal*'s striking force were ranged and ready by 1415. Captain Maund had hoped to add a few Fulmars to provide a 'synchronised diversion', but he had been compelled to abandon this idea because of the weather. He was still in some doubt about the identity of his target; the crews of Swordfish '2F' and '2H' had stuck to their respective stories and he had been unable to reach a definitive judgment on the matter. The striking force was prepared for either enemy; torpedo depth settings were adjusted to 30ft so that the Duplex pistols would be effective against the *Prinz Eugen* as well as the *Bismarck*. The launch sequence began at 1450, and at 1500 the striking force, now fourteen strong,[25] took its departure over the *Renown* and climbed away to the south. The range and bearing of the enemy was given as 195°, 52 miles.

This was to be a radar-assisted attack. With visibility in the target area poor and the cloud base low, the Swordfish formation climbed through the cloud, intending to establish contact by radar; it would then overfly the target, divide into sub-flights and dive through the cloud to make a coordinated sector attack. At about 1550 contact was duly established; it was the single contact that the strike leader had been briefed to expect. It was about twenty miles from the briefed position, a discrepancy worthy of note but not sufficient to cause alarm. The order to attack was given.

The *Sheffield* at this time was still closing the enemy, using the reports of the shadowing aircraft to guide her. She had yet to make contact. Captain Larcom had been expecting the striking force to overfly him but not to see Swordfish closing from all quarters and levelling as if for attack. He rang on full speed, ordered guns tight and put his wheel over towards the closest of his assailants. One or two weapons, he noticed, seemed to detonate on hitting the water; a few others exploded harmlessly in his wake. But half a dozen seemed to run true. With every eye watching for the moment of weapon release and searching the surface for torpedo tracks, he succeeded in threading his way between them. Not a single gun fired in reply.

The striking force returned to the *Ark Royal* mortified and confused. Diving through the murk to emerge over an angry sea with a target at close range, most crews had seen what they had expected to see. Only three had recognised the familiar shape of the *Sheffield*. More than two hours had elapsed since their departure and they now returned to find an admiral thirsting for news. Somerville asked whether an attack had been made. Maund replied:

> Yes. Eleven torpedoes fired at *Sheffield*. No hits. Afraid instructions to shadow not received in *Ark*. Aircraft left without this knowledge. Your [signal] not decoded and shown to me until striking force had taken its departure.[26]

The cause of this débâcle can be found in a single seemingly trivial omission. Somerville's order detaching the *Sheffield* for shadowing duties had been passed to the cruiser by light and had not been repeated to the *Ark Royal*. (The carrier had been operating independently to conduct flying operations.) Maund was first alerted to the risk of confusion in the target area more than two hours later when he was shown the decrypt of a situation report sent to him for information only. This message had received no special handling in his signal office. He had recognised the danger at once and had thrown caution to the winds in broadcasting an urgent warning to the striking force. But he had been too late.[27]

Maund's priorities now were to get his crestfallen air group to put this humiliating set-back behind them and to scrape together every available aircraft for a further attempt. There was, it seems, no hint of recrimination. Maund took the weight on his own shoulders. Swordfish were refuelled and rearmed from the *Ark Royal*'s dwindling stock of torpedoes and, following reports from the *Sheffield* that several weapons had detonated prematurely, the decision was taken to replace the Duplex firing mechanisms with contact pistols. Somerville, who would later accept his full share of responsibility for the afternoon's events, confined his report to the bare essentials. At 1800 he told the Commander-in-Chief, 'Striking force scored no hits and leaves again at 1830.'[28]

The wider implications of this new and frustrating delay were revealed in Tovey's response. It had been possible for some time to deduce his predicament, if only in general terms. He now made his worries explicit. The *King George V*, he told Somerville in a signal that was also read in Whitehall, had already reduced to 22kts in order to conserve fuel. He would thus no longer be overhauling the *Bismarck*; at best, he would be maintaining his position. Unless the *Bismarck*'s speed could be cut back, he would be forced to withdraw from the operation at midnight and return home for fuel. The *Rodney* could continue a little longer but she would have no escort.[29]

* * *

By 1900 Somerville was ready to make a second attempt. It had to succeed; this would be the last opportunity for a full-scale torpedo attack before daylight faded. Another bungled attempt was not to be contemplated.

The weather had shown no sign of moderating; it was still blowing hard from the north-west, the cloud base was at 600ft and violent rain squalls were sweeping across the area. Yet several factors had moved in Somerville's favour since the events of the afternoon. His hold on the enemy had become reasonably secure. His air shadowers, working in relays, had established firm contact with the enemy and were providing regular reports. They had succeeded in solving the riddle of enemy identity: this was the *Bismarck* – there could be no further doubt on the matter. Another Coastal Command flying-boat, Catalina 'M' of No 240 Squadron, had appeared in the contact area. (It had viewed the Swordfish with considerable mistrust and had reported, once or twice, that it was under attack by unidentified aircraft.) After her lucky escape, the *Sheffield*, too, had made contact with the enemy: she had taken up a shadowing position astern of the *Bismarck* at the limit of visibility, and she would be able to direct the attack.[30]

At 1915 fifteen Swordfish from 818, 810 and 820 Naval Air Squadrons, organised in six sub-flights, left the deck of the *Ark Royal* and formed up to take their departure. The enemy bore 167°, 38 miles. To avoid a repetition of the afternoon's events, the strike leader, Lieutenant-Commander T. P. Coode, took his formation southwards to join the *Sheffield*, keeping below cloud and steering on her radio transmissions. He found her towards 2000 and began to climb in a wide spiral above her to an approach altitude of 6,000ft.

Coode began his attack run at 2040, passing over the *Sheffield* with sub-flights in line astern. He had encountered heavy cloud during his climb and, once clear, had spent precious minutes marshalling his formation and re-establishing his position. Now, at last, prospects seemed good. Cloud cover was solid between 2,000 and 5,000ft and would conceal his approach; he knew the enemy's position to a fair degree of accuracy; and the *Bismarck* bore 110°, twelve miles. This would be a six-minute run. But, as the Swordfish formation settled into its approach, it ran into a dense wall of cloud covering the target's position.[31] Sub-flights quickly lost sight of the next ahead and took what action they thought best. The leaders, nearing the end of their timed runs, let down to make their attacks at once. Others, hoping to re-form above the cloud mass, attempted to climb through it. One aircraft lost its bearings altogether and returned to the *Sheffield* to start again. All synchro-nisation was lost and the attack degenerated into a formless mêlée. Sub-flights and a few aircraft acting on their own attacked piecemeal over a period of some thirty minutes.

The leading sub-flight let down through the mass of cloud to make an attack from the stern or quarter. It broke clear to find the *Bismarck* still four miles ahead and very much on the alert. Coode found himself under fire within seconds. He banked away and held to the cloud base while he repositioned his three aircraft for an approach from the target's port beam. He began his attack at 2055 and he was followed closely by a single aircraft ('5K' of No 3 Sub-Flight) which had lost its companion. As '5K' released its weapon and pulled away, the observer, Sub-Lieutenant (A) R. I. W. Goddard, saw a column of water 'half as high again as X turret' erupt from the *Bismarck*'s port quarter and collapse to leave wreaths of dense black smoke. His air gunner missed the water column but confirmed the presence of smoke.

Lieutenant D. F Godfrey-Faussett, leading the second sub-flight, had climbed into the wall of cloud and had reached clear air at 9,000ft. He had then located the target by radar and dived down to make his attack. He broke cloud at 2,000ft to find himself a mile on the *Bismarck*'s starboard beam. One of his aircraft had strayed during the descent. Fire was again prompt and

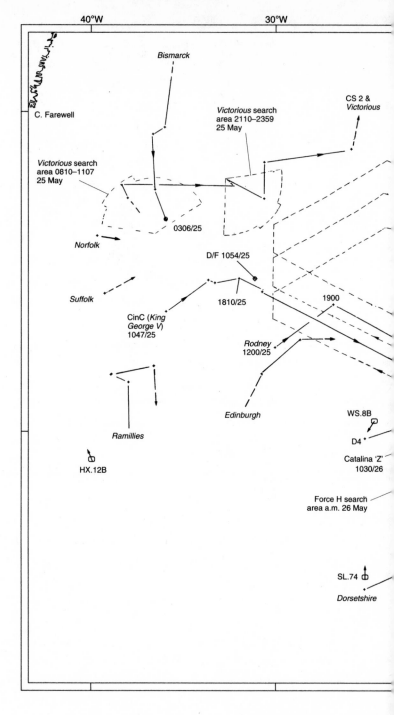

Search plans and movements a.m. 25 May to evening 26 May 1941. Times B (zone

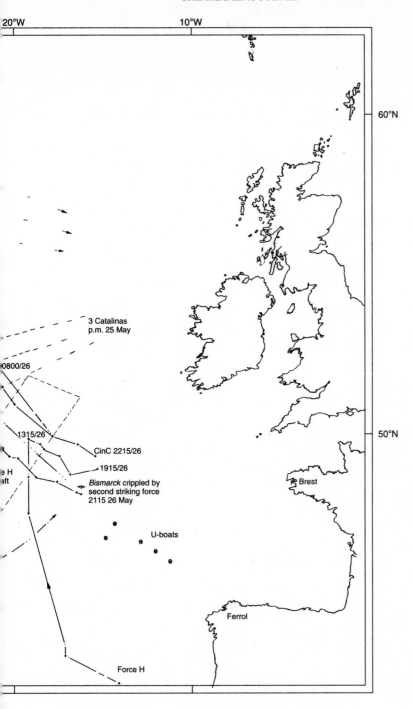

20°W

10°W

60°N

3 Catalinas
p.m. 25 May

0800/26

1315/26

CinC 2215/26

1915/26

e H
aft

Bismarck crippled by
second striking force
2115 26 May

50°N

Brest

U-boats

Ferrol

Force H

d on records of HM ships King George V, Victorious, Renown *and* Ark Royal.

intense. Godfrey-Faussett's two remaining Swordfish pressed home their attack, followed by a third ('4K' of No 5 Sub-Flight) which had been forced down by icing and which had found itself in a position to attack from the same direction. The crew of '4K' saw a water column erupt on the *Bismarck*'s starboard side between 'X' and 'Y' turrets as the leading pair made their getaway. The time was about 2115.

Sub-Lieutenant (A) A. W. D. Beale attacked at much the same time but from the opposite side. He had been a member of No 2 Sub-Flight but had become separated during the climb and had returned to the *Sheffield* for a new fix. He had broken cloud at 4,000ft to find the enemy at a range of 1,200yds. He and his observer, Sub Lieutenant (A) A. C. Friend, saw unmistakable signs of a hit on the port side amidships as they made their getaway. Both shadowing aircraft saw this hit as well.[32]

Other crews had different tales to tell, but there were no further claims of hits. As the Swordfish straggled back to the carrier, Captain Maund questioned each crew in turn in an attempt to establish what, if any, damage had been inflicted. Forming a clear and consistent picture proved difficult. Breaking cloud at ranges of a mile or less and fighting to meet the exacting height, speed and line criteria for a torpedo attack, crews had glimpsed the *Bismarck* for a few brief seconds and their vision had been obscured, as often as not, by smoke or driving rain. Defensive fire had been heavy and had included guns of all calibres. (Four aircraft had been damaged; one of these had 175 splinter holes and two members of its crew had been wounded.) There were no written records. Few could vouch for the sequence in which events had occurred. Maund found some of his young men still in a fever of excitement; he suspected that their accounts were slightly 'embroidered'.[33]

Maund was determined to release only the most objective of information. News filtered out slowly; it was nearly an hour before Somerville could be sure of one definite hit amidships and almost two hours before he knew of a possible second, this one on the target's starboard quarter.[34]

* * *

The *Bismarck*'s behaviour, meanwhile, had done little to encourage the idea that the strike had been successful. As the air attack subsided, look-outs on the bridge of the *Sheffield* had seen the *Bismarck* emerge from the gloom broadside on and within gun range. Captain Larcom had called for full speed and put down smoke, but his reaction had come too late. The first salvo of 15in shells had fallen short but the second had straddled, sending a hail of lethal fragments through the cruiser's unprotected structures. Four further salvos had fallen close. A dozen men had been wounded, three fatally, and the radar had been put out of action.

News of this incident found the fleet in pessimistic mood. A premature message from the strike leader had already indicated a 'nil' result; the *Bismarck*'s aggressive behaviour seemed to confirm it. Larcom's report that the enemy was steering 340° met open disbelief. Tovey remarked, famously, that Charles Larcom must have 'joined the reciprocal club'.[35] Corroborating evidence from the shadowing Swordfish made little impression. Reports that the *Bismarck* was making smoke and that her course was erratic were taken to mean that she was making a determined attempt to rid herself of her shadowers before night fell.[36]

The *Edinburgh* had reached her fuel safety margin. The 'no hits' report (2128) prompted Commodore Blackman to turn for home. An hour later he turned back; Somerville's latest signal had given him new hope. But there was little in the reports that followed to suggest that this single hit had impaired the *Bismarck*'s mobility. As midnight approached, Blackman made his final decision to break off. He estimated that he could make Londonderry with 5 per cent fuel remaining.[37] On board the *Rodney*, Dalrymple-Hamilton told his people that the last opportunity for a decisive gun action had slipped away and he reduced his state of readiness.[38] For Somerville, the night ahead remained full of uncertainty. At 2307 he asked Maund whether he was sending off another strike. The answer was:

No. May have 12 [torpedo-bombers] ready for dawn attack. Suggest dawn search. A probable second hit obtained on starboard quarter in last attack.[39]

The first solid evidence that damage to the *Bismarck* might be serious came at 2325 when the last of the Swordfish shadowers returned to the *Ark Royal*. It now became clear that, after one torpedo hit, the *Bismarck* had turned through two full circles and dropped to slow speed. The extravagant claims that the Maund had been inclined to dismiss gained added credence. It could now be inferred that the *Bismarck* had been out of control, temporarily at least.

Tovey, however, had mapped out his way ahead without the benefit of this new and conclusive information. When successive shadowing reports showed that the *Bismarck*'s easterly progress had been halted, he turned south, confident, at last, that he could bring about a decisive gun action at any time he chose. But the moment was not right. Darkness was coming on; the night ahead promised to be a foul one; and the situation in the target area was confused. Vian's destroyers were in intermittent touch with the enemy – that was now clear – but the *Sheffield* had lost contact after her brush with the enemy and the air shadowers had long since withdrawn. Rather than risk the uncertainties of a night encounter which could put friendly ships at hazard and which might easily prove inconclusive, Tovey decided to hold off till dawn. He would use the time remaining to resolve uncertainties in relative position, get the *Renown* and the *Ark Royal* clear of the scene of action and work round to the west of the *Bismarck* to gain the advantage of the early morning light.

Those who had little grasp of the conditions that prevailed that night, and those who feared that the *Bismarck* might recover her mobility and slip away, viewed Tovey's decision with grave misgivings.

Notes to Chapter 9

1   Tovey gives range estimates in his dispatches (PRO ADM 199/1188, p. 133). They seem, on the whole, to be underestimates.

2   PG48797, signals timed at 1152 and 1625, 25 May 1941.

3   *Ibid.*, Group West signal timed at 1148, 25 May.

4   Survivors from the *Bismarck* remembered Lütjens saying something on the following lines: 'Soldiers of the *Bismarck*! You have gained great honour. The sinking of the battlecruiser *Hood* was not a mere military victory; it was a victory of morale since the *Hood* was the pride of England. The enemy will now attempt to concentrate his forces and set them on us. Therefore, yesterday afternoon, I released the *Prinz Eugen* to begin independent cruiser warfare in the Atlantic. She has evaded the enemy successfully. We, on the other hand, have been ordered to run for a French port because of the damage we have received. On the way there, the enemy will concentrate and bring us to battle. The German nation is with you; we will fight till our gun barrels glow red and the last shell has left the breech. For us soldiers, it is now 'victory or death'. Despite reservations that these words were a fair reflection of what Lütjens had

said, they were included in Group West's reconstruction of the *Bismarck* War Diary. PG47897, entry for 1200, 25 May 1941.

5   Müllenheim-Rechberg, p. 183. Group West's reconstruction of the *Bismarck*'s War Diary (PG47897) notes simply that, after the Fleet Commander's address, 'morale – which up to then had been excellent – is alleged to have dropped somewhat'.

6   The statement to this effect in PG47895 (chronology for 25 May) is supported by Ballard's investigation of the *Bismarck* wreck; he found all anchors and cables missing. Müllenheim-Rechberg suggests (p. 191) that the matter was discussed by the command but not put into effect.

7   PG47897, Group West signals timed at 1239 and 1241 of 25 May.

8   PG47895, Group West and Group North closing summaries for 25 May 1941.

9   PG47897, Group West signals 1932 and 1952 of 25 May 1941.

10   HMS *Ark Royal* ROP, PRO ADM 199/1188, p. 159.

11   Force H Dispatches, PRO ADM 199/1188, p. 146.

12   Grenfell, pp. 114, 123. See also Kennedy, p. 177.

13   Admiralty signals 1414(B) and 1424(B) of 25 May.

14   Admiralty signals 0011(B) and 0036(B) of 26 May.

15   Admiralty signals 1220(B) and 1228(B) of 26 May. By this time the *Bismarck*'s position had been reported and she appeared to be well south of the expected route.

16   Grenfell, 1948, pp. 127–8; Vian ROP, PRO ADM 199/1188, p. 170.

17   Somerville, letter to wife, written late evening 25 May.*Somerville Papers*, No 159.

18   *Somerville Papers*, No 159.

19   HMS *Ark Royal* ROP, PRO ADM 199/1188, p. 159.

20   Catalinas had been supplied to Coastal Command under Lend-Lease. The US Navy had sent over a number of 'special observers' to assist with training.

21   The flying boat having been in the air for eight hours, the Catalina's navigational accuracy was suspect.

22   FO Force H dispatches, PRO ADM 199/1188, p.145.

23   Somerville had been pondering this question for some time and had concluded that he would need to be 'pretty artful'. In the event, he was told by the Admiralty – AM 1052(B), 26 May – that he should not become engaged with the *Bismarck* unless either the *King George V* or the *Rodney* was already heavily engaged. *Somerville Papers*, No 159.

24   Vian ROP, PRO ADM 199/1188, p. 170. Tovey supported Vian's decision and claimed later that he knew he would act in this way.

25   One Swordfish had returned to make an emergency landing as soon as the last aircraft had left the deck. PRO ADM 199/1188, p. 146.

26   *Ark Royal* signal 1746(B), 26 May.

27   Grenfell, pp. 146–7.

28   Force H signal 1800(B), 26 May. Somerville's account of the *Sheffield* incident is given in his ROP, *Somerville Papers*, No 161.

29 CinC signal 1821(B), 26 May 1941.
30 Somerville's report to CinC dated 4 June 1941, *Somerville Papers*, No 161.
31 It was later concluded that the *Bismarck* was lying under a weather front.
32 PRO ADM 199/1188, p. 149; *Somerville Papers*, No 161.
33 Analysis of torpedo attack, HMS *Ark Royal* ROP, PRO ADM 199/1188, p. 166.
34 Maund's final claim was two definite hits and a third probable. He could not state definitely that the first and second hits described in the narrative were not separate observations of the same event. Maund ROP, PRO ADM 199/1188, p. 166.
35 Grenfell, p. 155. A mildly scornful term describing people who fail to stick to the usual conventions for reporting bearings.
36 Force H dispatches, PRO ADM 199/1188, p. 149.
37 PRO ADM 199/1188, p. 219.
38 Grenfell, p. 155.
39 *Ark Royal* to FO Force H, 2312(B), 26 May 1941.

10

The Final Ordeal

Shortly before midday on Monday 26 May the comfortable assumptions that had gained currency in Group Headquarters overnight were shattered by the simultaneous arrival of two signals. One came from radio intelligence sources and was the transcript of an enemy report addressed by a British patrol aircraft to No 15 Group Coastal Command. It concerned a battleship, evidently the *Bismarck*, in 49°33′N, 21°47′W. The position was 'startling': it showed that British ocean reconnaissance was extending to unprecedented ranges. The other came from Lütjens: it was in the short-code format and indicated more immediate danger. It read, 'Enemy aircraft in contact; wheeled aircraft'. It could only mean that there was an aircraft carrier close by.[1]

In the hours that followed, Admiral Saalwächter was able to build up a tolerably accurate picture of developments in the approaches to Biscay. The weather had prevented the distant reconnaissance that the *Luftwaffe* had promised and close-in searches had found nothing; but a good deal could be gleaned from the reports of British aircraft. At midday one of these had sighted four unidentified contacts a little to the north-west of the *Bismarck*. (This was probably Vian.) Later, another had found a battleship some tens of miles to the north of the *Bismarck*'s position and had carelessly identified it as the *Rodney*. Traffic on British tactical wavelengths was on the increase once again and so was the volume of operational traffic from British shore stations. German D/F stations were beginning to make an input too; by early evening it was clear that a British cruiser had taken up a shadowing position. Admiral Saalwächter assumed (correctly) that this was the *Sheffield*.[2]

It was one thing to know what was happening in the approaches to Biscay, quite another to exercise any positive influence over the course of events. Saalwächter's options were limited. His battlecruisers were *hors de combat* and

193

his light forces stormbound; and the scene of action remained well beyond the *Luftwaffe*'s combat radius. He had eight U-boats at his disposal, but two of these were without torpedoes and one was damaged and unable to dive below periscope depth. He heard later that a battleship and a carrier had passed close to one of his 'lame ducks' at about 2000 that evening. The carrier had been at flying stations.[3] At 1954 Saalwächter directed *U-48* to operate against the *Sheffield* but the distance separating the two vessels can have given little hope of an early interception.

There seemed no end to the succession of unpleasant surprises. At 1903 Group West received a further signal from Lütjens. It read, 'Fuel situation urgent; when can I expect replenishment?' The limitations of the short-code format were not immediately appreciated ashore and the message was treated with considerable suspicion. Saalwächter quoted the text in his reply to Lütjens adding that he had received it on 24.9m, strength 3 to 4. 'Content not understood,' he said. 'Group assumes sufficient fuel.'[4] He had not appreciated the full extent of Lütjens' difficulties, but, again, there was little that he could do to remedy the situation. The tanker *Ermland* was still in harbour and would need twenty hours to reach the scene of operations; tugs would take forty hours; and neither would be of much use unless the *Bismarck* could hold on and gain the security of German air cover. Such hopes as remained rested on the weather. The noon forecast for Biscay had indicated force 5 to 7, increasing gale force 7 to 9, rain squalls and variable visibility. And the foul weather was expected to persist at least until the next day.[5]

Soon, even this last hope was extinguished. At 2054 Lütjens reported, 'Attack by carrier planes.' At 2105 he reported, 'Quadrant BE 6192, torpedo hit aft.' At 2115 he sent two signals, 'Ship no longer steering' and 'Torpedo hit amidships.' Saalwächter ordered all U-boats to make for the position given.

* * *

German accounts of the last and critical air attack on the *Bismarck* are no more reliable than those covering Esmonde's attack nearly forty-eight hours earlier. No single eye-witness had a complete grasp of the situation, and attempts by the command to produce a composite picture from the kaleidoscope of separate impressions resulted, once again, in gross overestimates of the enemy's strength.

Warning of the attack had come early. Anti-aircraft look-outs had spotted Coode's formation high overhead while it was still marshalling itself for the attack run. The alarm had been given, and gun crews, ready at their stations, had wondered at the lapse of time before the attack developed. Then everything had dissolved into confusion. Aircraft had appeared out of the clouds and attacked from every quarter, seemingly oblivious to the defensive barrage. There had been 35 in all; seven had been shot down.

Accounts differ as to the number of torpedo hits and the order in which they occurred. The Fleet Commander's reports to Group West suggest that the damage aft came early and that a second, less serious hit came later. This, in its essentials, squares well with British reconstructions. But Müllenheim-Rechberg's recollection was of two detonations forward of his gunnery control position early in the action and of a third well aft in the final stages of the attack. The ship had been under helm at the time of impact. He describes how he watched his rudder indicator, waiting for it to re-centre. It remained fixed at 12° to port.[6]

The effects of the fatal hit are not disputed. The shock wave from the explosion under the stern went through the ship like a whiplash, buckling deck plates in machinery spaces, lifting safety valves and knocking men down. The command was faced with an uncontrollable port turn and a partial, though temporary, loss of power. As it slowed, the ship developed a 5° list to port.

In the after part of the ship, flooding was rapid. Crews manning the steering rooms (a protected space in Compartment II at waterline level) were forced to leave their posts; damage control parties which tried to re-enter were held back by the spread of floodwater to adjacent spaces through split welds and damaged cable glands. These secondary problems had to be tackled first. When repair teams led by the Master Shipwright finally got to the armoured hatch above the steering mechanism they found the compartment below open to the sea. Torrents of water surged in and drained out as the stern of the ship rose and fell in the seaway. Relays of men, released from anti-aircraft and secondary batteries, tried to stem the inrush of water by hauling swathes of collision matting over the damaged area. The hole was too big. Despite many heroic attempts and periodic rumours of success, divers could not disconnect the steering motors and change to hand steering.

Lindemann had attempted, meanwhile, to gain control of the ship by using main engines. He tried all combinations of ahead and astern power but without success. Conclusions must remain tentative, but it can be inferred from the usual behaviour of warships in the conditions that prevailed that night that he could hold his bow into wind by going dead slow ahead. Alternatively, he could point his bow downwind (the direction he wanted to go in) by using stern power. In terms of directional control, there were no other possibilities.

At 2325 Lütjens sent the signal, 'Am surrounded by *Renown* and light forces.' As midnight approached, he sent, 'To the *Führer* of the German Reich: we fight to the last with firm faith in you, my *Führer*, and with rock-hard confidence in Germany's victory.' This was followed by, 'Armament and machinery fully operational; ship cannot be steered by engines.'[7]

Through the long night that followed, men took what comfort they could from promises of help from shore. Ocean tugs were said to be on their way and the *Ermland* was preparing for sea. FW 200 Condor reconnaissance aircraft would reach the *Bismarck*'s position at dawn and a *Luftwaffe* strike group – the first of three – would follow an hour or two behind them. By 0600 the *Bismarck* was sending regular weather reports to assist the planning of air operations and transmitting on the prescribed homing frequencies.

Messages from shore headquarters swayed uneasily between sympathy and the sterner call to duty. Saalwächter said, 'Our thoughts are with our victorious comrades.' Raeder added, 'We wish you success in your hard fight.' He later confirmed the award of the Knight's Cross to Adalbert Schneider, the *Bismarck*'s First Gunnery Officer and hero of the battle off Iceland. In a message to the men of the *Bismarck*, Hitler said, 'All Germany is with you. What can yet be done will be done. Your devotion to duty will strengthen our people in their fight for survival.'[8]

Whether these messages kept any spark of hope alive is difficult to say. Younger men, it seems, were ready to clutch at straws; those older and wiser had not the heart to disillusion them. Lütjens and Lindemann knew well enough what the future held. As it grew light, they ordered up one of the *Bismarck*'s Arado floatplanes to fly the Fleet War Diary ashore. The aircraft was manned and manoeuvred into position, and the engine was started, but pneumatic supplies to the catapult were found to have failed. The damage was beyond repair and the aircraft was ditched over the side where it drifted away, floats up. The aircrew, sullen and disillusioned, slunk back to their quarters.

Ashore, too, staffs were preparing for the worst. Raeder and Admiral Otto Schniewind, Chief of Naval War Staff, had already made contact with the Spanish naval authorities through their attaché in Madrid. It was now arranged that the cruiser *Canarias* and two destroyers would leave Ferrol during the morning of 27 May to render what assistance they could.[9]

* * *

It had been possible to chart Vian's progress towards the scene of action for some hours. Swordfish of the first striking force had sighted him to the west of Force H while returning from their abortive mission, and towards 1900 he had passed about ten miles south of the *Renown* and exchanged identities. Three hours later he had made contact with the *Sheffield*, and the cruiser, still nursing the injuries received during her recent brush with the *Bismarck*, had passed through his scouting line on a reciprocal course and given him her latest estimate of enemy position. Vian's timing was immaculate. He arrived on scene at a time when the results of the second air attack were far from clear, when it remained conceivable that the *Bismarck* might repair her damage and resume her easterly course and when the continuity of shadowing operations was very much in doubt. In the histrionic style that he cultivated, Vian told Tovey,

> I conceived my duty to be this. Firstly to deliver to you at all costs the enemy at the time you wished. Secondly to try and sink or stop the enemy with torpedoes in the night if I thought the attack should not involve the destroyers in heavy losses.[10]

Whether this piece of rhetoric aptly describes his subsequent behaviour is open to dispute.

The ships of the Fourth Destroyer Division worked that night in the foulest of conditions. Visibility was three or four miles at best, falling to a few hundred yards in squalls of driving rain. When the last glimmer of light had faded from the northern horizon, they felt their way through darkness that was as black as pitch, guided only by the flash of gunfire or the brief glow of a star shell. 'Tribal' class destroyers were among the first ships of their type to be fitted with automatic plotting tables; but defective log and gyro-compass inputs made them largely useless. Most captains submitted their record of the night's events with the gravest reservations.

The Polish destroyer *Piorun*, on the northern flank of Vian's scouting line, was the first to sight the enemy. The time was 2235. The *Bismarck* bore 145°, nine miles, and was pointing to the south-east. The line divided to take up shadowing positions, the *Piorun* and her subdivision leader, the *Maori*, making for a position north of the enemy while the remainder (the *Cossack*, the *Sikh* and the *Zulu*) skirted round to the south.

The two northern ships, silhouetted against the last of the light, soon found themselves under heavy and accurate fire. After two attempts to cross this arc of danger, Commander H. T. Armstrong of the *Maori* took the course of prudence and followed his consorts to the southward. The *Piorun* held on, however, and, on reaching a range of 13,500yds, returned fire with her 4.7in guns. By now heavy shells were falling uncomfortably close and the *Bismarck* seemed to be swinging to port to bring her broadside to bear. Commander Plawski checked his fire and retreated behind smoke. When he turned back, he found that the *Bismarck*, barely visible in the gathering darkness, had resumed her south-easterly course. The *Piorun* followed, still under accurate and rapid fire.

The unequal confrontation had been under way for about forty minutes when Plawski received Vian's orders to prepare for a coordinated torpedo attack. His consorts had long since disappeared from view. Plawski told his British liaison officer that he was 'not quite conversant with [Vian's] method' and that he would make his attack last. In the meantime he would hope to draw the enemy's fire while the others closed in. But visibility was growing worse and by midnight he could see nothing. He held his course to the south-east, hoping to maintain his relative position and make contact again.[11]

By 2330 the other ships of Vian's division were closing the *Bismarck* from the southward. Her shape was just discernible against the sun's afterglow; the destroyers believed themselves invisible against dark rain clouds behind them. At 2342, and without warning, the *Cossack* came under fire. The salvo was close and splinters took away Vian's main aerials. He put his wheel over and turned away. Moments later the *Bismarck*'s main batteries opened up on the *Zulu*. Commander Graham judged the range as 8,000 or 10,000yds but the first salvo was a straddle. There had been no searchlights and no illuminants. Precision of this kind could only mean that the *Bismarck*'s guns were firing under radar control.[12] The *Zulu* turned away as well; three men had been wounded by splinters.

The *Sikh*, a little to the south of her consorts and out of touch, was alerted by the flash of the *Bismarck*'s guns. She took over shadowing and reporting duties and for the next thirty minutes tracked the enemy to the north-west, holding contact by radar from a range of 7,000yds. At 0025 she became the next target for German guns. The salvo was on for range and only 30 to 50yds out for line. As he turned away, Commander Stokes ordered torpedoes but his control officer could not see the target and the opportunity was missed. The *Sikh* saw nothing more of the *Bismarck* for the best part of an hour.

As the flow of enemy reports dwindled, Vian realised that a concerted attack was impossible and told his destroyers to attack independently as opportunity offered. The *Zulu* was the first to regain touch. Feeling his way north-westward, Commander Graham sighted the *Bismarck* on his starboard bow. Her course was 340°. Suppressing the instinct to make an enemy report, he steered to pass up her port side and, at a range of 5,000yds, turned inwards to launch his torpedoes. The *Bismarck*'s secondary batteries came into action at once and the *Zulu* was again straddled repeatedly. At 3,000yds Graham fired a spread of four torpedoes with 10kts left deflection. There were no hits. At the moment of fire the *Bismarck* had appeared to turn away and it was assumed that the weapons had passed ahead of her.

The *Maori*, a little behind the *Zulu* and also probing to the north-west, had sown a line of starshell across the expected arc but had seen nothing. At 0107 Commander Armstrong saw the flash of gunfire as the *Bismarck* engaged his consort and turned towards. As the range closed, he fired more starshell. These illuminated the target perfectly; the *Bismarck* was now pointing north-east and the *Maori* was overhauling her on a parallel course. By 0137 Armstrong had closed to a position 3,000yds off the enemy's port bow, apparently undetected. He launched two torpedoes, keeping two in reserve for use on the opposite side. His salvo was followed by a flash which seemed to light the target's waterline from end to end; moments later a vivid glare appeared between bridge and stem. At their action stations, men cheered. But the *Bismarck* opened fire with her main and secondary batteries and with quick-firing guns. Armstrong increased to full speed and retreated into the night with the splash of shells erupting around him.[13]

As the *Maori* withdrew, the *Cossack* came in from the opposite side. Vian had seen the *Bismarck* in full silhouette against the flash of her guns and had fired three torpedoes from a range of 6,000yds. The effects of the *Maori*'s attack were, he thought, 'unmistakable'. Vian claimed a further hit of his own. The *Bismarck* now seemed to be stopped.

From now on the battle lessened in intensity. After evading the *Bismarck*'s fire, Commander Stokes had been misled by an inaccurate report and the *Sikh* had probed first to the east and then to the west before finding a target. She now approached with due caution and delivered an attack from a respectful range. It was 0230. An hour later Vian closed in once again to expend the last of his weapons. In response to orders from the Commander-in-Chief, whose heavy ships were stalking the perimeter, trying to get their bearings, the destroyers were now attempting to indicate the *Bismarck*'s position with starshell. It was a hazardous task which usually attracted return fire and it was gradually allowed to lapse. For Plawski, the night was a frustrating one. He spent it chasing phantoms in the dark. He saw the occasional glint of a starshell and, once or twice, found radar contacts at close range but nothing firm.

As dawn approached, the destroyers worked their way westward to remain concealed against the dark horizon. Vian, fearing that, with the coming of light, Plawski might find the *Bismarck* and put his ship at risk, ordered him to Plymouth for fuel. The *Piorun*, not to be deprived of her moment of glory, searched on for a further hour but without success. She caught one last glimpse of the *Bismarck* as she left the scene, but by now it was much too light to risk an attack. The *Bismarck*'s fire was still deadly. Towards 0700 the *Maori* closed to a range of 9,000yds to deliver the last of her weapons. She was straddled repeatedly and forced to take violent avoiding action. Like her consorts, she retired to a safe distance to await events.

The role of the Fourth Destroyer Division during the night of 26/27 May has since proved controversial. Tovey described Vian's conduct as a 'model of its kind'. Others were less certain. Grenfell saw torpedo attacks as incompatible with the shadowing task and accused Vian of following 'two antagonistic principles'.[14] That Vian accepted risks that earlier shadowers had been careful to avoid can hardly be disputed. Yet circumstances were different. Vian had been clear from an early stage that the enemy's mobility was seriously impaired and that interception by the battle fleet was no longer in question. The choice lay between prudent inaction and prudent initiative. Vian, the last man to accept a waiting game, chose initiative. His judgment was vindicated by events. His attacks failed – German evidence makes that clear beyond doubt – but his destroyers came to little harm and casualties were light. Those who believe that Fate deals kindly with those who err on the side of initiative will find their justification here.

* * *

The passage of time had done little to resolve the uncertainties of the heavy ships gathering round the scene of action. It had been difficult to generate any consistent plot from the reports of Vian's destroyers and D/F had done little to help. Somerville, feeling his way round the western flank to take up a position south of the *Bismarck*, had seen the flash of gunfire on his port bow and had altered away to give himself a wider margin of safety. He could now estimate the *Bismarck*'s position to a fair degree of accuracy but he had little idea of where Tovey was or when he would begin his attack. The uncertainty was making him anxious: daylight would bring the *Luftwaffe*, and he had no wish to linger in the area too long. Soon after 0300 he asked the *Ark Royal* when her torpedo-bombers would be ready, suggesting that, 'with any luck,' they might finish off the *Bismarck* before the CinC arrived. Maund replied that his striking force was ready now but urged delay until it was light enough to 'differentiate friend from foe'.[15] His concern was legitimate. A dozen British ships were now circling the scene of action and their positions and movements could only be guessed at. Force H was making for a position south of the *Bismarck*. If Tovey was sticking to plan he would be working his way to the west. The *Sheffield*, presumably, would be somewhere to the west as well. The *Norfolk* would be joining from the north; Wake-Walker had just reported that he would arrive in time for the finish and that he would act as flank marker for the CinC. And it was now clear that a new player would be arriving on scene: when news of the Catalina sighting had been broadcast by Whitehall the heavy cruiser *Dorsetshire* had left her convoy (SL.74) under the charge of an armed merchant cruiser and steered for the Bay of Biscay at 25kts. She would be joining from the south-west.

Towards 0600 the first hint of light appeared on the north-eastern horizon. The weather was as bad as ever. Somerville described it as 'a horrid dawn, overcast, thick, and blowing like the Devil from the W.'[16] The prospects for a third air strike seemed far from promising. Gusts over the deck of the *Ark Royal* were now reaching 60kts, and, with the sea abeam, the carrier's giddy roll was raising fears for the security of aircraft parked on deck. Visibility remained appalling; a spotter plane launched to locate the *Bismarck* and make contact with the CinC returned to the deck having accomplished nothing. Maund warned Somerville that, in the prevailing conditions, the torpedo-bombers 'might be a menace to our ships' and asked for permission to strike them down.[17] Somerville agreed though with some reluctance. He was influenced, it seems, by renewed uncertainty about the *Bismarck*'s position. Reports from some of Vian's destroyers were beginning to suggest sizeable errors in his estimate and he needed to resolve them if the risk to friendly forces were to be minimised.[18] When the *Ark Royal* had finished moving aircraft, Somerville turned north to make contact.

He succeeded much sooner than he expected. At 0810 he sighted the *Maori* and established the *Bismarck*'s position as seventeen miles north of his own. Thus reassured, he turned to a (relatively comfortable) southerly course and gave the order to range aircraft. He was tempted to stay in touch with the *Maori* so that he would be ready to support the CinC when he began his attack, but wiser councils prevailed. With visibility at the scene of action as poor as it was, the presence of the *Renown* might be more hindrance than help, and, besides, his first concern had to be for his vulnerable carrier. He decided to stay with the *Ark Royal*, at least until the *Sheffield* re-joined.[19]

* * *

Tovey had faced similar difficulties in establishing relative position. He had seen no sign of Vian's starshell, although, from 6 o'clock onward he had been able to deduce a good deal from D/F. He was not going to be hurried. He knew from Vian's signals that the *Bismarck*'s armament and fire control arrangements were still intact and he was determined to select the direction and timing of his approach to suit himself. Wind, sea and light indicated an approach from west-north-west. Fighting to windward, he concluded, would be very difficult. And he wanted to approach his victim as nearly as

202

possible end-on. A narrow inclination would make his ships difficult to hit and help him to close to a decisive fighting range quickly.[20] If the *Bismarck* maintained the north-westerly trend reported by Vian's destroyers, he would then deploy to the southward and engage the enemy on opposite courses. Beyond that, little could be foreseen.

At 0737 – it was now fifteen minutes after sunrise – Tovey turned to a course of 080° to make his approach. He gave the *Rodney* a loose station to the north that would ensure adequate separation between the two ships and allow Dalrymple-Hamilton the freedom that he would need to avoid the enemy's salvos and to open his firing arcs.[21] The best estimate of enemy position (based on the *Maori*'s radio transmissions) was 120° at 21 miles. The latest report of enemy course and speed was 300°, 10kts.

Tovey kept to the eastward, adjusting his course from time to time to avoid rain squalls and to allow for reported changes in enemy movement. For forty minutes he saw nothing. Then the masts of the *Norfolk* came in sight he was able to establish that first – and vital – visual link with the enemy. Persistence had received its reward. After a chase which must often have seemed hopeless, Wake-Walker had arrived on the scene in the nick of time. He had sighted the *Bismarck* just twenty minutes earlier and had at first mistaken her for the *Rodney*. He was now standing back in order not to 'irritate her'.[22] With all doubts resolved, Tovey turned 30° to starboard. At 0843 his look-outs made out the shape of the *Bismarck* fine on the starboard bow. She was pointing directly towards them. The flagship's Type 284 radar gave the range as 25,000yds.

* * *

The action opened at 0847 with a salvo from the *Rodney*'s 'A' and 'B' turrets. The *Bismarck* returned fire at 0850 and for twelve tense minutes the antagonists closed one another, bow to bow, at a combined speed of 25kts. At one point there were signs that the *Bismarck* might be swinging to starboard to bring her broadside to bear. Tovey hoisted the preparatory signal for a deployment to port; but the enemy soon veered back to his former course. Tovey was able, therefore, to keep to the plan that he had formulated.

The *Bismarck*'s fire, concentrated on the *Rodney* during these early minutes, did much to confirm the fearsome reputation of German gunners for finding the range quickly. Her third salvo was a straddle, the nearest shell falling a mere 20yds short of the *Rodney*'s bridge and covering the battleship's decks with a cascade of evil-smelling water. It was a lucky escape. Dalrymple-Hamilton made full use of the discretion that Tovey had given him, turned to port to open his firing arcs and began a series of carefully timed course alterations to spoil enemy computation. Captain Coppinger, a passenger in the *Rodney* and an important witness of the morning's events, believed that these evasive manoeuvres had been a vital factor in saving the ship from damage.[23]

British fire in this opening phase was less accurate and certainly less consistent. The *Rodney* straddled the *Bismarck* with an early salvo and believed that she had scored a hit; but a false range reading had then spoilt her aim and she was not back on target for ten crucial minutes.[24] The *King George V* made an uncertain start too. Poor visibility frustrated the efforts of visual range-takers and obscured the fall of shot. Radar operators, failing to appreciate the rapid rate of closing, searched for the *Bismarck*'s echo at the range of first detection and squandered several precious minutes. But at 0853 they got a firm reading at 20,500yds. A double salvo was ordered, spread 200yds either side of the target; it produced a straddle and a definite hit. The 14in projectile struck home at the base of the forward superstructure, port side, causing a fire which continued to burn for some time.[25]

As the range closed, the weight of fire put down by the British ships began to tell. By 0859 both battleships were on target and firing steadily. (Recalling practice firings from the past, Captain Coppinger was amazed at the cool deliberation of the *Rodney*'s command team.) Heavy salvos were landing around the *Bismarck* at the rate of four per minute, raising fountains of water as high as her foretop. Secondary batteries were coming into action as well. And from her marking position to the north-east of the *Bismarck*, the *Norfolk* had opened a brisk fire with her 8in guns. To British observers, the target appeared as little more than a storm of smoke and spray through which return fire – desultory and erratic now – appeared as a dull orange glow.[26]

As the range fell to 16,000yds Tovey executed the emergency turn to starboard that would bring the full weight of his firepower to bear as his battle line passed the *Bismarck* port to port. The flagship began her turn at 0859 and the *Rodney*, keeping loose formation, followed a few minutes later. The effects of their combined fire had been hard to assess so far – armour-piercing shell revealed little to the external observer – but at 0902 an event occurred which was visible to all and which many found significant. A 16in shell from the *Rodney* struck the *Bismarck* well forward and appeared to engulf the whole forepart in a sheet of livid flame. Later speculation suggested that it was this salvo which disabled the *Bismarck*'s forward turrets. The *Norfolk*, which had closed to 16,000yds to fire torpedoes, certainly gained this impression. And it was about this time that Müllenheim-Rechberg, manning the *Bismarck*'s after fire control station, got word that the forward guns and the main (foretop) control position were out of action and that he was to take charge of the after batteries.[27]

As the two battleships settled on their new course, gun directors found their view obscured by cordite smoke and funnel gases. The *King George V* checked the fire of her dual-purpose 5.25in batteries in an attempt to ease the problem, but she remained almost wholly reliant on her gunnery radar. She was now coming under fire for the first time, but the dragon's teeth had been drawn and the threat was diminishing. There was a worrying moment when, despite the deafening cacophony of her own fire, the whistle of heavy shells was heard on the bridge. The salvo was long but not by much. Captain Patterson altered course towards the splashes and waited for the fall of the next salvo 'with interest'.[28] When it came, it was longer still and poorly grouped. Patterson concluded that the enemy was no longer following the spotting rules and that further avoiding action was pointless. He turned back to his southerly course.[29]

By 0917 the *Rodney* was passing the *Bismarck*'s beam. With enemy fire now directed at the flagship, Dalrymple-Hamilton seized the moment and swung his ship back to the northward. He steadied on a converging course which, over the next twenty minutes, would reduce the range from 8,600 to 4,000yds. By 0919 his 16in batteries were back in action, directing salvo after salvo into the *Bismarck*'s battle-scarred port side. And he was beginning to engage with torpedoes. Only one main turret, 'Caesar', returned his fire. Before this too fell silent, it put a salvo close off the *Rodney*'s bow, jamming the sluice-valve door of the starboard torpedo tube and causing other minor damage.[30]

The *King George V* followed the *Rodney* round and steadied on a course of north. Her starboard battery of 5.25in guns opened a rapid fire. They seemed to have a devastating effect on the *Bismarck*'s lighter structure. The flagship's main armament, on the other hand, was beginning to suffer from break-downs of the kind that had plagued her sister-ship the *Prince of Wales* three days before. A series of mechanical failures, fourteen in all and the majority affecting ammunition supply, put 'A' turret out of action for thirty minutes and 'Y' for a shorter, though significant, period. Even 'B' turret went down briefly.[31] For much of the period 0920–0950 the *King George V*, a modern battleship six months into her commission, could produce 14in salvos of one or, at best, two guns. Her gunnery radar had gone down as well, and not a single enemy projectile of any calibre had come aboard.

But the *Bismarck* was now blowing off steam, and a thick, oily smoke, welling up from the base of the funnel, was masking the entire after end of the ship. The main and secondary batteries were silent. The guns of 'Anton' turret were at full depression, as if the elevating mechanism had failed. 'Bruno' turret was trained to port with one barrel pointing skywards. A fierce fire was blazing in the hangar area. The port list was plainly visible.

The British battleships were now free to come in to any range they chose. The two heavy cruisers were also attempting to get in close, looking for an opportunity to fire torpedoes. By 0950 the *King George V* and the *Rodney* were manoeuvring off the *Bismarck*'s port and starboard bow respectively, holding her in a devastating cross-fire. She was stopped, burning fore and aft and wallowing heavily; but the effects of the heavy salvos remained difficult to assess and the violent event that everyone hoped would signal her end seemed increasingly elusive. Tovey urged Patterson to 'Get closer, get closer; I can't see enough hits.'[32] He had every reason for wanting to bring matters to a swift conclusion. The Admiralty had given notice that heavy air attacks were to be expected shortly. A Condor reconnaissance aircraft had already been seen over the fleet and air raid warnings were in force. The flagship's air warning radar which had been providing ranges for the guns was reverting to its primary role. The 5.25in batteries were preparing for air attack and anti-aircraft crews were leaving their shelter positions to man their guns.[33]

As the range closed to 3,000yds and less, observers in the British battleships began to witness some of the more dramatic effects of their fire and to see sights that could only disturb them. At this range it was possible to follow the flight of a heavy projectile all the way to the target. Soon after 1015 a pair of heavy shells from the *King George V* entered the base of the *Bismarck*'s forward superstructure and produced a firestorm that swept upwards to bridge level and ignited the pyrotechnics stowed there in a cascade of stars. A third shell from the same salvo went through the face of 'Bruno' gunhouse and blew the armoured plate which formed the back of the turret over the side.[34] The dimmest of imaginations could begin to envisage the gruesome events taking place inside the ship. For some minutes now, small parties of men had been seen jumping from the quarterdeck. By 1020 the trickle had become a flood and at 1021 the cease-fire was given.

Tovey was now certain that the *Bismarck* could never get back to harbour. Unwilling to expose his ships to further risk, he turned for home and ordered the rest of his force to follow him.

* * *

The *Ark Royal*'s torpedo-bombers, arriving to join the action, came on a scene of confusion and uncertainty. They found a heavy cruiser lying close to the *Bismarck*'s smoking hulk and were forced to withhold their attack. They tried to attract the attention of the flagship but could get no reply and were fired on for their pains.[35] Somerville, who had left the *Ark Royal* in the care of the *Sheffield* and who was hurrying north to lend a hand, could make no sense of the situation. At 1025 he asked the CinC, 'Have you disposed of [the] enemy?' A few minutes later he got the reply, 'Have had to discontinue action for fuel.' After what seemed an interminable delay, he got the message, 'She is still afloat,' followed by 'Any ships with torpedoes are to use them on [the] *Bismarck*,' and then by, 'Cannot sink her with guns.'

To those dependent on Tovey's terse signals for their understanding of developments, the outcome seemed extraordinarily untidy. It had been difficult enough during the last twenty-four hours to divine what Tovey's intentions were. Flag and commanding officers gathering at the scene of action had been left to follow their own instincts. They had received little by way of information or direction. Now it seemed that the CinC was going off with the job half done, leaving a vacuum behind him. In London, surprise bordered on indignation and Somerville, usually one of the Admiralty's sternest critics, seems, for once, to have been in sympathy with them. 'T[heir] L[ordships],' he noted when it was all over, 'have got a bit crapulous with Jack Tovey this morning and asked what the hell he was doing going off and leaving her still afloat. Must confess,' he added, 'I was rather surprised. It was old Wake-Walker who told *Dorsetshire* to go in and torpedo her at close range.'[36]

Somerville had been speculating on the scale of the task left to him and drafting instructions for his striking force when signals from the *Dorsetshire* had put his mind at rest. Seeing that the *Bismarck* was, as he put it, '*in extremis*', Captain Martin had fired two torpedoes into her starboard side. He had then crossed her bow and fired a third.[37] At 1036 the *Bismarck*, colours still flying, had heeled over to port, turned turtle and gone down stern first. The recorded position was 48°09´N 16°07´W; the charted depth was 2,500 fathoms.

Notes to Chapter 10

1 PG20418, p. 23 (original text); PG47897, *Bismarck* War Diary, entries for 1154 and 1225, 26 May 1941.

2 PG47897, *Bismarck* War Diary, entries for 1711, 1732 and 1955, 26 May 1941.

3 Lt-Cdr Herbert Wohlfarth (*U-556*) claimed later that he had been in an ideal position to attack the *Renown* and the *Ark Royal*, but he was returning from patrol low on fuel and with no torpedoes remaining. Group West signal 2117 of 26 May 1941; Müllenheim-Rechberg, p. 230.

4 PG47897, *Bismarck* War Diary, Group West signal 1925, 26 May 1941.

5 Although the weather might help solve the *Bismarck*'s immediate problems, it complicated arrangements for her reception in St Nazaire. There were fears that if the swell became worse and the *Bismarck*'s draught exceeded 11.5m, the ship would not clear the St Nazaire mine barrier. She might have to go to Brest instead. PG47897, entry for 1501, 26 May.

6 Müllenheim-Rechberg, p. 208.

7 PG 47897, *Bismarck* War Diary, Lütjens's signals of 2325, 2358 and 2359, 26 May 1941.

8 Sent by Group West at 0153(B), 27 May 1941.

9 When this became known in London, the Admiralty sent a stern remainder to the Spanish Ministry of Marine that, under the Geneva Convention, survivors could not be repatriated.

10 D4 ROP, PRO ADM 199/1188, p. 170.

11 *Piorun* ROP, PRO ADM199/1188, pp. 182–5.

12 This diagnosis was wrong. Müllenheim-Rechberg (pp. 217–19) shows that the *Bismarck*'s optical rangefinders were fully effective even in the dirty conditions that prevailed that night.

13   Armstrong's claims, supported by Vian and others, were mistaken. A starshell
     had landed on the *Bismarck*'s foredeck and had burnt there for a minute or so.
14   Grenfell, p. 173.
15   *Ark Royal* signal 0320(B) of 27 May 1941.
16   Somerville, letter to his wife, *Somerville Papers*, No 159.
17   *Ark Royal* signal 0637(B), 27 May 1941; *Ark Royal* ROP, PRO ADM 199/1188,
     pp. 163–4.
18   Some reports were suggesting that the *Bismarck* might be up to 60 miles to the
     north of his position. *Somerville Papers*, No 161.
19   *Somerville Papers*, No. 161. The *Sheffield*'s position was unknown; Somerville
     assumed that she would be re-joining from a position somewhere close west
     of the *Bismarck*.
20   Tovey, Dispatches, PRO ADM 199/1188, pp. 138–9. Grenfell makes it clear
     that the end-on approach was a Tovey fetish, his pet theory (derived from
     observation of practice firings) being that errors in line were likely to exceed
     errors in range. Tovey also hoped that the sight of two battleships steering
     straight towards them would shake the nerves of German range-takers and
     control officers.
21   The contrast between this and the more rigid formation adopted by Holland
     in the Denmark Strait will be noted.
22   CS1 ROP, PRO ADM 199/1188, p 208. At precisely the same moment, the
     Cossack, thirty miles to the south-east, was providing a similar visual link for the
     Dorsetshire.
23   Coppinger's records are in PRO ADM 199/1188, pp. 221–2.
24   German eye-witnesses were quick to comment on this sub-standard perform-
     ance. PG 47897, *Bismarck* War Diary, citing evidence of survivors. See also
     Müllenheim-Rechberg, p. 248.
25   *King George V* narrative (gunnery annex), PRO ADM 199/1188, p. 143. It was
     later suggested that this hit might have jammed the *Bismarck*'s 'Bruno' turret
     in training.
26   *King George V* ROP, PRO ADM 199/1188, p. 140.
27   Müllenheim-Rechberg, p. 250.
28   *King George V* narrative, PRO ADM 199/1188, p. 141.
29   It seems probable that the after fire control station was now out of action and
     that 'Caesar' and 'Dora' turrets were in local control. See Müllenheim-
     Rechberg, pp. 251–2.
30   The *Rodney* fired ten torpedoes in all and claimed one hit, though this is not
     supported by German sources. Torpedoes were widely fitted to capital ships
     of her generation but there can be few other examples of their use during a fleet
     action.
31   *King George V* ROP, gunnery annex, PRO ADM 199/1188, p.143.
32   Grenfell, p. 184.

33 *King George V* ROP, PRO ADM 199/1188, p. 142.

34 *Ibid.*

35 Grenfell tells the story that when Captain Patterson asked the officer of the quarters whether he had not seen the aircrew waving, he got the reply, 'I thought they were Huns shaking their fists.'

36 Somerville, letter to wife, *Somerville Papers*, No 159.

37 HMS *Dorsetshire* ROP, PRO ADM 199/1188, p. 187.

11

The Search for Lessons – and Scapegoats

By midday on 27 May the German naval leadership had resigned itself to the inevitable. Group West had heard nothing from the Fleet Commander since 0729, when, in a request strangely characteristic of the man, he had asked for a U-boat to save the Fleet War Diary, the document that would explain his actions to his peers. Thereafter, repeated requests for information had remained unanswered. At 1322 Saalwächter had sent what was to be the final message addressed to the *Bismarck*. 'Reuters reports *Bismarck* sunk,' it read, 'report situation immediately.'[1]

News reaching Group West in the hours following the sinking did little to soften the impact of the disaster. The British, it seemed, had brought matters to a close with brutal efficiency and had left few hostages to fortune. A handful of aircraft from the *Luftwaffe*'s first strike wave had reached the scene of action at about 10 o'clock in the morning. They had attacked a number of ships, one of them an aircraft carrier, but with little apparent success. This was not the Aegean; there was no precedent for massed air operations against ships at ranges like these. A second wave had left at noon and a third in the early evening. Both had been fifty-strong, but neither had found anything; the British fleet seemed to have melted away. It was twenty-four hours before returning aircraft began to bring better news. From dawn on 28 May the *Luftwaffe* had spread its searches further afield and had found a number of British units, mostly isolated destroyers, making for their bases. This was compensation of a kind.[2]

Nor had rescue operations brought much by way of reward. British ships had picked up a hundred men or so before suspending their rescue attempts; that was clear from British communiqués. *U-74* and the weather trawler *Sachsenwald* had found another five, but the *Canarias* and her destroyers and the other U-boats that had scoured the area had found no soul alive. The tally of survivors, 115 in all, formed a pitifully small proportion of the 2,200 officers and men who had sailed from Gotenhafen with such fanfare seven days before. There were few officers' names in the lists; Lütjens, it seemed, and the entire fleet staff had perished.[3] It remained to be seen whether the *Prinz Eugen*, still at large in the Atlantic, could salvage something from the wreckage of 'Rheinübung'.

* * *

When Lütjens had released him on the evening of 24 May, Brinkmann had rejected the option of refuelling in the north, believing that the rendezvous off Cape Farewell might soon become compromised, and, instead, had begun the thirty-six-hour passage to the mid-Atlantic fuelling area, hoping, fervently, that he would find the tankers on station.

At dawn on 26 May he had made contact with the *Spichern*. His tanks were nearly empty and he had spent the rest of the day fuelling, a passive witness to the critical developments that were taking place in the Biscay approaches.[4] Thereafter he had found it impossible to adopt any settled plan. His first idea had been to create a diversion on the Halifax route but he had soon thought better of it. By evening, he had decided to postpone action until the two scouts, *Kota Penang* and *Gonzenheim*, both diverted from the north, had reached his area. Then he had got wind of an enemy hunting group forming in the Bay of Biscay and evasion had come to seem the better course.[5] The evening of 27 May had found him making further ground to the southward in search of the oiler *Esso Hamburg*, determined, above all else, to maintain a healthy margin of fuel in his tanks. All thought of seizing the initiative had gone; the main thing, now, was to keep the enemy in the dark. He was keeping strict radio silence, and turning tail whenever a puff of smoke appeared on the horizon.

With the destruction of the *Bismarck*, the need for diversionary action on the northern convoy routes lapsed. On 28 May Group West decided to open a new area of operations in the remote expanse of ocean west of the Canaries and began to move his tankers in that direction. The objective, from now on, would be single ships; action against convoys would be postponed for the moment. Little was known of traffic patterns in the area. Brinkmann drew up an ambitious search plan for his scouts designed to identify the routes favoured by shipping coming from the South Atlantic. He passed his orders to the *Kota Penang* by hand message and told her to deliver a similar set of orders to the *Gonzenheim*. Scouts were given strict instructions to make their shipping reports to Group West and never to address the *Prinz Eugen* directly.

While the scouts were on passage to their new stations, Brinkmann decided to rest his crew and seize the opportunity for some essential maintenance. Worries about the condition of the cruiser's main machinery were beginning to assert themselves. A leaky flange on a main steam line was preventing the development of full power. Noise from a chipped propeller blade (the damage was attributed to ice in the Denmark Strait) was interfering with sonar. There were unexplained rumblings from the port turbine; misalignment was suspected, the result, possibly, of the mine damage that had delayed the start of '*Rheinübung*'. A good deal of investigation was clearly necessary. What seems to have worried Brinkmann most of all was advice from his engineering department that, in order to carry out the necessary inspections and repairs, he would have to shut down an engine, possibly for an extended period.[6]

By the evening of 29 May Brinkmann had reached his decision. In an obscure and rambling analysis of his situation, he concluded that the 'unprecedented encircling tactics adopted by the English' (tactics that he had witnessed at first hand) made his margin of speed advantage more important than ever. He had lost this; his speed was restricted to 28 or 29kts. Yet if he shut down a powerplant to effect repairs his powers of evasion would be limited and he might be observed and reported by any merchant ship that appeared on the horizon. British hunting forces poised to exploit just such an opportunity would then converge on his position. He decided, with 'the heaviest of hearts' – a phrase that seems to ring a little hollow – to make for a Biscay port.[7] Two days later, when past Cape Finisterre and, as he judged, free from the danger of interception by Force H, he told Group West of his decision.

By 1 June he was safely in Brest. Whatever the merits of his case, his cruise had been, at best, undistinguished. Although the staff echelons which examined his war diary decided, generally, to give him the benefit of the doubt, it was hard to conclude that Brinkmann had been anything other than a fugitive on the high seas. There was nothing in the record to give comfort to the exponents of cruiser warfare in the Naval High Command.[8]

* * *

213

Grand Admiral Raeder met Hitler at the Berghof on 6 June. He had prepared his case with special care. His tone was magisterial and a little pained. He began by observing that from the very beginning the Navy had been obliged to wage war with inadequate means. Eighteen months on, the balance of naval power had moved even further against him: the British had commissioned three aircraft carriers and two fast battleships, and others were building. British sea power stood in the way of the *Führer*'s most cherished projects and, as he had long argued, it could only be smashed by the combined efforts of the German armed forces as a whole. Yet his repeated demands that the *Luftwaffe* should concentrate its bombing campaign against enemy building and ship repair yards had fallen on deaf ears. The *Führer* agreed and 'promised to instruct the *Luftwaffe* accordingly once again'.[9]

Raeder went on to remind Hitler that his objective, all along, had been to mount an unbroken campaign of disruption against British supply lines, a campaign that had some hope of producing a decisive outcome in the short term. The adverse naval balance made mobility rather than the concentration of combat power the key to success. He rejected the idea that the operations based on single ships or small task groups were 'wrong in principle', although in the light of recent experience he was looking again at the way they were being planned and conducted.

It is clear from the record of this meeting that the Naval Staff had pinpointed three main topics for further investigation: the break-out phase for ships departing from home waters; questions arising form the enemy's (unexpected) possession of radar; and the question of aircraft carriers. The first of these was a compound problem. The Navy had failed, in the first instance, to cover its intentions with sufficient care. The enemy had got wind of the *Bismarck*'s movements. Thereafter, inadequate air reconnaissance, coupled with a failure on the part of radio intelligence to detect any sign of enemy reaction, had bred a false sense of security. The Fleet Commander had committed himself to the operation believing, wrongly, that he retained the element of surprise.

As a result of these failures, Lütjens had encountered enemy cruisers in the narrows. This, in itself, was neither unexpected nor serious. It had happened before. The novel and 'decisive' feature on this occasion was that the cruisers had possessed a highly efficient radar system. This had enabled them to keep in touch with the German task group in conditions of poor visibility and, ultimately, to bring a superior force into contact. The Fleet Commander, Raeder suggested, would certainly have avoided an action if he had been able to do so. He had been correct in his decision not to press the action against the *Prince of Wales*; as it was, the damage received, although comparatively minor, had forced him to change his plans. The battle had shown, on the other hand, that, ship for ship, German battleships were the equal of their opponents. There were thus good prospects that a ship of the *Tirpitz* class would achieve success against a convoy protected by some single elderly battleship. It would no longer be necessary to 'avoid such an encounter'. (Here, surely, was self-deception on a monumental scale!)

Raeder's analysis of the final phases of '*Rheinübung*' were a little sketchy, but he emphasised the important part played by aircraft carriers, adding, pointedly, that, if Lütjens had possessed a carrier of his own, 'the whole picture might have been entirely different'.

Raeder then outlined a range of measures that he believed would help to overcome the problems that he had identified. To avoid giving the enemy advanced notice of a break-out he would deploy heavy ships to Trondheim and keep them there for several weeks until the right moment came. He would continue to use the French Atlantic ports as a base for operations; easy access to the supply routes outweighed the danger from the air. Ferrol and Dakar would be better still.[10] He had asked Group West to investigate the use of the Channel route, at least by cruisers and pocket battleships, although, given the weakness of the *Luftwaffe* in the West[11] and the shortage of escorts, he was not yet persuaded of its advantages.

Turning to the question of radar, the Grand-Admiral acknowledged that this was an important increment to enemy capability. It seemed to rule out future use of the narrow waters of the Denmark Strait and it might well have implications for existing replenishment arrangements; but it did not mean fundamental change. There were technical solutions to the problem. A radar warning device had been developed and was now being fitted to ships of the surface fleet. The influence of radar, he acknowledged, deserved careful examination but, 'on no account should it be allowed to render this type of naval warfare impossible'.

As for the future, the pocket battleship *Lützow* (ex-*Deutschland*) would be ready to make her break-out in July. He would move her to Trondheim shortly and, during this interim period, she would act as a deterrent to British actions on the Norwegian coast. The *Admiral Scheer* would be moved north in July or August and the *Admiral Hipper* in September. The *Tirpitz* would be held at Kiel during the opening phase of '*Barbarossa*', where she would be secure against air attack; she could go to Trondheim any time after that. Meanwhile the *Prinz Eugen* and the *Scharnhorst*, both in Brest, would be ready by mid-June. A joint operation by these two ships could be considered as soon as the battlecruiser had completed a short period of sea training. A decision would be taken as soon as the situation in the Atlantic became clearer. The *Gneisenau* would not be ready before the autumn.

While waiting for these operations to start, Raeder went on, the Naval Staff had been reviewing options for making the war against merchant shipping more effective. They had decided against an extension of the existing area of operations in favour of giving ships greater freedom of action within the present zone. He was now seeking the *Führer*'s approval to begin action against United States shipping under the prize rules.

If Raeder's object was to deflect criticism, he was largely successful. Hitler asked a few perfunctory questions about the action in the Denmark Strait but did not pursue matters further. But on future plans for cruiser warfare he was entirely non-committal. Everything would depend on the impact of '*Barbarossa*' and on political developments in Britain. Britain was in a bad way and a collapse could occur suddenly. By the middle of July, he would be able to judge how the Eastern Campaign was progressing and how it was going to affect the war as a whole. Until then, it would not be expedient to take great risks with the surface fleet unless there were definite prospects of major success. If Britain were on the point of collapse, he might, for instance, want to seize a naval base in a lightning attack.[12] The surface fleet would then have an important part to play. Hitler agreed to the transfer of the *Lützow* to Trondheim but asked to be kept informed of any further plans. He could accept no change to the present rules governing operations against American shipping. The matter could wait until the fleet was ready to begin operations.

* * *

Later attempts by the German naval authorities to pinpoint the factors that had contributed most to the débâcle of May 1941 tended to follow the agenda that Raeder had set in this early meeting. Worries about operational security

216

were widespread, and towards the end of July Admiral Fricke, newly appointed as Chief of Naval War Staff, published the results of an investigation into the matter. Although suspicions continued to centre on enemy agents watching the Great Belt and reporting to London via the British Naval Attaché in Stockholm, there were numerous alternative possibilities. The *Bismarck*'s departure had become known to a wide circle of people. The ship had left Gotenhafen with the band playing the anthem*Muss i Denn*, a sure and quite unnecessary clue to her intentions. Her sailing had been common knowledge in Berlin; an officer's wife had spread the news after missing her daily telephone call. Plans had been widely known within the supply organisation. Because of the hurry to get the ships away, the numerous staff organisations at home and abroad had made their arrangements on insecure telephone lines, some of which ran through occupied territory. Some telephone exchanges were manned by foreign nationals. But there was little solid evidence to go on; nor was it clear what specific action should be taken. The report concluded, somewhat lamely, that security had to be the business of everyone.[13] On the credit side, the investigation identified one important area of success. Group North's management of signal traffic before and during the departure stage had been masterly. It seemed most unlikely that the enemy would have been able to derive useful information from traffic analysis.

Although there was general agreement among operational staffs that the origins of the recent disaster could be traced back to decisions made during the break-out phase, there was little immediate consensus on how things should be managed from now on. Commenting on the *Prinz Eugen* War Diary, Admiral Schmundt, CinC Cruisers, suggested (with some justification) that, almost from the start, there had been ample evidence to show that the enemy was aware of German intentions. The proper course would have been to put into Trondheim or withdraw to the Arctic Ocean and await the results of air reconnaissance.[14] Admiral Carls, scenting criticism of his own part in the affair, took exception to this view and suggested that Schmundt was being wise after the event. He [Carls] had been looking for evidence in enemy signal traffic but this had now dwindled to a 'paltry minimum'.[15] Schniewind, Lütjens's successor as Fleet Commander, argued that, in future, ships should leave from the Elbe to avoid observation in the Great Belt and the Kattegat.[16] Carls warned of delays in the Kaiser Wilhelm Canal and pointed to the increased risk of observation from the air. If there was any common ground between the admirals it was this: that, with enemy strength in Iceland on the increase, the covert break-out through the northern exits was becoming untenable as an operation of war. If a movement through northern waters was unavoidable, they would have to treat it as a major operation, calling, if need be, on the full resources of the Navy and the *Luftwaffe* to accomplish it. Schniewind spoke in terms not simply of air escort but of 'air superiority'. Carls warned that reconnaissance had to be improved 'at all costs' and that the weather service rested on 'feet of clay'. If U-boats had to be withdrawn from the Atlantic campaign to meet these requirements, then so be it. There could be no half-measures.

There was a minority, in the immediate aftermath of the *Bismarck* operation, which still rejected the idea that the unprecedented efficiency of British shadowing had been based on radar. Brinkmann's rather curious views on the subject have been mentioned already. Surprisingly, they found enthusiastic support in quarters that should have known better. In a stubborn rearguard action, the Head of the Naval Intelligence Service (no less) argued that:

> Shadowing in thick weather and at great range does not necessarily indicate the presence of radar on the English side ... There is the possibility too of efficient sound-detectors, for which the conditions in the cold water zone of the Denmark Strait are most suitable. Also, it is still an open question whether the enemy was able to shadow the [*Bismarck*/*Prinz Eugen*] combat unit by picking up the German radar impulses or VHF [radio] transmissions.[17]

What was missing from this general review of lessons learned was any authoritative judgement on whether, once all the problems connected with departure and break-out had been overcome, cruiser warfare on the high seas could be made effective. Exponents had seen a vision of cruisers on the rampage, probing for weaknesses in the enemy's defence, striking when opportunity offered, melting away before a heavy-footed enemy could bring his forces to bear and, what is more, sustaining the process over an extended period. But the concept had yet to be proved. On any objective measure, the achievements of 'Berlin' had been modest. 'Rheinübung' had ended in disaster and it was becoming abundantly clear that the heavy cruisers of the *Hipper* class were unequal to the task. The reasons behind this yawning chasm between concept and reality were there in the war diaries; the inadequacy of

German ocean reconnaissance arrangements; and the psychological pressures on commanders who knew that machinery break-down or action damage, however minor, could bring their operations to an abrupt end or deprive them of the mobility on which their safety depended. Brinkmann's records gave a glimpse of what it was really like for the cruiser commander as, isolated and uncertain, he tried to put together a coherent plan from the fragments of information available to him. The operational commands seem not to have grappled with these questions. Some were blind to them. Admiral Carls' summary of the issues was typically robust but largely unhelpful. This was a war, he told Raeder, of 'midgets against giants'. Unless the Navy were prepared to act as a fleet-in-being (a concept which he rejected), operations 'would always entail risks and always lead to losses'. Whether those risks were acceptable could only be judged in relation to the objective in view. There was no sense in risking the fleet on missions that were 'unnecessary or of little weight'. But where the objective had genuine potential to affect the outcome of the war, then the Navy had to grit its teeth and throw everything – ships of the *Bismarck* class included – into the balance.[18] But could ocean warfare be made to work? That was the key question, and no one offered an answer to it.

* * *

The admirals had hardly come to grips with the events of May 1941 before they found new problems crowding in on them. A week after Raeder's meeting with the *Führer*, the *Lützow* left the Baltic to make her passage to Trondheim. An attack by Coastal Command torpedo-bombers, pressed home in the mid-summer twilight off Lindesnes, the southern tip of Norway, left her dead in the water and listing heavily. In the lull following the storm, she managed to restore power and turn for home. Her air escort, hastily reinforced, kept follow-up attacks at bay, and in the afternoon of 14 June she limped into in Kiel. Disaster had been averted; it was clear, nonetheless, that operations would have to be postponed for several months.[19]

At the end of June, British bombers resumed their offensive against Brest after an interval of more than two months.[20] Damage received during the night of 1 July put the *Prinz Eugen* into drydock and raised new fears for the safety of the battlecruisers. The three-month programme to replace the

Scharnhorst's superheaters was approaching completion and the decision was taken to move her south to La Pallice as soon as she was ready to begin trials and training. She sailed during the night of 21 July. Thirty-six hours later Royal Air Force Halifax bombers made an unprecedented daylight raid on her new berth and registered five hits. Two bombs which penetrated the armoured deck failed to explode but damage was extensive. Several major compartments were flooded and fire caused serious damage to the ship's electrical ring main. The *Scharnhorst* returned to Brest during the night of 24 July and was docked immediately. She faced another lengthy period under repair. The forward programme that Raeder had put before Hitler only six weeks earlier was beginning to unravel. It was hard to avoid the conclusion that in the weeks following 'Rheinübung' the enemy had seized the initiative.

Nor were these the only set-backs to Raeder's plans. It had become clear soon after 'Rheinübung' that German auxiliaries in the Atlantic were facing new and perplexing difficulties. Looking back, the problem seemed to have started with the disappearance of the trawler *München* in early May. She had been on weather patrol off Jan Mayen and her loss was still a mystery. By the end of the month two more weather ships, the *Heinrich Freese* and the *August Wriedt*, had also gone missing. Then, on 3 June, the tanker *Belchen*, tasked after 'Rheinübung' to support U-boats of the Western Group, had been surprised and sunk by British cruisers at her rendezvous in the Davis Strait. (*U-93* had taken her survivors on board.) On 4 June the scout *Gonzenheim*, returning to Biscay in the wake of the *Prinz Eugen*, had scuttled herself when intercepted by British forces, and, a thousand miles to the southward, the tanker *Esso Hamburg* had come to a similar fate. On the very next day, the same thing had happened to the tanker *Egerland*. By the end of June the German naval authorities were having to account for the sudden disappearance of twelve ships, half of them tankers, in three widely separated areas of the Atlantic. It was clear that the enemy could have achieved this unprecedented run of success only under 'exceptionally favourable circumstances'.[21]

What lay behind it all? Those charged with investigating the matter could not rule out the possibility that the trawlers had fallen into the hands of the enemy. They might have been located by D/F or betrayed by Norwegian agents; they might have been caught at night or in low visibility by a British patrol. It was entirely possible that the operation orders, charts and code-books that they carried had been compromised. But to accept a link between missing trawlers and accidents further afield was another matter. As far as could be seen, the *München* and her consorts had carried nothing which could throw light on the operations of other ships. (They had no reason to know about such things.) The run of losses in the Atlantic was attributed, initially, to the heightened state of alert after '*Rheinübung*', to American reconnaissance, to the unfavourable time of year, to the activities of secret agents and to 'unlucky circumstances'. When, somewhat later, information reached Berlin showing that the tankers *Gedania* and *Lothringen* had been taken by the British, the answer became obvious. Their orders had included the coordinates of the Atlantic fuelling areas, the positions assigned to weather ships and the routes taken by prizes and blockade-runners. At least five of the losses could be explained in this way. It was hardly necessary to look further.

The true reasons behind this extraordinary run of bad luck remained hidden from German eyes. A compromise of naval ciphers was considered but rejected; the idea that the Admiralty might have initiated a systematic campaign to capture the necessary material seemed too far-fetched to merit serious investigation.[22] 'After a new and very thorough inquiry', Admiral Fricke reported at the end of July, 'the possibility of the enemy being able to read signals by deciphering them has been unanimously discounted all the experts.[23] Rather as the Intelligence Division of the Naval War Staff had resisted the notion that enemy ships might be fitted with radar, so now the Communications Service dug itself in to defend the idea that its codes and ciphers were inviolable. The broader conclusion was this: that if the loss of auxiliaries could be attributed to the unusual set of conditions that had followed '*Rheinübung*', existing afloat support arrangements would remain viable.

* * *

British preoccupations in the weeks following '*Rheinübung*' centred primarily on questions of *matériel*. The loss of the *Hood* was an uncomfortable reminder of Jutland and left the Admiralty vulnerable to the accusation that lessons of that battle had not been learned. Signs of public disquiet were quick to surface. A leader in *The Times* of 28 May hinted at continuing design weaknesses in the Royal Navy's capital ships, and Pound found himself obliged to enlist the help of his distinguished predecessor Lord Chatfield in an attempt to set the record straight. In a letter to the Editor, Chatfield drew attention to the relative ages of the *Hood* and the *Bismarck*, outlined the advances in capital ship design that had been made since the 1920s and put the blame for the disaster on those who, until 1937, had opposed the rebuilding of the British battle fleet. But this could only be a holding action. Fearing that the events of 24 May might provoke a public outcry and damage morale in the fleet, the Admiralty set up a Board of Inquiry under Vice-Admiral Sir Geoffrey Blake[24] and sent it north to establish the facts and establish them quickly.[25]

Blake presented his findings to the Secretary of the Admiralty on 2 June after what had clearly been a lightning tour of the Scottish bases. Drawing on the accounts of the principal eye-witnesses, among them Captain Leach and Lieutenant-Commander G. W. Rowell, the Navigator of the *Prince of Wales*, he concluded that the cordite fire first observed in the *Hood*'s midship section had been superficial in its effects and that the probable cause of the disaster had been the direct penetration of one or more of the ship's after magazines. The Admiralty was not impressed. There were other possibilities and Blake had done little to investigate them. Leading the attack on the report, Sir Stanley Goodall, the veteran Director of Naval Construction, drew attention to the anomalies that had yet to be resolved and particularly to the distance between the *Hood*'s after magazines and the apparent site of the explosion. He thought it at least plausible that a direct hit on one of the torpedo warheads, stowed in its armoured box or 'mantlet' in the ship's midship section, might have been the cause – a view seemingly shared by Tovey, who had already ordered the removal of torpedoes from similar upper deck stowages in the *Repulse* . The Controller, Rear-Admiral B. A. Fraser, was inclined to let matters rest; Phillips and Pound were not. This was a lightweight report when measured against the scale of the disaster and one that would never stand public scrutiny. A new inquiry was therefore ordered.[26]

The second Board of Inquiry, under the presidency of Rear-Admiral H. T. C. Walker, a former captain of the *Hood*, met in late August. This was a much more searching investigation. It took detailed statements from dozens of eye-witnesses, weighed the advice of naval architects and experts in ballistics and made a serious attempt to establish the chemical origins of the explosion. It was hesitant in its conclusions, perhaps inevitably so: the Board had heard too much contradictory and inconclusive evidence to allow otherwise.[27] Yet its findings were accepted as authoritative.

The balance of probability suggested a sequence on the following lines. A shell from the *Bismarck*'s third salvo had struck the *Hood* on the boat deck close to the mainmast. The resulting fire had spread rapidly to cover a large part of the midship area, had pulsated for a few moments, and then died down. According to a survivor from the *Hood*, it had sounded like a Chinese fire cracker – a sequence of sympathetic detonations. Everything pointed to a fire among ready-use 4in and UP ammunition, large quantities of which were stowed on the upper deck.[28] There was little evidence, on the other hand, to support the idea that the fire could have spread to the ship's main magazines through the 4in ammunition supply train. The survivor had been certain that upper-deck ammunition hatches had been shut. And officers who had left the *Hood* in recent months had been able to confirm that orders were clear and drills firmly enforced.[29]

The fatal explosion itself had followed the *Bismarck*'s fifth or sixth salvo. One shell had struck home in the midship section, throwing up a quantity of dark-coloured debris, and others had fallen just short. After an interval of two or three seconds, witnesses had seen a 'fierce upward rush of flame in the shape of a funnel'. It had come from a position just forward of the mainmast and, according to Captain Leach, it had looked like 'a vast blow lamp'. The view from the bridge of the *Prince of Wales* had then been obscured by volumes of dense smoke. Other eye-witnesses placed the seat of the explosion much further aft. Some had seen huge pieces of debris, even whole turrets, flying through the air; others described the whole after part of the ship as being reduced to a mass of twisted framework. There was little unanimity in these matters. There was general agreement, on the other hand, that there had been no noise, no shock, no loss of speed – just that single gush of flame.

How, then, had the disaster occurred? Mr D. E. J. Offord, representing the Director of Naval Construction, argued the case for a torpedo warhead. The detonation of 500lb of TNT, he suggested, would have destroyed the main structural deck over a considerable width and blown out the hull plating to a position well below the waterline. With the ship travelling at 28kts, the inrush of water would have carried away bulkheads in the after part of the ship and broken her back. The Board was not persuaded. The effects

223

described by eye-witnesses were not consistent with Offord's hypothesis. The explosion of a torpedo warhead could not be ruled out, but it was not seen as the direct cause of the sinking.

The Inquiry now centred on whether a 15in shell fired from a range of 16,500yds and striking the *Hood*'s belt armour at an angle of incidence of 50° could penetrate to the after magazine group. It would all depend on muzzle velocity, and the figures for German guns were uncertain. There seemed little doubt that velocities of 3,050ft/sec, a figure towards the top end of the range, would achieve the necessary penetration. It was less easy to say how a slower projectile might have behaved; the *Hood*'s scheme of armour protection appeared, generally speaking, to provide a good defence against these. There were, perhaps, two narrow zones of vulnerability. The first had been discovered in a skeleton model put together by naval constructors; there appeared to be an area of weakness (40ft long and 18in deep) that, under certain conditions of roll or heel, would allow a slower shell to penetrate the comparatively light (7in) armour of the upper belt, break through the armoured deck close to the ship's centreline and explode near the forward 4in magazine. A penetration of this kind, possible in theory, was judged highly unlikely. It implied a fusing delay greater than any in British use. The second zone of weakness appeared to lie below the waterline and had come to light as a result of damage to the *Prince of Wales*. Here a 15in shell, falling a little short, had passed under the armoured belt and penetrated to a depth of 15ft before coming to rest against a bulkhead. (It had failed to explode.) The total distance travelled from the moment of water entry had been some 90ft, and calculation showed that, under certain narrowly defined conditions, a shell following a similar trajectory might have penetrated to the *Hood*'s main magazines. This, too, would have been a 'lucky shot', but it could not be dismissed out of hand; there had been no sign of damage to the Hood's main belt.

Penetration of the main deck by a shell passing over the side armour, a matter of special interest to the Board in view of the *Hood*'s known weaknesses, was ruled out. The ranges were too short. Specialist advice suggested that a shell striking the armoured upper deck would have tended to ricochet upwards; even if it had penetrated the deck, its subsequent trajectory would have taken it well above the magazine spaces. The relative weakness of the *Hood*'s horizontal protection had not, in the event, contributed to her loss.

The findings of the second Board did not differ much from those of the first. The loss of the ship was attributed to the explosion of a 15in shell in or close to one of the after magazines. It was possible that one of the 4in magazines had gone up first. There was no solid evidence to suggest that a torpedo warhead had exploded, but the Board could not rule out the possibility altogether. The fire on the boat deck had not been the cause of the disaster.

The findings of the Walker Board were widely accepted. The DNC described their report as containing 'all that will ever be known' on the loss of the *Hood*. But he held to his view that upper-deck torpedo tubes should be removed from capital ships. As a result of the Board's work, additional armoured bulkheads were fitted to the battleships of the *Nelson* class and steps were taken to improve magazine protection in the older *Queen Elizabeth* and 'R' classes. The newer battleships of the *King George V* class received additional splinter protection to alleviate the problem of hits below the waterline. Little more seemed necessary. The Inquiry had produced no evidence that the system of flash-tight doors between gunhouse and magazine introduced in the post-Jutland era was in any way defective, and made no case for a change from bagged to cased propellant for the Navy's heavy guns.

* * *

The search for strategic and tactical lessons that occupied German minds in the wake of '*Rheinübung*' found no echo in Britain. (The Royal Navy had, after all, found the measure of its opponent.) But the margin of success had been narrow and the tension, at times, almost unbearable. Charity was not in the air.

There had been signs almost from the beginning that the Admiralty was going to judge the conduct of its admirals and captains by very exacting and very traditional standards. Wake-Walker had been among the first to feel the weight of Admiralty scrutiny. Leach, too, had sensed that his conduct during the battle off Iceland would invite 'the most critical examination'.[30] (His premonitions were right.) For some time Tovey had remained immune; the authority of a commander-in-chief was not to be challenged lightly. But on that last tense evening, when Somerville's attack had failed and when Tovey had intimated that a second failure would leave him no option but to break off for fuel, patience in Whitehall had come near to breaking-point. It was then – and possibly at Churchill's instigation[31] – that admirals in London, beside themselves with anxiety and frustration, had first considered the option of a signal that would require the CinC to remain on station until the job was done, regardless of the consequences. Pound had been reluctant to cross this rubicon, but the idea had ceased to be unthinkable. Signs next morning that the CinC was leaving the scene with the *Bismarck* still afloat removed what few inhibitions remained. The Admiralty's message read:

> We cannot visualise the situation from your signals. *Bismarck* must be sunk at all costs and if to do this it is necessary for the *King George V* to remain on scene then she must do so, even if it subsequently means towing *King George V*.[32]

Tovey's immediate reaction to this message was defensive; resentment came later. By 30 May (the day following his arrival in Loch Ewe) he had put together a detailed account of his operations and a full justification of his actions during the final phase. He had assumed, he told the Admiralty, that every serviceable U-boat and destroyer on the west coast of France would be sent to the *Bismarck*'s aid. The *King George V* had been the only effective capital ship in home waters; she had been close to safe fuel margins and he had not been prepared 'to expose her unscreened at low speed to almost certain attack by U-boats unless there was very good prospect of achieving a result commensurate with the risk'.[33]

He went on to defend his decision to postpone the gun action until dawn and then to wait for full light. He had been ready to force an action earlier; but light conditions had been 'most unfavourable' and he would have given the enemy an 'excessive advantage'. The risk of misidentification in the contact area had been grave; D/F had done little to resolve his uncertainties; and he had made due allowance for 'differences in reckoning' between forces that had been widely separated and which had been given few opportunities to take sights. On the untidy end to the gun action, Tovey made it clear that he had left the *Bismarck* a smoking wreck and that her sinking could only have been a matter of time.

The tone of this letter was conciliatory. Tovey admitted that his signals to Somerville might have been 'unfortunately phrased'. He was careful to acknowledge the Admiralty's contribution to the success of his operations. Dispositions ordered in London had saved the day when contact had been lost and when his own forces had been too few to cover all possibilities. The speed and accuracy of the Admiralty's enemy information had been 'beyond praise'. But, in a hint of things to come, he gave equal credit to the skill and understanding of his subordinates. 'Flag and commanding officers of detached units,' he told the Admiralty, 'invariably took the action I would have wished before or without instructions from me.'[34]

The letter seems to have choked off further criticism of Tovey's part in the affair. But the conduct of some of his junior flag officers and captains was still under investigation. When Pound and Phillips showed that they were going to leave no stone unturned in their search for errors and omissions, the stage was set for some sharp differences of opinion between the Admiralty and the CinC. There was a minor scuffle over the conduct of the *Rodney* . In his official dispatches, issued on 5 July, Tovey had described her blocking position on the route to Brest as 'extremely well chosen'.[35] Pound, who had gone through the records with extraordinary diligence, thought it 'very ill judged'.[36] There was right on his side. Dalrymple-Hamilton's diagonal movement across the cone of courses leading to Biscay had offered little prospect of success and had condemned him to a stern chase which, but for the intervention of Force H, must certainly have ended in failure. Yet it was Tovey's version which went to the printers. Exchanges on the conduct of Leach and Wake-Walker were sharper still. To Pound and Phillips the bare facts of the case meant automatic court-martial; this was the path of orthodoxy. Outside White-hall, their attitude smacked of mindless zealotry. Tovey, sensing an injustice and, no doubt, smarting at his own treatment, dug his toes in. (There was substance in his reputation for bullish obstinacy.) When told that the Admiralty would start proceedings under its own authority, he threatened to haul down his flag and act as 'prisoner's friend'.[37] Nothing more was heard of the matter. In its formal comments on Tovey's dispatches, the Board accepted that Leach's decision to break off the action (and Wake-Walker's decision not to renew it) had been 'entirely correct having regard to the circumstances of the case . . .'[38]

* * *

227

The Navy's formal observations on the events leading to the sinking of the *Bismarck* contained nothing which could re-ignite earlier controversies. Tovey's position remained fixed in all essentials. Success, he suggested, had come from the skill and understanding of flag and commanding officers who, acting alone and usually without orders, had grasped and even anticipated what was in their admiral's mind.

The Admiralty broadly agreed with him. Admirals were given credit for their accurate appreciations and 'skilful anticipation' of enemy movements. Somerville's arrival could 'hardly have been better judged'; Tovey's tactics during the final battle were 'a model for similar operations'. Their Lordships had been impressed by the 'ability, determination and sea sense displayed by Commanding Officers'. The work of naval aircraft deserved 'special tribute' and so did the dedication of engine-room departments.

It seems, looking back over an interval of nearly sixty years, that these findings captured an important truth. This was no longer Jellicoe's navy. The fleet that had caught the *Bismarck* had not waited tamely for directions from its Commander-in-Chief; it had developed the habit of thinking for itself and had come to revel in it. The thinking may have been imprecise, messy, sometimes wayward; but it had seldom been rulebound and, at its best, it had produced moments of brilliant creativity. A culture had changed.

But was it the whole truth? The obsessive focus on individual conduct and the personal antagonisms that had followed seem to have diverted attention from the serious deficiencies that remained – the fleet's dismal weapon training standards, the complete absence of afloat support, command arrangements that encouraged external interference in the conduct of operations, boundaries of responsibility that were ill-defined. These short-comings were left out of the reckoning; they survived to cramp the Royal Navy's operations in the testing years that still lay ahead.

* * *

The set-backs which followed hard on the heels of *'Rheinübung'* did not shake Grand-Admiral Raeder's strategic convictions, though they did make him change his arguments. On 25 July (the damage to the *Scharnhorst* was fresh in all minds) he told Hitler that the prime function of the Brest Squadron was to keep the British on the defensive and thus to relieve pressure on other key theatres of war. The great sacrifices that the enemy was making to keep the ships immobile was a sure indication of how much he feared a renewal of operations on the high seas.[39]

Raeder continued to press for more vigorous action against the United States. After the US occupation of Iceland in August 1941, and again after Roosevelt's 'active defence' speech in early September, he announced that he could no longer see any distinction between British and American ships and demanded a change to existing rules. He found Hitler preoccupied with events in the East, anxious about the security of his western sea frontiers and critical of the mounting losses to Axis supply and transport shipping in the Mediterranean. His demands were rejected pending the 'great decision' in the Eastern Campaign.

As autumn drew on, a new threat appeared on the horizon. Raeder found his monthly allocation of fuel oil reduced to levels that were well below projected rates of expenditure; he would have to dig deep into scarce naval reserves. To add insult to injury, he was facing mounting demands for a transfer of stocks to the Italian Navy which had been reduced (by oil shortage) to 'operational and tactical impotence'. The situation, he told Hitler, was fast becoming intolerable. He would be forced to abandon plans to use the *Tirpitz* in the Atlantic; he would send her to Trondheim as soon as she became ready and develop a role for her on the Norwegian coast.

Through the autumn of 1941, Raeder fought a dogged rearguard action to keep the two battlecruisers and the *Prinz Eugen* on the Atlantic coast and thus to keep the option of cruiser warfare alive. The international situation, he told Hitler in mid-November, was extremely fluid. A success in Russia would have a marked influence on political attitudes in Spain and Japan; decisions on the future employment of the three ships should await the course of events. Although shortage of oil and lack of afloat support would prevent protracted operations, there were still important strategic targets to be found on Britain's north–south lines of communication.[40]

The outbreak of war in the Pacific seemed, momentarily, to give new force to his arguments. American preoccupations in the western hemisphere would, he thought, create new and exciting opportunities nearer home. His hopes were short-lived. In mid-December the Royal Air Force resumed its bombing and mining offensive. For the rest of the year the bombers appeared over Brest nightly; and from time to time they came in daylight, too, accompanied by swarms of fighters. The attack seemed unremitting.

A visit by Vice-Admiral Fricke to Hitler's East Prussian headquarters while this offensive was at its height marked the beginning of the end. The situation called for deft handling; Fricke, an uncompromising cruiser warfare zealot, failed to read the signs. After listening politely to the familiar exposition of the naval case, Hitler's patience snapped. He raised the spectre of an Anglo-American invasion of Norway and declared that it could have decisive consequences for the outcome of the war. The Navy's main task was the defence of Norway and he wanted the heavy ships brought home. Differences over the best means of accomplishing this withdrawal opened the rift still wider. Hitler made it clear that he favoured a surprise move through the English Channel; Fricke raised objections. Hitler declared that, if the Channel break-through was impracticable, it would be best to lay the ships up and use their guns ashore. He even went so far as to cast doubts on the value of heavy ships in modern warfare! According to notes of this meeting, this statement 'met with sharp and detailed opposition from the Chief, Naval Staff'. In the end Fricke asked for time to review the whole question before a final decision was made. This was the only concession that he could get.[41]

On 11 January 1942 Raeder brought the plans for Operation *'Cerberus'* before Hitler and senior members of the Armed Forces High Command. He could not, in all conscience, take on the role of advocate himself, though he would support the plan if a decision to go ahead was made. (He left the presentation to Vice-Admiral Ciliax, CinC Battleships, and Commodore Ruge, Flag Officer Western Defences.) Although Hitler now declared an open mind on the conduct of the operation, he left no room for doubt about his basic objective. He was prepared to accept that the Brest Squadron performed a useful diversionary function so long as it remained seaworthy. In a damaged state, it performed no useful function whatever; and he was no longer prepared to leave it exposed to chance hits day after day. Bringing the ships home would involve risk, but the Squadron was like a patient with cancer: if it were to survive, it had to submit to an operation however drastic that might be. The threat to Norway was acute; this was the decisive point for a naval concentration and he was determined to bring it about.

The plan put forward by Ciliax was simple yet daring. The Squadron would sail by night, make a fast passage up the English Channel and pass the narrows in daylight. Success would depend on secrecy, surprise, careful timing and, from dawn onwards, strong *Luftwaffe* support. Although Lieutenant-General Jeschonnek, *Luftwaffe* Chief of Staff, refused to guarantee the level of support that the Navy demanded, the plan was approved. In summing up, Hitler expressed the view that the British were incapable of 'making and carrying out lightning decisions'. They would fail to concentrate their bomber and fighter formations in time.[42]

The *Scharnhorst*, *Gneisenau* and *Prinz Eugen* left Brest during the night of 11/ 12 February 1942 and sailed for home, leaving the war against Atlantic shipping to Admiral Dönitz and his U-boats.

Notes to Chapter 11

1 PG47897, *Bismarck* War Diary, 27 May 1941.

2 The destroyers *Mashona* and *Tartar* took the brunt of the attacks. They had formed part of the *Rodney*'s escort and had delayed their departure too long. They were returning home at economical speed and by the morning of 28 May were trailing 100 miles astern of the CinC. The *Mashona* was sunk with heavy loss. The *Piorun* also had an eventful passage home: she fought off ten air attacks before reaching Plymouth Sound.

3 British rescue operations were suspended when a 'suspicious smoking discharge' was seen from the bridge of the *Dorsetshire*. It was assumed to be a U-boat exhaust. German sources have tended to discount this possibility. At this point, the *Dorsetshire* had recovered 85 men and the *Maori* 25.

4 The *Prinz Eugen* had 250 cubic metres of fuel remaining – about 8 per cent – when she met the *Spichern*. PG47895, Section E, *Prinz Eugen* War Diary for 26 May 1941.

5 PG47895, Section E, *Prinz Eugen* War Diary, 27 May 1941. According to Group West's signal 1850(B) of 27 May, an Italian submarine had reported five battleships in quadrant BE 5568 (about 400 miles north-west of Cape Finisterre). Course and speed were given as 220° fast. These vessels were possibly Force H en route to Gibraltar.

6 *Ibid.*, 28 May 1941. Brinkmann's account leads to the suspicion that the mine damage to the *Prinz Eugen* on 25 April was more serious than was admitted at the time. The authorities may even have accepted certain machinery limitations – for example, the inability to uncouple and recouple the starboard shaft – in order to avoid further delay.

7   *Ibid.*, 29 May 1941.

8   Comments on the *Prinz Eugen* War Diary by CinC Cruisers and the Group Commanders are given in PG47895, Sections G to K. The diary is an odd document. A translator's comment gives the general flavour. 'The language,' he says, 'is stilted, grammar is complicated, and the overall impression is that the Captain is attempting to make his entries sound "momentous" and "impressive".

9   The account of this meeting is missing from the published edition of *Führer* Conferences (a surprising omission). The summary given here is taken from the (US) Navy Department version issued at the end of the war.

10 Negotiations with the Vichy regime concerning the use of Dakar had already taken place; it was expected that facilities would be ready by mid-July.

11 *'Barbarossa'* was a mere two weeks away; much of Göring's strength was deployed in the East.

12 Raeder would probably have taken this as a reference to the Azores.

13 Naval War Staff memorandum dated 24 July 1941, PG20418, pp. 33–5 (German text).

14 PG47895, Section F.

15 *Ibid.*, Section K.

16 *Ibid.*, Section H.

17 PG20418, p. 16 (German text).

18 PG47895, Part K, 'Comments and Conclusions by CinC Group North'.

19 The *Lützow* remained in Kiel until January 1942.

20 There had been a fierce debate on bombing priorities between the Admiralty and the Air Staff. The weight of effort had tended to ebb and flow according to the latest assessments of German readiness.

21 PG20418, p. 36 (German text). The Head of the Communications Service issued an initial report on 24 July 1941. The inquiry was reopened when it became clear that two tankers, the *Gedania* and the *Lothringen*, had fallen into British hands. The second report, issued in July 1942, confirmed the findings of the first one.

22 For an account of the Admiralty's campaign, see Hinsley, Vol. 1, pp. 337–8. The capture of the *München* (7 May) provided the Enigma settings for June 1941 and enabled Bletchley Park to read the widely used *Heimische Gewässer* code for June 1941 in near-real time.

23 Memorandum, 'Operational Security', dated 24 July 1941, PG20418, p. 34 (German text).

24 Blake was a gunnery specialist and former Battle Cruiser Squadron commander. He had been placed on the retired list (on health grounds) before the war but had been recalled to serve in the Admiralty as ACNS(F). He had recently been appointed as liaison officer to the USN Mission in London.

25 A record of the exchanges between Admiralty Board members is to be found in PRO ADM 116/4351.

26 PRO ADM 116/4351. It may be of interest that the reports into the loss of the *Hood* were withheld from public scrutiny for twenty years.

27 Eye-witnesses had differed on the site of the explosion, on the behaviour of the main hull sections, on the volume of debris thrown into the air and on the colour of the smoke and flame generated by the explosion.

28 Following the ship's 1940 refit, the *Hood*'s secondary armament consisted of fourteen dual-purpose 4in guns in twin mountings. Ready-use ammunition was provided on the scale of 80 rounds per gun. The UP (unrotated projectile) was an early and unsuccessful anti-aircraft rocket device. More than nine tons of UP ammunition was also stowed in upper deck lockers.

29 PRO ADM 1/11726.

30 PRO ADM 199/1188, p.127.

31 See Roskill (1977), p. 125.

32 Admiralty message 1137(B), 27 May 1941. Roskill (1977) p. 125; Kennedy, p. 225.

33 Letter to Admiralty, 'Report of Operations in pursuit of the *Bismarck*', 30 May 1941. PRO ADM 199/1188, p.14. The Admiralty was puzzled by this letter; it looked like Tovey's formal report on the recent operation but he had clearly not consulted other commanders. Pound made it clear that he was looking for something more.

34 CinC letter of 30 May 1941, PRO ADM 199/1188, p. 18.

35 CinC Home Fleet letter of 5 July 1941, later published as CB 04164, Tovey's official dispatches on the sinking of the *Bismarck*.

36 Letter to CinC, 1 August 1941; PRO ADM 199/1188, p. 25.

37 Roskill (1977), p. 125.

38 Admiralty letter to CinC, 10 September 1941, PRO ADM 199/1188, p.32.

39 Conference of 25 July 1941, *Führer Conferences*, p. 223.

40 Conference of 13 November 1941, *Führer Conferences*, pp. 235–43.

41 *Führer Conferences*, pp. 246–9.

42 Memorandum on the planned passage of the Brest Group through the Channel, 12 January 1942, *Führer Conferences*, pp. 256–61.

APPENDIX

A Technical Controversy: The Plotting of D/F Bearings

In the wake of the *Bismarck* affair, no one in authority was much interested in how Tovey's staff had come to misinterpret the D/F data sent to them on the morning of 25 May. There were larger issues to be resolved; this was chicken-feed and largely unintelligible except to the specialist. No formal investigation was made. Historians who looked into the matter after the war found plenty of unsubstantiated opinion an a good deal of obfuscation. It may be worth peering above the parapet to see if we can get a glimpse of the truth.

A brief word on chart projections. Most of the charts used at sea are based on the Mercator projection. (So are the diagrams reproduced in this book.) The Mercator is usually described as a cylindrical projection. The layman is invited to imagine a light source located at the centre of the Earth projecting an outline of geographical features onto the internal surface of a cylinder. Lines of longitude (meridians) appear as parallel straight lines. They are crossed at right angles by lines of latitude to form a right-angled grid. Direction (measured in degrees clockwise from any meridian) remains constant across the surface of the chart. To lay off a course or to plot a bearing, the navigator aligns a parallel rule to the required direction using the nearest convenient compass rose and slides it to the point or feature concerned. It is simplicity itself.

The Mercator chart has a number of peculiarities of which the navigator has to be aware. The most obvious of these is that the scale of latitude (and distance) expands progressively towards the poles until, at the poles, it becomes infinite. The navigator has to measure distance at the latitude of interest and avoid selecting it at random from the chart's latitude scale. A second and related problem is that beyond a certain latitude (75°–80° for practical purposes) the distortion of the Mercator chart renders it unfit for use. In polar regions the navigator has to use a different projection.

But there is a further peculiarity that has immediate relevance to the problem under discussion. The navigator who draws a straight line between (say) Southampton and New York and who steers along it will arrive at his destination. But he will not do so by the most direct route. The shortest distance between two points on the Earth's surface lies on the circumference of a circle whose plane passes through the centre of the Earth – the so-called great circle. This appears on a Mercator chart as a curve. Over short distances, the difference between great circle and straight line (rhumb line) can be ignored, but over ocean distances it becomes significant; the difference measured in mid-Atlantic is well in excess of 100 nautical miles. The navigator using a Mercator chart for long-distance route planning is thus presented with the problem of constructing a curve (or, to be more exact, a series of short lines or chords approximating a curve), a task which is tedious and time-consuming.

A similar problem arises if the navigator wants to plot the bearing of a distant radio source on a Mercator chart. The radio signal has travelled over a great circle and must be treated accordingly. Rather than constructing the curve, the navigator applies a correction to the raw data so that he can plot it as a straight line. It is known as a 'half-convergency' correction and it varies with latitude and with the angular distance between the observer's meridian and that of the source. Half-convergency tables are (and were) readily available in a number of Admiralty publications.

In practice, of course, the navigator sailing a great circle route (or plotting a long-range D/F bearing) will prefer an alternative chart projection in which great circles appear as straight lines. The gnomonic chart has this property: geographical features are projected on to a flat surface which touches the Earth at a selected 'tangent point'. Meridians converge on (or radiate from) the poles; lines of latitude appear as curves. Scale remains constant across the surface of the chart but direction does not. Direction, in this instance, has to be measured at the meridian of interest and is valid only for geographical points that lie on that meridian.

But to return to the events of May 1941. The Admiralty's Operational Intelligence Centre (OIC) had been set up before the war to act as a focal point for the collection and dissemination of intelligence and reconnaissance data. Under the leadership of a few dedicated individuals, it had evolved into what amounted to an Admiralty command centre. The function of the OIC and its permanent staff remained advisory rather than executive, but the service provided had become essential to decision-makers. D/F fixing and tracking was one of its more important functions. The OIC's D/F plotting cell, led by Lieutenant-Commander Peter Kemp, had done much to pioneer the technique. They regarded themselves, rightly, as experts in the field at a time when the Fleet was still exploring the technical and procedural problems involved.

Sometime prior to the events described in this book (the exact point is difficult to establish) discussions took place between the Fleet Staff and the OIC on the format to be adopted when D/F information was signalled to ships at sea. The decision agreed (for better or worse) was that the OIC should provide the Fleet with raw (i.e. uncorrected) data. The reasons are obscure; they may simply reflect the natural preference of operational commanders for unadorned fact rather than for something processed by unknown (hence unreliable) persons in an obscure office. The most important consideration was uniformity. Provided that the Fleet knew what it was getting, the exact format did not matter too much.

Now to the issue itself. Towards 0900 on the morning of 25 May the Scarborough D/F station (the controlling station for the British D/F chain) passed the OIC a set of readings on an HF radio source that had opened up to the west of the United Kingdom. The characteristics of the transmission were very similar to those recorded during the extended period of shadowing which had just ended. There was every reason to assume that this was the *Bismarck*. Kemp plotted the data, such as it was, and reached the considered opinion that the source of the transmission had been in 55° 0′N and somewhere between 30° and 32°W. Although the various position lines produced a poor 'cut', Kemp's superiors in the OIC (Denning and Clayton) accepted his findings.

The raw material was then passed on to Tovey in accordance with agreed procedures and it was assumed that he would reach similar conclusions. He did not. His signal to the fleet timed at 1047(B) reached the Admiralty at 1116 and showed that he put the enemy in 57°N 33°W, a difference of at least 90 miles. By this time the OIC had received further D/F data which tended to corroborate their earlier findings.

The instant reaction of the OIC specialists was that Tovey's flagship had plotted the fix on a Mercator chart without applying the necessary (half-convergency) corrections, a charge that cast serious doubt on the competence of Captain Frank Lloyd, Tovey's Master of the Fleet. Patrick Beesly, a member of OIC staff at the time, describes how Kemp transferred the uncorrected data to a Mercator chart and found 'sure enough' that it produced an apparent fix several degrees north of his own.[1] (What he neglects to add is that the uncorrected data tends to produce a fix that is substantially further north even than the one promulgated by the CinC.)

Nevertheless, the charge stuck. And it gained credence from claims, again emanating from the OIC, that the *King George V* had not been supplied with the gnomonic charts which would have made the process of D/F plotting so much easier. According to Beesly, Denning recalled having had to arrange a special issue for the flagship. Tovey's recollections lent weight to the case. Writing to Roskill (after an interval of twenty years) he admitted, 'Our own interpretation [of the 0854 D/F data] was inaccurate, owing to the lack of the requisite special charts'.[2] But we should not regard Tovey's evidence as conclusive; he was not a notably reliable witness in old age and he may never have probed too deeply into the methods used by his navigation specialist. (He had more important things to think about.) The phrase 'requisite special charts' is itself misleading. Any chart would have served the purpose if it had been used properly.

Does the charge stick? The issue before the jury is whether a navigation specialist of many years' standing could have plotted radio bearings on a Mercator chart without applying half-convergency corrections, It must be admitted that Captain Lloyd was under extreme pressure to produce a result. Could he, perhaps, have assumed that the errors arising from the use of uncorrected data would be too small to matter? Well, perhaps. But we are dealing with a specialist, not with some callow youth. The use of radio stations for navigational purposes had been common practice for decades, at least during times of peace. The process now required was exactly the same. The theory of half-convergency occupied a prominent place in the navigation manuals of the time; conversion graphs and tables were readily available.[3] It was part of the navigator's stock in trade.

It is hardly surprising that Captain Lloyd should have denied these allegations. (He did so with a good deal of indignation.) He told Ludovic Kennedy:

No one but a fool would have thought of plotting D/F bearings direct on to a Mercator chart. [Very true.] Of course we had gnomonic charts on board. But the gnomonic charts didn't have compass roses printed at the position of most of the stations from which bearings were taken. [True again.] One had to lay off the bearings with a protractor set to true north at each station; but the graduations on the protractor didn't correspond with those of the missing [compass] roses.[4]

Taking the issue of gnomonic charts first. Gnomonic charts were available to the Fleet for a number of applications – great circle sailing, polar navigation, plans of harbours and anchorages. They were available though chart depots; navigators would have needed no guidance from the OIC on how to get them. Those issued routinely may not have been ideal in terms of scale or coverage for the D/F plotting task, though some would have served the purpose. The OIC may well have had useful advice to offer on the best available chart to use or been able to point navigators to unofficial sources of supply such as the Air Ministry.

But the rest of Lloyd's statement is puzzling; it suggests either a deliberate attempt to confuse or a serious lapse of memory. He refers to a protractor, evidently the Douglas Protractor, a square, transparent instrument graduated in degrees, not unlike the thing in a schoolboy's geometry set. Aligned to a meridian, it is the proper instrument to use on a small-scale (wide area) gnomonic chart to measure (or plot) direction. There is nothing wrong with its graduations; degrees are degrees wherever you find them. But if Lloyd used a Douglas Protractor as he implies, why his emphasis on compass roses? The Douglas Protractor makes them irrelevant. (They are largely irrelevant on the small-scale gnomonic chart anyway.) The suspicion must be that Lloyd constructed his fix not with a Douglas Protractor but with a parallel rule aligned to the nearest convenient compass rose, hoping that the angular difference between rose and D/F stations was insufficient to induce large fixing errors. Had he lost his Douglas Protractor? We shall never know; but it is a mean thing, not much used at sea and easily mislaid. His results, as promulgated to the Fleet, are consistent with the use of a compass rose centred on a meridian about 5° west of the stations concerned.

If this interpretation is correct, Lloyd's mistake was scarcely less elementary than the one which Kemp and Denning had pointed to. It must be said, however, that the small-scale gnomonic chart would have been unfamiliar to him (certainly less familiar than the Mercator) and its quirks and pitfalls less firmly fixed in the mind. Unfamiliarity and extreme pressure – the two together produce mistakes in the best regulated organisations.

Notes to the Appendix

1 Beesly, pp. 81–2.
2 Cited in Kennedy, p. 278.
3 See, for example, *Admiralty Manual of Navigation*, Vol. I (1938), Chapter V, 'Fixing by W/T-D/F'.
4 Kennedy, p. 278.

Bibliography

German documents

PG20418: *The Atlantic Operation of the Combat Group Bismarck and Prinz Eugen,*
Naval High Command, Berlin, 1942. (Part of series 'Operations and Tactics;
Evaluation of Important Experiences of the War at Sea'.) Post-war transla-
tion by Naval Historical Branch.

PG34677: *Gneisenau* War Diary, 16 January 1941 to 22 March 1941, covering
period of Operation *'Berlin'.*

PG47895: *Atlantic Operation of Combat Group Bismarck and Prinz Eugen under
command of Admiral Lütjens,* May 1941. Collected papers relating to the operation, including:

Part A: Operational Directive of Group West.

Part B: Task Force Commander's Intentions.

Part C: Chronology (based on war diaries and signals of Group
           Commands):

      I   Joint operations to evening of 24 May.

      II   24 May to final engagement.

      III Further operations of *Prinz Eugen.*

Part D: Abbreviated report by Task Force Commander.

Part E: Experiences of *Prinz Eugen.*

Part F: Comments on *Prinz Eugen* War Diary by CinC Cruisers.

Part G: Group North's comments on Part F.

Part H: CinC Fleet's comments on *Prinz Eugen* War Diary.

Part J: Group West's conclusions and lessons.

Part K: Group North's conclusions and lessons.

Part M: Summary by Naval High Command.

PG47897: *Bismarck* War Diary for the period 28 February 1941 to 27 May 1941.
(The period 19–27 May is a reconstruction by Group West based on all
available records.)

Führer Conferences on Matters Dealing with the German Navy, Office of Naval Intelligence, Washington D.C., 1947.

Führer Directives and Other Top Level Directives, 1939–1941, Naval Intelligence
Department; Washington D.C., 1948.

241

British Documents
PRO ADM 116 (Admiralty & Secretariat Cases):
>4351: Loss of HMS *Hood*: Report of first Board of Inquiry.
>4352: Loss of HMS *Hood*: Report of second Board of Inquiry.

PRO ADM 199 (War History Cases & Papers):
>1187: Pursuit and destruction of German battleship *Bismarck*.
>1188: As above; original papers and records.

PRO ADM 205 (First Sea Lord's Papers):
>10: Correspondence with Prime Minister and related papers.

PRO ADM 234 (Navy Reference Books); Directorate of Training and Staff
>Duties (Historical Section), 1942:
>321: Battle Summary: The Chase and Sinking of the *Bismarck*.
>327: Battle Summary: Home Waters and Atlantic 1940–41.

Books and publications

Admiralty Navigation Manual, Vol. I, 1938 (London: HMSO, 1939).

Barnett, Correlli, *Engage the Enemy More Closely: The Royal Navy in World War II* (London: Hodder & Stroughton, 1991).

Beesly, Patrick, *Very Special Intelligence: The Story of the Admiralty's Operational Intelligence Centre 1939–45* (London: Hamish Hamilton, 1977).

Behrens, C. B. A., *Merchant Shipping and the Demands of War* (London: HMSO, 1955).

Bekker, C. D., *Hitler's Naval War* (London: Macdonald & Jane's, 1974).

Broome, Jack, *Make a Signal!* (London: Ian Allan, 1955).

Brown, D. K. (ed.), *The Design and Construction of British Warships* (Greenwich: Conway Maritime Press, 1995).

Churchill, W. S., *The Second World War*, Vol. II (London: Cassell, 1966).

Deist, Wilhelm, 'The Rearmament of the Wehrmacht', *Germany and the Second World War*, Vol. 1 (Oxford: The Clarendon Press, 1990).

Friedman, Norman, *Battleship Design & Development 1905–1945* (Greenwich: Conway Maritime Press, 1978

Fuehrer Conferences on Naval Affairs 1939–45 (London: Greenhill Books, 1990).

Grenfell, Russell, *The Bismarck Episode* (London: Faber, 1964).

Grove, Eric J. (ed.), *The Defeat of the Enemy Attack on Shipping 1939–45* (Aldershot: Ashgate Publishing, for Navy Records Society, 1997).

Hancock, W. K., and Gowing, M.M., *The British War Economy* (London: HMSO, 1949).

Hillgruber, Andreas, *Germany in the Two World Wars* (Cambridge, Mass.: Harvard University Press, 1981).

Hinsley, F.H., *British Intelligence in the Second World War: Its Influence on Strategy and Operations*, Vol. 1 (London, HMSO, 1979).

Howse, Derek, *Radar at Sea: The Royal Navy in World War 2* (Annapolis: Naval Institute Press, 1993).

Kennedy, Ludovic, *Pursuit: The Chase and Sinking of the Bismarck* (London: Collins, 1974).

Lenton, H. T., *German Warships of the Second World War* (London: Macdonald and Jane's, 1975).

Messerschmidt, Manfred, 'Foreign Policy and the Preparation for War', *Germany and the Second World War*, Vol. 1 (Oxford: The Clarendon Press, 1990).

Müllenheim-Rechberg, Burkard, Baron von, *Battleship Bismarck: A Survivor's Story* (Annapolis: Naval Institute Press, 1990).

Raeder, Erich, *My Life* (Annapolis: Naval Institute Press, 1960).

Rohwer, J., and Hummelchen, G., *Chronology of the War at Sea 1939–1945* (London: Greenhill Books, 1992).

Roskill, S. W., *Churchill and the Admirals* (London: Collins, 1977).

——, *Naval Policy between the Wars*, Vol. 2 (London: Collins, 1976).

——, *The War at Sea 1939–45*, Vol.1 (London: HMSO, 1954).

Rössler, Eberhard, 'U-boat Design and Development', in Howarth, Stephen (ed.), *The Battle of the Atlantic, 1939–45* (London: Greenhill Books, 1994).

Salewski, M., *Die deutsche Seekriegsleitung 1939–45. Band III: Denksschriften und Lagebetrachtungen* (Neustadt: Bernard & Graefe Verlag, 1973).

Schmalenbach, Paul, *Kriegsmarine Bismarck* (Warship Profile 18) (Windsor: Profile Publications, 1971).

Schofield, Brian B., *The Loss of the Bismarck* (London: Ian Allan, 1972).

Simpson, B. M. (ed), *The Development of Naval Thought: Essays by Herbert Rosinski* (Newport, RI: Naval War College Press, 1977).

Simpson, M. (ed.), *The Somerville Papers* (Aldershot: Scolar Press, for Navy Records Society, 1995).

Stephen, Martin, *The Fighting Admirals: British Admirals of the Second World War* (Annapolis: Naval Institute Press, 1991).

Thomas, Charles S., *The German Navy in the Nazi Era* (London: Unwin Hyman, 1990).

Wegener, Wolfgang, *The Naval Strategy of the World War* (Annapolis: Naval Institute Press, 1989). First published 1929.

Glossary

AA. Anti-aircraft.

'A' arc. The arc over which a gun or gun turret can traverse before coming on to the stops. Thus, the arc over which a weapon is effective.

ASV (radar). An airborne radar designed to detect ships. The type referred to is the ASV IIN. This was first fitted to Swordfish aircraft in the spring of 1941.

Battle ensign. An additional ensign (or ensigns) traditionally worn by British ships during a surface action. Richly symbolic.

B-Dienst. German radio-intelligence organisation responsible for monitoring and interpreting enemy signal traffic.

Bletchley Park. The Government Communications and Cypher School (GC&CS) in Buckinghamshire.

Boom defence. A system of nets suspended from buoys for the protection of harbour entrances.

Bulkhead. A watertight wall dividing a ship's hull into sections. Bulkheads usually lie athwartships, but larger ships may be divided longitudinally as well.

Cable. A unit of measurement commonly used for the stationing of ships, 1 cable being 200yds, or one-tenth of a nautical mile.

Challenge. A coded signal made by light or by pyrotechnics demanding a ship's identity. The ship replies with the code of the day.

Coaming. A shallow screen or lip (as round a hatch) designed to keep the weather out.

Conning position. The position from which the movements of a ship are directed. Usually the bridge or compass platform, but warships may have emergency conning positions to allow for the possibility of action damage. Before the advent of the 'operations room' or 'combat information centre', the position from which the command exercised its function.

Convoy. A group of merchant vessels moving in formation. The term usually implies that the group is under escort.

Cordite. The explosive propellant used in the Royal Navy's guns.

Datum, datum position. A lost contact position formally promulgated to assist in search planning.

Displacement (standard). As defined by the Washington Naval Treaty of 1922. Broadly, deep displacement less liquids.

Degaussing. A system of electrical coils designed to reduce the strength of a ship's magnetic field and thus to provide protection against the magnetic mine.

D/F. Direction-finding. The term describes the process used to determine the position of a ship at sea from the direction of its high frequency (HF) radio transmissions.

DNC. Director of Naval Construction.

Duplex (pistol). A torpedo firing mechanism, the warhead being triggered by the change in the target's magnetic field as the weapon passed underneath the keel.

Enemy report. A brief signal message in standard format reporting enemy identity, position, course and speed. Under British rules, always transmitted *en clair*. Initial reports were given 'emergency' precedence to ensure that they received absolute priority in ships receiving them.

Evaporator. An installation for producing fresh water, particularly feedwater for use in boilers.

Feedwater. Water free from impurities (particularly salt) and fit for use in a ship's boilers.

Fighting top. At this date, the term denoted a gun direction and observation platform occupying a commanding position an the foremast of a warship.

FOIC. Flag officer in charge.

Furthest-on circle. The circle centred on an enemy's last known position showing his maximum (or most probable) movement since loss of contact.

HA. High angle. Generally used to describe guns or directors with a dual anti-aircraft and anti-surface function.

Heave-to. To bring a ship to a stop; usually implies head to wind.

Hydrophone. An underwater listening device designed to detect propeller noise.

IFF (IFF beacon). Identification friend or foe. An electronic beacon triggered by an 'interrogator' showing the identity of a unit (usually an aircraft) on a radar screen.

Intercept course. The course needed to 'head off' a moving enemy and thus to provide the highest possible closing rate.

Interior lines. A military term expressing the advantages of occupying a central position.

Marker (flank marker). A ship providing gunfire corrections to a consort from a position where it can observe errors in range.

MF. Medium frequency (radio).

Obersalzburg. The mountain in the Bavarian Alps where Hitler had his retreat, the Berghof.

OIC. Operational Intelligence Centre. A section of the Admiralty's Naval Intelligence Division providing intelligence and reconnaissance information to Naval Staff decision-makers and operational commanders ashore and afloat.

Operational (of signal traffic). An expression used by the German Navy to distinguish signals issued by higher headquarters (Admiralty or major shore command) from 'tactical' signal traffic between ships at sea.

Plain language. A message transmitted *en clair*, i.e. without encryption.

Point (of compass). The compass card was traditionally divided into 32 points. (A point is thus 11.25°).) While the Royal Navy usually gave direction in degrees, points were still used when manoeuvring ships in formation. (The simplicity of the flag signal '2 Blue' meaning 'prepare to turn two points to port' explains the survival of this archaic form.)

Quarter, quarter line. The angle between beam and stern. Ships in quarter line take station 45° abaft the beam of the next ahead to form an echelon.

Ready use (ammunition). Term describing ammunition stowed in lockers close to the guns rather than in a magazine.

RDF. Radio direction-finding; an early term for radar.

Salvo. Strictly, a group of shots, spread in range, used for ranging purposes. More generally, any group of shots fired simultaneously.

Sight. A position or fix obtained by astronomical measurement.

Sperrbrecher. Literally, 'barrier breaker'. A vessel used by the German Navy to lead the way though a minefield.

Stability. Tendency of a ship to return to the upright after external forces (usually the effects of weather or turning moments) are removed. A high degree of stability becomes particularly important after action damage.

Standard distance. The distance between ships assumed in the absence of other orders. Ships stationed at double standard distance are said to be in 'open order'.

Starshell. A shell releasing a parachute flare to illuminate targets at night.

Stem. The main upright structure at the bow of a ship.

Straddle. The term used to describe a salvo which is 'on' for range. (The fall of shot 'straddles' or 'brackets' the target.)

Superheater. A second stage of heating designed to raise steam temperatures and thus to increase energy.

Traffic analysis. An intelligence-gathering process which seeks to determine an enemy's intentions from patterns in his signal traffic. The volume of traffic may itself indicate that something is afoot; a knowledge of who is originating the signals and to whom they are going, and the priority attached to them, may provide further clues.

Trim. A term describing the relationship between the longitudinal axis of a ship and the horizontal. A 'bow down' angle may reduce propeller and rudder efficiency.

Turbo-generator. A steam turbine used for the generation of electrical power.

UP. Unrotated (or unrifled) projectile. A primitive anti-aircraft rocket device. It was quickly withdrawn from service.

Uptake. Usually funnel uptake. The trunking or duct carrying smoke and other combustion products from the furnace to the top of the funnel.

W/T. Wireless telegraphy (Morse)

Index

A

Admiral Graf Spee (German *Panzerschiff*), 26–7, 174
  scuttled, 28
Admiral Hipper (German cruiser), 29, 36, 41, 43, 44, 47–8, 49, 52, 56, 63, 64, 68, 79, 90, 216
  and SLS 64, 62
  recovery of, 64, 65, 70, 82, 91
Admiral Scheer (German *Panzerschiff*), 16, 29, 41, 68, 216
  recovery of, 64, 65, 70, 82, 83, 91
Admiralty, 164
  air plans, 98
  reinforces CinC, 99–102
  and Crete, 134
  dispositions after *Hood*, 136–8
  logistic arrangements, 147
  and D/F intercepts, 163, 165–7
  and Coastal Cmd patrol areas, 177
  and aftermath, 226–7, 228
Alexandria, 65
Altmark, (German oiler), 27, 178
Anglo-German Naval Agreement, 19
Arethusa (British cruiser), 63, 103, 177
Ark Royal (British carrier), 56, 63, 69, 129, 135, 169, 176, 179, 180, 189, 190, 201–2, 207
  reconnaissance sortie, 179–80
  erroneous attack on *Sheffield*, 182–3
  attack on *Bismarck*, 184–8
Armstrong, Cdr H. T., (*Maori*), 198, 199
Aurora (British cruiser), 103, 148
Azores, 56, 64, 68, 134

B

Battle Cruiser Squadron (BCS), 99, 103, 111ff, 133, 135
B-Dienst, 36, 107, 122, 143, 161–2
Beale, Sub-Lt(A) A. W. D., 188
Bergen, 83, 96ff
Berghof, 214
Birmingham (British cruiser), 99, 103, 177
Bismarck (German battleship), 19, 23, 25, 29, 64, 68, 77, 80, 82, 84ff, 91, 92, 93ff, 113ff, 132ff, 147ff, 172ff, 193ff, 211, 212
  first contact with British ships, 104–5
  in action with BCS, 119–20
  damage in action with BCS, 125–6, 128, 133, 140–1
  attacked by *Victorious'* aircraft, 148–51
  located by Coastal Command, 179
  crippled by *Ark Royal's* aircraft, 185–8
  extent and effects of torpedo damage, 195–6
  attacks by Fourth Destroyer Division, 197–201
  final action, 203–8
  sinks, 208
  see also 'F', Ship
Blackman, Commodore, (*Edinburgh*), 189
Blake, V-Adm. Sir Geoffrey, 222
Blücher (German cruiser), 13
Bovell, Capt. H. C., (*Victorious*), 150–1
Bowhill, A.M. Sir Frederick, (CinC Coastal Cmd), 176–7, 179
Brest, 79, 158, 165, 168, 175
  Prinz Eugen arrives at, 213

Briggs, P.O. O. D., 179
Brinkmann, Capt. Helmuth, (*Prinz Eugen*), 96, 141, 218
    assumes break-out successful, 106
    during battle off Iceland, 124–5
    actions on release, 212–13
    decides to make for Brest, 213
Britannic (British transport), 92, 137, 158, 177

C
Cairndale (British tanker), 177
Canarias (Sp. cruiser), 197, 211
Canary Islands, 56–7, 59, 63, 64, 78, 212
Cape Verde Islands, 56, 59, 78
Carls, Gen.-Adm. Rolf, (CinC Gp North), 94, 95–6
    advises against Denmark Strait, 43
    'Rheinübung' orders, 83–4
    proposes U-boat trap, 129
    reviews lessons, 175, 217–18
Chatfield, Adm. of the Flt Lord, 221–2
Ciliax, V-Adm., (CinC Battleships), 230–1
Churchill, W. S., 226
Clayton, Capt. J., 163
Convoys,
    HX.108, 44
    HX.109, 45
    HX.111, 49
    HX.112, 49, 50
    HX.114, 67
    HX.115, 67
    HX.127, 137, 138
    HX.128, 138, 177
    SC.22, 45
    SC.32, 177
    SL.67, 56, 67, 68, 80
    SL.68, 56
    SL.69, 60
    SL.74, 201
    SLS.64, 62, 90
    SLS.68, 56
    SLS.69, 60
    WS.8B, 99, 135, 172, 178
Coode, Lt-Cdr T. P., 184–5, 195

Coppinger, Capt. C., 204
Cossack (British destroyer), 178, 198–200
Curteis, R-Adm. A. T. B., (R-Adm. 2CS), 148, 157–8, 163

D
Dakar, 133
Dalrymple-Hamilton, Capt. F. H. G., (*Rodney*), 158, 164, 168, 189, 204, 205, 227
Daniel, Capt. C. S. (D Plans), 166
Denham, Capt. H. W., (BNA Stockholm), 97, 98
Denmark Strait, 84, 90ff, 103, 105ff, 133, 161–2, 215
Denning, Lt-Cdr N., 163, 166
Deutschland (later *Lützow*) (German *Panzerschiff*), 17, 26–7, 28–9
Dönitz, R-Adm. Karl, (BdU), 231
Dorsetshire (British cruiser), 201, 208

E
Edinburgh (British cruiser), 136, 158, 164, 172, 176, 181, 189
Edwards, Capt. R. A. B., (D. of Ops [H]), 166, 178
Ellis, Capt. R. M., (*Suffolk*), 144
    enemy reports, 116
    loss of contact, 154–5
    search plans, 163–4
Emden (German cruiser), 92
Emerald (British cruiser), 46
Esmonde, Lt-Cdr E., (825 NAS), 99, 148–50, 152–5, 194

F
'F', Ship,
    design, 17–19
Fancourt, Capt. H. St J., (RNAS Hatston), 98, 102
Faulknor (British destroyer), 63
Ferrol, 133, 158, 197
Fleet Air Arm, *see* Naval Air Squadrons
Force H, 48, 56, 57, 60, 68, 127, 138, 158, 164, 169, 174, 197, 201

sails to join convoy WS.8B, 135
Forester (British destroyer), 63
Fraser, R-Adm. B. A., (Controller), 222
Freetown (Sierra Leone), 60, 63
Fricke, R-Adm. Kurt, (Hd *Seekriegleitung* Ops. Div.), 217, 230
Friend, Sub-Lt(A) A. C., 188
Furious (British carrier), 63

G
'G', Ship, 19
Galatea (British cruiser), 103, 148
Gibraltar, 45, 48, 59, 63, 73, 74, 129, 137
Gick, Lt P. D., 150
Gneisenau (German battlecruiser), 17, 26, 28, 29, 77, 85, 91, 176, 216
sinks *Rawalpindi*, 27
and Operation *'Berlin'*, 34ff, 55ff
damaged at Brest, 80
and Operation *'Cerberus'*, 231
Goddard, Sub-Lt(A) R. I. W., 185
Godfrey-Fawcett, Lt. D. F., 185–8
Goodall, Sir Stanley, (DNC), 222
Göring, Hermann, 16, 75
Gotland (Sw. cruiser), 93–4
Graf Spee, see *Admiral Graf Spee*
Graham, Cdr H. R., (*Zulu*), 198–9
Great Belt, The, 82–3, 93, 95
Group Command North, 82, 84, 95, 96, 97, 127, 128–9, 142, 217
Group Command West, 44, 48, 50, 56, 59, 61, 64, 69, 78, 142, 151, 159, 174, 194, 195, 211, 213, 215

H
'H', Ship, 23, 24
Halifax (Nova Scotia), 44, 48, 49, 64, 67, 138, 177
Hatston, RNAS, 93, 98, 102, 103
Hermione (British cruiser), 103, 148
Heye, Cdr Helmuth, 20
Heye Memorandum, 20–4
strategic concept, 20–1
role of the U-boat, 21–2
geopolitical issues, 22–3

material questions, 23–4
Hipper, see *Admiral Hipper*
Hitler, Adolf, 220
and naval rearmament, 24,
approves 'Z Plan', 24
and *'Weserübung'*, 13
and *'Seelöwe'*, 14–15, 16
and *'Barbarossa'*, 72
and *'Felix'*, 73, 74
rejects maritime strategy, 73–4
message to *Bismarck*, 196
meets Raeder after *'Rheinübung'*, 214–16
and Brest Squadron, 228–30
Hoffmann, Capt. (*Scharnhorst*), 46–7, 48, 50, 57, 61
Holland, V-Adm. L. E., (V-Adm. BCS), 99, 103, 111ff
tactical constraints, 113–16
general assessment, 120–2
Home Fleet, 48, 93, 95, 127, 133, 134, 163
Hood (British battlecruiser), 68, 70, 91, 99, 116ff, 129, 173, 221
design, 111–12
loss, 119, 136
Boards of Inquiry, 222–5
Hvalfjord (Iceland), 39, 99, 103

I
Icarus (British destroyer), 121
Iceland, US occupation of, 229

J
'J', Ship, 23, 24
Jan Mayen, 84, 92
Jasper, Cdr., 123
Jeschonnek, Col-Gen. Hans, (*Luftwaffe* Ch. of Gen. Staff), 231

K
'K', Ship, 24
Kattegat, 82, 93
Kemp, Lt-Cdr. P., 162–3, 166
Kenya (British cruiser), 103, 148
Kiel Canal, 82
King George V (British battleship), 17, 18,

67, 68, 103, 112, 129, 148, 157, 167, 173, 176, 225, 226
  meets up with *Rodney*, 182
  conserves fuel, 184
  action with *Bismarck*, 204–7
Köln (German cruiser), 92
Korsfjord (Norway), 94, 95, 103
Kristiansand, 99

L
'L', Ship, 24
La Pallice, 220
Larcom, Capt. C. A. A., (*Sheffield*), 180, 182–3, 189
Leach, Capt. J. C., (*Prince of Wales*), 93, 112, 113, 119–20, 132, 140, 222, 223, 225, 227
Lindemann, Capt. Ernst, (*Bismarck*), 81, 150, 173, 196
Lloyd, Capt. F., 163, 165
'Lolo', point, 55
London (British cruiser), 137
Luftwaffe, 74, 75, 79, 96, 134, 168, 201, 211, 215, 218, 231
  reconnaissance, 92, 95, 159–60, 174, 193, 196
  support for *Bismarck*, 83, 175, 196
Lütjens, V-Adm. Günther, (Fleet Commander), 33ff, 90ff, 134, 141–2, 159, 172, 193, 194, 196, 211, 212, 214
  characteristics, 33–4
  evades British cruisers, 35–8, 39–40
  plans and convoy schedules, 41–3, 44–5
  meets *Ramillies*, 46–7
  reprimands Hoffmann, 47
  meets *Malaya*, 61–3
  takes prizes, 65–6
  meets *Rodney*, 68
  evades Force H, 68–70
  orders for 'Rheinübung', 80–1
  meets Raeder, 85–6
  briefs commanding officers, 86–7
  enters Bergen, 94
  attempts to shake off pursuers in

  Denmark St., 106
  handling of Denmark St. action, 124–5
  decides on St Nazaire, 128, 151
  detaches *Prinz Eugen*, 141–3, 159, 162
  breaks radio silence, 160
Lützow (ex-*Deutschland*) (German *Panzerschiff*), 13, 91, 92, 215–16, 219

M
'M', Ship, 24
Malaya (British battleship), 61–3, 67
Manchester (British cruiser), 99, 103, 177
Maori (British destroyer), 178, 198–200, 202
Marschall, Adm., 27–8, 82
Martin, Capt. B. C. S., (*Dorsetshire*), 208
Maund, Capt. L. E. H., (*Ark Royal*), 176, 180, 182–3, 189, 201
Merchant ships (British and neutral):
  Bianca, 65, 69
  Chilean Reefer, 67, 68
  Harlesden, 51
  Kantara, 51
  Lustrous, 51
  Marathon, 65
  Polycarp, 66, 68, 69
  San Casimiro, 66, 69
  Simnia, 66
  Trelawny, 51
Modoc (USCG cutter), 153
Müllenheim-Rechberg, Burkard, 106, 173, 195, 205

N
'N', Ship, 24
Naiad (British cruiser), 39
Naval Air Squadrons (NAS):
  800Z, 99, 149
  810, 184
  818, 184
  820, 184
  825, 99, 169
  848, 98, 102
Naval War Staff (*Seekriegsleitung*), 76–9, 214, 216

'Rheinübung' directive, 77–9
Nelson (British battleship), 38, 70, 177, 225
Noble, Adm. Sir Percy, 178
Norfolk (British cruiser), 92, 104, 119, 132–
3, 139, 143, 149, 153, 157, 176, 181,
201
  final action with Bismarck, 204–5
Northern Patrol, 91

O

Offord, D. E. J. (RCNC), 223–4
Operations and plans:
  'Barbarossa', 72, 216
  'Berlin', 34ff, 55ff, 76, 77, 78, 82, 84, 91,
    125, 142, 177
  'Cerberus', 230–1
  'Felix', 73
  'Gelb', 13
  'Rheinübung', 72ff, 211ff
  'Seelöwe', 14–15, 16, 29, 30
  'Weiss', 24, 26
  'Weserübung', 13, 14, 29

P

Patterson, Capt. W. R., (King George V),
  205
Phillips, V-Adm. Sir Tom (VCNS), 97–8,
  135, 222, 227
Piorun (Polish destroyer), 178, 181, 198–
  200
Plawski, Cdr E., (Piorun), 181, 198, 200
pocket-battleships,
  role of, 23
  commence operations, 26–7
Pound, Adm. Sir Dudley, (1SL and CNS),
  120, 135, 166, 221, 222, 227
Prince of Wales (British battleship), 93, 99,
  113ff, 129, 143–4, 163, 206, 215, 222ff
  design features, 112
  condition of, 112–13
  damage to, 132
  role after Denmark St. action, 138–40,
    153–4, 157
Prinz Eugen (German cruiser), 25, 29, 64,
  77, 78, 80, 83, 85ff, 91, 93ff, 104, 122,
126, 151, 154, 161, 162, 174–5, 177,
182, 216, 217, 220, 229
  in action, 119, 123–5
  released, 141–4, 159
  when released, 212–13
  damaged at Brest, 219
  and Operation 'Cerberus', 231

Q

Queen Elizabeth (British battleship), 68, 70,
  225

R

Raeder, Gr-Adm. Erich, (CinC Navy), 13–
  14, 126, 141, 172, 196, 220
  and naval rearmament, 24–5
  and Anglo-German Naval Agreement,
    19–20
  and Heye memorandum, 23–4
  reflections on start of war, 15, 25–6
  initiates ocean campaign, 26–7
  on German strategy, 17, 29, 73, 74–6
  on relations with USA, 72–3, 75–6, 85,
    229
  opposes 'Barbarossa', 72
  defends 'Rheinübung', 214–16
  and Brest Squadron, 228–31
Ramillies (British battleship), 44, 46–7, 49,
  137, 147, 158, 164, 177
Rawalpindi (British AMC), 27
Read, Capt. (Ramillies), 137
Renown (British battlecruiser), 56, 63, 129,
  135, 176, 180, 182, 190, 196, 197, 202
Repulse (British battlecruiser), 38, 39, 63,
  99, 103, 134, 147, 148, 157, 222
Revenge (British battleship), 44, 137, 177
Rodney (British battleship), 38, 39, 67, 92,
  137, 147, 158, 164ff, 172, 173, 176, 177,
  181, 184, 189, 193
  meets up with King George V, 182
  action with Bismarck, 203–7
Roosevelt, President F. D., 135, 229
Rotherham, Cdr. G. A., 102–3
Rowell, Lt-Cdr G. W., 222
Royal Air Force, 74, 229

Coastal Command, 79, 98, 99, 102, 176–7, 179–80, 193, 219
  raids on Brest, 79–80, 219–20, 229–30
Ruge, Commodore, (FO Western Defences), 230

S

Saalwächter, Gen-Adm. Alfred, (CinC Gp West), 105, 129–30, 142, 159, 160, 162, 174–5, 193–4, 196
St Nazaire, 128, 151, 159, 161, 173, 175
Scapa Flow (Orkney), 37, 39, 48, 93, 102
  reconnaissance of, 92, 95, 96, 159–60
Scharnhorst (German battlecruiser), 17, 19, 28, 29, 91, 176, 216, 228
  and Operation *'Berlin'*, 34ff, 55ff
  sinks *Rawalpindi*, 27
  damaged at Brest, 220
  and Operation *'Cerberus'*, 231
Schmalenbach, Lt-Cdr. Paul, 123–4
Schmundt, Adm., (CinC Cruisers), 217
Schneider, Cdr. Adalbert, 196
Schniewind, V-Adm. Otto, (Ch. Naval War Staff), 197, 217
Scott, R-Adm. R. J. R., (FOIC Iceland), 133
scouts, German,
  Gonzenheim, 212, 213, 220
  Kota Penang, 212, 213
Severn (British submarine), 177
Sheffield (British cruiser), 129, 135, 164, 176, 180, 184–5, 188, 190, 193, 194, 197, 201, 202, 207
  attacked in error, 182–3
Sikh (British destroyer), 178, 198–200
Skagerrak, 83
Smith, Ensign Leonard B., 179
Somerville, V-Adm. Sir James, (V-Adm. Force H), 138, 158, 164, 166, 174, 178–80, 184, 189, 225, 226
  supports SL.67, 63
  locates German prizes, 69
  evaded by Lütjens, 69
  sails from Gibraltar, 135
  air plans against *Bismarck*, 176, 179–80

  detaches *Sheffield*, 180
  during Tovey's approach, 201–2
  on Tovey's withdrawal, 207–8
Stokes, Cdr. G. H., (*Sikh*), 199, 200
Suckling, P.O. M., 98
Suffolk (British cruiser), 92, 103–4, 113ff, 121, 138ff, 143–4, 149, 154–7
Supply and support ships (German):
  Adria, 36, 38
  Belchen, 220
  Brehme, 48
  Egerland, 220
  Ermland, 55, 65, 194, 196
  Esso Hamburg, 48, 212, 220
  Gedania, 221
  Lothringen, 221
  Schlettstadt, 44, 48
  Uckermark, 55, 65, 66, 67
  Wiessenburg, 84, 96
  Wollin, 95

T

Thorshaven, 99
Tirpitz, Gr-Adm. Alfred von, 17
Tirpitz (German battleship), 19, 23, 25, 29, 86, 98, 229
  see also 'G', Ship
Tovey, Adm. Sir John, (CinC Home Fleet), 38–9, 68, 99–103, 133, 135, 140, 147–8, 181, 184, 190, 200, 222, 225, 228
  and dawn encounter (Jan. 1941), 39
  at close of *'Berlin'*, 70
  and standing patrols, 91–2
  initial dispositions, 92–3, 99
  sails BCS, 99
  sails Fleet, 103
  detaches *Victorious*, 148
  search orders, 157–9
  response to D/F fixes, 163–4, 165ff
  orders for final action, 202–3
  withdraws from action, 207–8
  defends conduct, 226–7
  defends subordinates, 227
Trondheim, 40, 95, 99, 127, 215, 216, 219, 229

U

U-boat arm, 74, 76
  deployment, 60–1, 78–9, 141, 175
U-boats:
  U-48, 194
  U-74, 211
  U-93, 220
  U-105, 62
  U-124, 59, 61

V

Versailles, Treaty of, 18
Vian, Capt. P. L. (Capt. D4), 178, 181,
  193, 197–201, 202
Victorious (British carrier), 92, 103, 142,
  148
  assigned to Home Fleet, 99–102
  attack on *Bismarck*, 148–51
  search plans, 157–9, 163

W

Wake-Walker, R-Adm. W. F., (R-Adm.
  1CS), 103–4, 121, 143–4, 153, 201, 208,
  225, 227
  action policies, 132–3, 136, 138–40, 164
  loses contact, 155–7, 158
Walker, R-Adm. H. T. C., 222
Washington, (US battleship), 17, 18
Washington Naval Treaty, 17, 112
Weather trawlers, German:
  August Wriedt, 220
  Heinrich Freese, 220
  München, 220, 221
  Sachsenwald, 211

Z

'Z Plan', 24, 25
Zulu (British destroyer), 178, 198–9